MORALE

MORALE

A Study of Men and Courage

The Second Scottish Rifles
at the
Battle of Neuve Chapelle
1915

by JOHN BAYNES

LEO COOPER
LONDON

First published by Cassell & Company Ltd, 1967
Re-issued 1987 by Leo Cooper Ltd
Leo Cooper is an independent imprint of
the Heinemann Group of Publishers,
10 Upper Grosvenor Street,
London W1X 9PA
LONDON MELBOURNE JOHANNESBURG AUCKLAND

Printed in Great Britain by
Biddles Ltd, Guildford and King's Lynn

To my father

LIEUTENANT-COLONEL R. M. S. BAYNES

LATE THE CAMERONIANS (SCOTTISH RIFLES)

Joined the Regiment 1908

Wounded Festubert 1915

Commanded 2nd Battalion (2nd Scottish Rifles)

1933–1937

Came back from retirement to the active list

1939–1945

Acknowledgements

I am indebted to the following:

Correlli Barnett for an extract from *The Desert Generals*; John Betjeman for an extract from his *Collected Poems*; Mrs John Brophy and Eric Partridge for extracts from *The Long Trail: What the British Soldier Sang and Said in the Great War 1914–1918* by John Brophy and Eric Partridge; Sir Arthur Bryant for an extract from *English Saga 1840–1940*; Messrs Jonathan Cape for extracts from *Mental Seduction and Menticide* by J. A. M. Meerloo and *Soldiers and Soldiering, or Epithets of War* by Field-Marshal the Earl Wavell; Charles Carrington for extracts from *Soldier from the Wars Returning*; Alan Clark for extracts from *The Donkeys*; Messrs William Collins Sons for extracts from *Wavell, Scholar and Soldier* by John Connell; Percy Croney for an extract from *Soldier's Luck*; Mrs Rose Elton and Messrs Chatto and Windus for extracts from *Disenchantment* by C. E. Montague; *Encyclopaedia Britannica* for extracts from their entry on 'Children's Literature'; Major-General Essame for an extract from his article 'Second Lieutenants Unless Otherwise Stated' (*United States Military Review*, May 1964); Stephen Graham for extracts from *A Private in the Guards*; Sir Alan Herbert, Messrs Methuen and A. P. Watt and Son for extracts from *The Secret Battle*; Messrs Hutchinson for extracts from *My War Memories 1914–1918* by General Ludendorff; Major S. H. F. Johnston for an extract from *The History of The Cameronians (Scottish Rifles), Volume I, 1689–1910*; the executors of the T. E. Lawrence Estate and Messrs Jonathan Cape for an extract from *The Seven Pillars of Wisdom*; Sir Basil Liddell Hart for extracts from *A History of the World War 1914–1918*; Messrs Macmillan for an extract from *The Day of Reckoning* by Mary Clive and *The Collected Poems of Thomas Hardy*; Lord Moran for extracts from *The Anatomy of Courage*; Odhams Books, Ltd. for an extract from *Great Contemporaries* by the Rt. Hon. Sir Winston S. Churchill; the Oxford University Press for extracts from *Edwardian England 1901–1914* (Ed. Simon Nowell-Smith); Margery Perham for an extract from *Lugard: The Years of Adventure 1858–1898*; A. D. Peters and Co. for an extract from *Poems of Many Years* by Edmund Blunden; Siegfried Sassoon for extracts from his *Collected Poems*; Messrs Secker and Warburg for an extract from *Portrait of an Officer* by P.-H. Simon (translated by H. Hare); Messrs Sidgwick and Jackson and Dodd, Mead and Co., New York for an extract from *The Collected Poems of Rupert Brooke*; Field-Marshal the Viscount Slim for extracts from *Defeat into Victory*; Averil Stewart for extracts from *'Alicella'*, *a Memoir of Alice King Stewart and Ella Christie*; Colonel H. H. Story for extracts from *The History of The Cameronians (Scottish Rifles) 1910–1933*; John Terraine for an extract from *Douglas Haig: the educated soldier*, and extracts from *General Jack's Diary 1914–1918*; A. P. Watt and Son for extracts from *Goodbye to All That* by Robert Graves; the editor of *The Journal of the Royal United Service Institution* for an extract from 'Writers and the Great War' (August 1964) by Barrie Pitt, and extracts from 'Writing about Soldiers' (August 1965) by John Connell; the editor of *The Covenanter, the Journal of The Cameronians (Scottish Rifles)* for an extract from 'How It Was In The Army' (February 1963) by Robert Leggatt, and 'A Salute to Malta' (Poem, March 1965) by J. C. Horne; the editor of *The British Army Review* and the Controller, Her Majesty's Stationery Office, for extracts from 'Discipline and Enthusiasm' (April 1965) by Lieutenant-Colonel A. A. Hanbury-Sparrow.

Contents

Illustrations

Maps and Diagram

● ● ●

Preface

MY MOTIVES IN writing this book are largely explained in the Introduction. However, I want to stress in this Preface that it does not reflect my ideas on how a modern Army should be run. At times it will be found that I use the present tense, especially when writing of matters which seem to me to have an unchanging application to human affairs, and at times I compare favourably the way things were done in the early years of the century with modern methods. For all this, my approach to military problems at the time of writing (1966) is in most respects radical rather than traditional, as indeed is that of most of my contemporaries. Therefore I want to establish that this is an historical study to be judged on its own merits as such: I admire at a distance the achievements of the pre-1914 Army, but do not hanker in any way for a return to its way of life.

In writing this book I have been fortunate to receive advice and assistance from many different people. To start with I must mention retired officers and soldiers of The Cameronians (Scottish Rifles). Among many who have answered questionnaires and given me information I would like to list the following who have given me special help, or whose words I have quoted (mostly anonymously) at some stage in the book.

Brigadier C. N. Barclay, C.B.E., D.S.O.
Mr J. Cosgrove, M.M.
Lieutenant-Colonel D. A. Foulis, D.S.O., O.B.E.
Brigadier-General W. D. Croft, C.B., C.M.G., D.S.O.
Lieutenant-General Sir Alexander Galloway, K.B.E., C.B., D.S.O., M.C.
Captain M. D. Kennedy, O.B.E.
Major R. McGuinness, M.C., M.M.
Lieutenant-Colonel D. G. Moncrieff, M.C.
Major-General R. C. Money, C.B., M.C.
Mr J. W. Noble
Brigadier A. C. L. Stanley Clarke, C.B.E., D.S.O.
Mr H. Smith
Mr F. W. Woods

For the sketch map and the diagram I must thank Mrs George Stephen (Caroline), who has drawn them most clearly and skilfully. Mr D. D. Bell gave me the supplement to the *Daily Mail* on which the picture map is based.

Those who have been kind enough to look at and comment upon various chapters are Sir William Robieson, one-time editor of *The Glasgow Herald* and an important figure in the life of Glasgow University; John Terraine, the historian, broadcaster and prolific writer on the First World War; Brigadier John Oldfield, for whom I am working at the time of writing as Brigade Major; Mrs A. Stewart of Murdostoun, from whose book *Alicella* I quote at length in Chapter 7; two of the officers mentioned earlier, Brigadier Stanley Clarke and Captain Malcolm Kennedy; and my father, to whom the book is dedicated.

I have received encouragement from two Colonels of The Cameronians (Scottish Rifles), General Sir Horatius Murray, G.C.B., K.B.E., D.S.O., and Lieutenant-General Sir George Collingwood, K.B.E., C.B., D.S.O.; from Sir Basil Liddell Hart, from Captain The Earl Haig and Major-General Frank Richardson, C.B., D.S.O., O.B.E., M.D. My wife, having four sons, knows just how much affectionate goodwill is required to encourage the male in his activities without letting him upset the household completely.

Almost last, but very far from least I must thank my agent, Jamie Kinross, himself at one time an officer of The Cameronians (Scottish Rifles), for putting the book in the path of Cassell and Co., and Kenneth Parker and the other directors of that famous publishing House for being good enough to take notice of it.

For much accurate and careful typing I am indebted to Miss Margaret Ross-Taylor, Miss Audrey Green, and Miss Lynne Crosley: I must thank Margaret in particular for nearly three years of help and encouragement.

Finally, I must record a debt to my contemporaries in my Regiment, who have served the essential purpose of ensuring that my attempts at writing should not give me a swollen head. Their indifference to my efforts has been both necessary and salutary. At a Regimental Dinner early in 1966 I found myself next to an old friend with whom I have not served for some years. About half-way through the meal he said: 'What's this about you writing a book?' But this opening led nowhere. Before I could say anything he finished the discussion. 'I bet it's a bloody awful book.' It seems to finish this Preface on a good note as well.

JOHN BAYNES

Preface to the Second Edition

Some twenty years after it was first published in 1967 *Morale: A Study of Men and Courage* is being re-issued. Reading it through again after all these years I find that there is little that I want to add to what I wrote then on the main theme of the book. However, I am anxious to cover two matters in this short preface. First, to elaborate on the vital, but perhaps not entirely obvious, connection between command and morale: second, to write about the sad events in the 1960s which saw the Regiment forming the core of my study reduced from that great body, which in 1914 consisted of several thousand regular and part-time officers and men as described in Chapter One, to only two Territorial Army companies.

My first introduction to the subject of morale came when I was an Officer Cadet at the Royal Military Academy, Sandhurst and had to learn the 'Principles of War'. Among these, remembered by means of a mnemonic no longer recalled, was 'Maintenance of Morale': words which in those days meant little to me. It required personal involvement as an officer to learn their significance. People without experience of warfare are unlikely to put as much emphasis on this aspect as those who have seen active service themselves, or have made a deep study of military history.

On first reflection command seems concerned with using and directing military force: a matter of strategy and tactics; of the handling of troops in battle; of communications and gaining intelligence about the enemy; of making plans to defeat him; of advance, attack, withdrawal and defence. Only on looking deeper does it become clear that a major task of a successful commander is to ensure that the men he leads have high morale.

Perhaps one reason why this aspect of command is less discussed than some of the others mentioned above is that so many of the factors connected with it involve administration —a much more mundane subject. Yet one of Britain's greatest, if not luckiest, soldiers had no doubt about its importance.

Many years ago, in 1939, Field-Marshal Earl Wavell, at the

time a Lieutenant-General, delivered three lectures at Trinity College, Cambridge under the title 'Generals and Generalship'. In the first he quoted a passage, attributed to Socrates, describing the qualities in a general, which starts:

'The general must know how to get his men their rations and every other kind of stores needed for war.'

The passage ends:

'He should also, as a matter of course, know his tactics; for a disorderly mob is no more an army than a heap of building materials is a home.'
Commenting on this point, Wavell stated:

'Now the first point that attracts me about that definition is the order in which it is arranged. It begins with the matter of administration, which is the real crux of generalship, to my mind; and places tactics, the handling of troops in battle, at the end of his qualifications instead of at the beginning, where most people place it.'

Throughout history there are of course examples of tattered, starving soldiers achieving great feats when deprived of almost everything needed to sustain them, but such occasions tend to be isolated events. To fight well in a long drawn-out campaign, and survive the hardships of active service for prolonged periods, troops must be provided with 'the stores needed for war,' and the General must see they get their rations. Even the finest and best led soldiers cannot hold on for ever without proper supplies. So it is not by chance that administration is always clearly linked with morale in military circles, and indeed in examinations for entrance to the British Army Staff College a major subject is called 'Administration and Morale'.

Though morale must be fostered at the higher levels of command, it is largely created at the regimental or battalion level. A General must regard the maintenance of high morale in the large formation under his control as one of his main priorities, but he relies to a great extent on the Colonels who command regiments and battalions to produce the results he needs.

At the very end of *Morale*, in Chapter 12, I describe the five most important factors which I believe sustained the 2nd Scottish Rifles at Neuve Chapelle, and first I place . . . 'Regimental loyalty; the pride in belonging to a good battalion, in knowing other people well and being known by them; in having strong roots in a well-loved community.' The importance of this particular loyalty has become clearer to me since the sad day when the last links with the 2nd Scottish Rifles in the regular British Army disappeared on 14 May 1968.

To tell the full story of how this came about would be too laborious, but it must be sketched in briefly. Up until 1947 the two regular battalions described in Chapter 1 of the book still existed, though by then the old feuding between them had more or less died away during the war years 1939 to 1945. In 1947, at the start of a long and continuous process of contraction in the British armed forces, the two battalions were amalgamated, and given the title of 1st Battalion The Cameronians (Scottish Rifles). (It was just after this amalgamation that I was commissioned into the Regiment.) Up until 1964 we still kept our regimental Depot, although this was shared with another regiment, and also our Territorial Army battalion, the 6th/7th. Then in 1964 the Depot closed and our recruits were moved to a more centralised establishment. Next, in 1966 the 6th/7th Battalion was reduced to Company size. Finally, in 1967, having just returned to Edinburgh at the end of an exceptionally successful operational tour in Aden we received the shattering news that the regular 1st Battalion itself was to go within a year.

So on 14 May 1968, on the same day and on the same spot at Douglas in Lanarkshire where it had been raised by the young Earl of Angus in 1689, the 1st Battalion The Cameronians (Scottish Rifles) was disbanded. The words of the Rev. Donald McDonald, D.D., the renowned former regimental padre who came back from retirement to address and bless the parade on this sad day, rang out as the last moments in the two hundred and seventy-nine year life of the regiment approached:

'You now move out of the Army list because of changes of emphasis in our defence systems coupled with economic duress—and political expediency. But be not disheartened. The Army list is a document of temporary significance, liable to amendment or excision according to the whim and swing of governments. So put pride in your step, Cameronians. As you march out of the Army list, you are marching into history, and from your proud place there, no man can remove your name and no man can snatch a rose from the chaplet of your honour. Be of good courage, therefore! The Lord your God is with you wherever you go, and to His gracious mercy and protection I now commit you.'

The full value of what has been lost became steadily clearer to me in the years that followed the sad events of 14 May 1968 at Douglas. Apart from the problem of losing a clearly understood identity, which affected in a particularly personal fashion all of us who were despatched to join other Regiments, I have often tried to establish in my own mind what were the most vital qualities that were destroyed. The most obvious loss was that of a long tradition, but what this word means must be more fully explained.

After the disbandment of the battalion the Commanding Officer, Lt-Colonel L. P. G. Dow, O.B.E., recorded his feelings for inclusion in the final volume of the Regimental History, and wrote this about the last days:

'At the risk of sounding almost childish, I believe that the battalion in its last months was especially supported by its ghosts. Not for nothing—whatever the reflection on methods of command—did a field officer from another regiment serving with the battalion for the final eighteen months of its life maintain that often all that was needed at a Commanding Officer's conference was an executive nod; the action, even of an intricate nature, then followed promptly and efficiently without any visible co-ordination whatsoever. 'All done by mirrors' he said. What in fact he referred to were reactions and procedures acquired over generations of service.'

This is one of the best explanations I have ever read of the practical value of tradition. No better reason can be found for supporting the old maxim that 'if change is not absolutely necessary, it is absolute necessary not to change'. People who struggle to run efficient and happy human organisations, whether regiments, schools, businesses, or whatever, know only too well the value of familiar and well-tested procedures.

Often the desire to make changes seems to come over those who work well away from the places where things are actually done; it appears that they are frequently instigated by those who are attempting to make their own reputations rather than generate real improvements.

The other side of tradition is what might be called the spiritual, or perhaps emotional. Since so much is made of this factor in the main body of the book it is not necessary to say more about it at this point, except to stress the great importance to a British regiment of long family connections. Many of us in the 1st Battalion The Cameronians (Scottish Rifles) in 1968, both officers and men, were sons of the regiment. In an article in *The Sunday Telegraph* on 25 November 1984 Peregrine Worsthorne wrote about:

. . . 'the fascinating question of how an institution acquires a corporate character, capable of evoking love and loyalty; the crucial contribution in this process that can be made by families whose connection is particularly close and long-standing; the value of having some members whose feelings for the institution have been fostered from infancy onward. Such considerations do not only enrich schools, colleges or regiments. They also enrich trade unions, businesses, and, indeed all human organisations—countries, of course, in particular.'

Two of the prominent characters in *Morale* are Carter-Campbell and Ferrers. At the Disbandment Parade the former's son was present among the retired officers in the form of Lt-Colonel D. M. Carter-Campbell, O.B.E., who had commanded the 1st Battalion as recently as 1957. Colonel Ferrers, as he became, had no family to follow him, but among the fourteen living regimental Generals who were there, mostly retired, many freely admitted that much of their later success in the Army sprang from the training he gave them during his tenure of command of the 1st Cameronians in the 1920s. And if I can add a personal note, I can clearly remember Ferrers staying with us when I was about eight and my father was commanding the 2nd Scottish Rifles in Bordon in the 1930s. So such an outstanding figure was somebody I remembered and revered from childhood. How do you place a value on contacts such as this?

Apart from the two great assets discussed above, a long-service, regular, military unit has another, which is the close personal knowledge gained by the officers of their brother officers, of their non-commissioned officers, and of the majority of their private soldiers. Needless to add, the same process works upwards through the rank-structure as well as down it! The value of this knowledge is inestimable when the moment comes for action: the Commanding Officer knows exactly who among his subordinate commanders can be trusted and left on his own, who needs guidance, who has to be encouraged and who has to be held back. Of course in a battalion formed in time of war at short notice everyone will soon learn about each other in much the same way, but nothing can replace the really deep, close understanding found in a regular one.

Although the last links with the 2nd Scottish Rifles have disappeared from the regular British Army, there are two Territorial Army Companies which still wear the Douglas tartan and carry the regimental name. There is little chance now of a regular battalion ever being formed again, but it is not beyond possibility that in the troubled days ahead a complete part-time battalion might be formed, and the members of these two companies would form its nucleus. Referring again to the great body of men who formed the regiment in 1914—two regular battalions, two Special Reserve battalions, four Territorial battalions and a Regimental Depot—what is left in 1985 is not much. But, thank God, it is something!

MORALE

Introduction

THIS BOOK IS an attempt to fill a gap. In all the mass of histories, studies, memoirs, biographies and novels which have been published about the First World War little has been done to investigate the most interesting field of all—the morale of the front-line soldier. Commenting on all the people to whom war has recently become big business, John Connell wrote just before his death in an article 'Writing about Soldiers':

Too many of them, however, have concentrated on the enormousness—and the enormity—of war itself: too few have troubled themselves overmuch with the minds and spirits of the men involved, and those who have done so have tended to simplify, and thus distort, complex motives, beliefs, aspirations, anxieties and aims, in order to argue a case and bolster a prejudice. The soul of man, in all its majesty and mystery, has been dwarfed by the war game.[1]*

To do something to rectify this situation is my primary object. Such other aims as I have will, I hope, become clear in this introduction.

I have been fascinated by the First World War for many years. I think it must have been reading Siegfried Sassoon's George Sherston trilogy which started me off, and my thirst for information about the First World War remains unquenchable. This interest also covers the history, particularly social history, of the decade before 1914. Obviously there are numerous other people who share my fascination with this period and its devastating culmination, and it is intriguing to speculate why. One of the reasons is well described by Barrie Pitt in an article published in August 1964:

At this remove the Great War stretches across time like a curtain; beyond it is history, this side is the world we live in. The strands of the life we live today can be traced backwards through these early sixties with comparative ease, through the fifties and forties—a

---

* Superior numbers throughout the book refer to source notes listed at the back of the book, starting on page 271.

few tangles in the early forties but these can be quite easily unsnarled—clearly from this distance through the thirties (though God knows life was bewildering enough at the time) on through the pale and diminishing twenties as far as the end of 1918. There the strands end. They have reached the curtain—the Great War, the most prodigious historical event since the followers of Mahomet carved an empire from Cordova to the gates of Samarkand.[2]

There is also the consideration that the curtain closed on the scene in which Great Britain had enjoyed a period as the most powerful nation in the world. To a few people it was clear even as the War was being fought that it signalled the end of Britain's supremacy in world affairs, but for the majority of the nation it took many years for the fact to become clear that between 1914 and 1919 the descent started to the stature of a second-class power on the international scale.

Another intriguing point is that although life before 1914 seems so distant, one can know well people who in that year were already fully mature, and yet are still busy in contemporary life. My own father was twenty-nine when he went to France in 1915, and yet as I write he is active in many fields, and has as lively a mind as anyone I know.

In this book my interest is not so much with the broad aspects of strategy and operations from 1914 to 1918, as with the reactions of individuals to the conditions and dangers they had to face in fighting the War. I have always found the personal side of military history the most enthralling. Perhaps this is because the other side, the chronicling of actions and movements, can be so dull. Few subjects can be quite so boring as history badly written, or badly taught; no branch is more open to this than military history. A few people seem able to derive a satisfaction from studying the moves and deployments of armies without concern for the men who made and undertook them. While often wishing in the past for examination purposes that I could find a little interest in such matters, I must admit that nothing sends me to sleep quicker than bald statements about the so-and-so division advancing along a certain axis, and passing through endless places which are rarely shown on any map. My concern is always to discover what the men taking part in the operation thought of it. The First World War is particularly rich in this field of personal experience, not only because of the wealth of reminiscence that has been published about it, but because of the number and diversity of the men who fought. Further, the battles were so similar, in Europe at least, and the tactics so stereotyped, that attention is inevitably turned from what men did towards the way in which they did it. The achievement of the British Army was not so much winning the War as enduring it. My concern is to find out why the infantry, which suffered the most as it always must, was able to show such courage and determination. My search is for all the influences that made men go so bravely over the top to face the machine-guns, the artillery barrages, the mud, and the less than fifty-fifty chance of survival which characterized First World War battles.

In starting this quest I have come up against many difficulties. The first is the mass of material that has been published about it. A. P. Herbert wrote in *The Secret Battle*:

So many men have written descriptions of trench life in France; there have been so many poems, plays and speeches about it that the majority of our nation must have a much clearer mental picture of life in the Western Front than they have of life at the Savoy, or life in East Ham.

That was written in 1919, and of course the picture is slightly different now. Even so, there can be few people who have read at all widely who have not read something about the First World War. Professor Cyril Falls published a bibliography in 1930 in which he described briefly all the books he had studied when writing his official history. This is quite a big book in itself, and lists 546 books published in English alone up to that date.[3] Since then at least another three hundred books must have appeared on the subject if Regimental and formation histories are counted. Call it a round total of nine hundred books available to the student of the War and one would not be far out. Add books in other languages and the total might near two thousand.

Apart from the difficulties inherent in choosing a theme from amidst such a mass of material, there is the awkward fact that those who fought in the War varied in their reactions to it from sharp and real enjoyment through different frames of mind to utter loathing of every moment of every day. They probably varied within themselves many times during the course of each week they were in France. Satisfaction, boredom, elation, misery, eagerness, frustration would follow each other in quick succession. In times of stress these emotions are very strong, and also transient. Within an hour a man could easily say 'This is fun', and 'This is hell', and genuinely mean it both times. Furthermore, there is the problem of looking at something in retrospect. The normal tendency for human beings is to forget the bad moments and remember only the good. At the same time there are those who brood and build up an image of only their unhappiness. Perhaps the slightly introverted type of mind, which seems to be common to a number of men who have written reminiscences of the War, has this tendency. It must be admitted, however, that there are a number of personal records which do seem to be amazingly sane and balanced in their description of what life was really like in the trenches. What great calmness and good sense, for example, one finds in a book like Frederick Manning's *Her Privates We*. But even with the aid of this and other books with the same stamp of truth on them, the task of gauging the feeling of men in 1914 and the following years is not easy.

The length of time that the War lasted is another cause of difficulty. It went on long enough for most of the participants to change over not once but many times, and by the end those who were fighting were generally far removed in outlook, background and training from those who filled the front line at the start. This aspect is important. Those who bore the brunt in 1914 and 1915 were Regular soldiers; by 1918 there were scarcely any of them left, and the Army was very much a citizen force. Also, the men at the start were older. The average age in an infantry battalion at the start of the War could have been about thirty; by the end it would be ten years younger.

Coupled with this difficulty is that of the size of the Army: 5,399,563 men went out to fight in France and Flanders alone during the course of the War. That is equivalent to the entire population of Scotland today. These men were scattered from the front-line trenches, through the rest area, and the training and reinforcement units, along the lines of communication, and back eventually to the base areas along the Channel coast. Even though the administrative 'tail' was not as greedy of men as it is today it still absorbed three to every one who ever fired a rifle in the line. This was well understood by many a reluctant hero who managed to wangle a 'cushy billet' along the lines of communications. But even with two-thirds of the Army drawn out of the scope of this study there are still some two million to be considered who endured to a lesser or greater extent the harsh conditions of trench warfare. And this is a vast field of human experience to explore.

Faced with all these difficulties it was hard to know where to lay the foundations of this study; I thought at one time of trying to encompass the whole field of morale in the infantry in the First World War. But the subject is too big. I decided that I would rather stick to something small and try to get near the truth, and being a Regular serving officer in The Cameronians (Scottish Rifles) I naturally chose to study my own Regiment. I decided to look at one battalion in one battle—the 2nd Battalion at the Battle of Neuve Chapelle, 9 to 15 March 1915. This battalion, which always referred to itself as the 2nd Scottish Rifles and did not normally use the name Cameronians, started the battle about nine hundred strong on 9 March. Six days later it came out of action. By this time the hundred and fifty men left were commanded by the sole surviving officer, a 2/Lieutenant. Throughout the battle the battalion gave not only a wonderful example of courage but also of the other human qualities, such as loyalty, generosity, unselfishness, and endurance, which are only found in a unit in which morale is at its peak.

In confining myself to the study of one battalion and one battle I am accepting many limitations. These will be explained. It may be that they will render what I want to say too narrow, though every effort will be made to demonstrate the wider influences which affected the relatively small number of men being looked at. What I hope is that by keeping to one regiment which I have not only served in but was born in, my chance of misjudgement will be smaller than if I covered a wider field. On this point, I would mention Lord Moran's *The Anatomy of Courage*. Those who know it might well think that he has already said all that needs to be said in its pages on the subject of infantry morale. But I not only want to acknowledge its excellence and the help I have had from reading it, but to point out that the main impact of the book comes from Lord Moran's own detailed observations of one battalion of The Royal Fusiliers which he knew really well. For me, the sections in which he deals with Bomber Command pilots are less effective because less intimate. The men whose problems come home to me are the soldiers; the pilots and their problems I find a little remote.

Of the limitations of my study, the first and most important is that the battalion concerned was a Regular battalion. After Neuve Chapelle it was to change, and its old structure was never to be seen again. But at the time that it went over the top on 10 March 1915 it was a professional unit with scarcely a man in its ranks with less than five years' service. It was very much a battalion of that Army which was referred to by the Germans as 'a perfect thing apart'. This particular limitation has troubled me a lot in preparing the book. Obviously one of the most fascinating aspects of morale in the First World War is the courage and endurance of those who served as temporary soldiers. It could well be argued that for the Regular the War merely provided an outlet for all the things he had been trained to do over the years. It was his job to fight well and show courage, and no credit was due to him for doing his duty, but only obloquy for failing in it. The answer to such criticism will, I hope, develop in this book. Although in the end it was the same sort of courage which sustained the New Army battalion as had held together a battalion of the old Regular Army, the two types of unit were of such different background that they cannot really be examined together. I am interested as much in the paths they followed to reach their high morale as in the morale itself, and their paths were essentially divergent.

The second limitation is that the 2nd Scottish Rifles at Neuve Chapelle were in their first major action. Much more will be said later about the importance of freshness in battle but there is no doubt that it is a lot easier to be brave the first time over the top than the second or third time. On this score, there is only one answer, and that is that units did not go more than once into battles like Neuve Chapelle. Individuals went back again for the second, third, or fourth time, but battalions did not. They carried on in name, but the men were entirely different. For example the 2nd Scottish Rifles were in action again at Aubers Ridge on 9 May 1915. But by then nearly eight hundred new men had joined the battalion. I am searching for those factors which gave the whole unit its morale at Neuve Chapelle. Whatever they were, they did not apply by the end of the battle. This is not to say that much of the spirit of the battalion did not live on to be absorbed by new men, but that the myriad threads and influences which made the original battalion what it was had been broken and lost in the enormity of its sacrifice.

The final limitation is that the Battle of Neuve Chapelle lasted only a few days. For many of those who fought it lasted only a few minutes. Many people would say that morale at its highest is only seen when men face danger and discomfort for long periods. There is certainly much to be said for this view but it does not seem to me to detract from the fact that the 2nd Scottish Rifles at Neuve Chapelle gave a superb example of high morale. Furthermore, there is a great danger in overestimating the time that units did fight in the front line. Reading both official history and personal reminiscence can be most misleading. Obviously a writer does not chronicle all those days which in a personal diary go down as: 'Cold and wet. Dull day.' It is therefore easy for him to give the impression that warfare is all battles, actions, or gruelling activities of some kind. But for even the hardest used units in the First World War, there was a great deal of time spent in billets or rest areas. *Her Privates We* gives the soundest impression of what life was really like. Frederick Manning does not pretend that it was pleasant, but he shows that there was a lot of time for rest and relaxation of a sort when out of the line.

Having mentioned some of the difficulties and limitations of my study I must now state clearly what my aim is. My aim is to study a good Regular battalion of the pre-1914 Army in its first major action in the First World War, and to look for those factors which gave it such morale that it was able to suffer appalling losses with no weakening of its spirit.

Although the book is very much concerned with the 2nd Scottish Rifles, it will be found throughout that there are references to, and quotations from, books and writings of many people who had nothing to do with the battalion. A soldier certainly lived a life centred on his own unit to a very great extent in 1914—much more so than today—but he was still part of the nation, and took up the attitudes of the society in which he had his roots.

Throughout the book I have quoted from many different sources. These fall into three groups. First there are the published and unpublished books connected with The Cameronians (Scottish Rifles). The two published ones are *The History of the Cameronians (Scottish Rifles), 1910–1933*, by Colonel H. H. Story, M.C.—referred to as the official Regimental history from this point on—and *General Jack's Diary 1914–1918*, edited by John Terraine. Jack did not fight at Neuve Chapelle, being with the 1st Cameronians at the time, but he joined the 2nd Scottish Rifles in August 1915 and stayed with them for a year before going to command the 2nd West Yorks. The unpublished book is called *The Turn of an Era*, and has been lent to me by the author, Captain M. D. Kennedy, O.B.E., with permission to use it as freely as I like. Kennedy fought at Neuve Chapelle, and so his record of the battle is of immense value.

The second group of sources includes all the other books, shown in my bibliography, which have seemed to me to cove·

aspects common to all units and men serving in the War. The third group comprises the letters, notes, answers to questionnaires, and spoken comments sent or given to me by all the different people to whom I have turned for help and advice. I am most grateful to them.

Since my concern is with the civilian background of all ranks of the 2nd Scottish Rifles almost as much as with the influence upon them of the Army, it is obviously necessary to refer at times to the classes from which they came. I have divided British society in the years up to 1914 as follows:

Upper Class—the nobility and big landowners and members of their families;
Upper-middle Class—small landowners and professional people of all sorts including the Church, the Law, and Medicine; also successful businessmen; and all those in the higher grades of the Civil Service and Government;
Middle Class (this class had the fewest connections with the career of arms)—yeomen farmers, small businessmen and prosperous shopkeepers;
Lower-middle Class—shopkeepers, clerks and white collar workers of all descriptions; also very highly skilled artisans;
Working Class—a wide bracket from the artisan to the farm labourer, the criterion being that the man had to be in regular employment;
*Real Lower Class**—the casual labourer; the sort of person who lived in the slums of the big industrial cities.

Of these classes, the upper-middle and the working class are the most difficult to delineate. At the top of the upper-middle class it is difficult to know just where people became pure upper class and where they still retained a suspicion of 'middle' about them. In the same way, at either end of the

---

* *I have borrowed the term 'real lower class' from Vance Packard's study of American class structure* The Status Seekers. *Sir William Robieson of Glasgow has suggested a more accurate term would be 'the lower stratum of the working class'. Although I think he is probably correct I have continued to use Packard's term because it is shorter and to my mind more vivid.*

working class the line of demarcation with the classes above and below was very blurred.

To close this chapter I will echo Richard Hoggart in his Preface to *The Uses of Literacy*: 'I have thought of myself as addressing first of all the serious "common reader" or "intelligent layman". . . .'[4] Although my prime purpose is to study men and their actions of fifty years ago as an historical exercise, leaving it to anyone who wishes to judge for themselves if there is any relevance to modern problems, I believe that three comments on the First World War might be appropriate.

First, I believe one must try to see it in perspective. It was a terrible war—to quote General Jack, who fought right through it, it involved 'hardships and perils beyond even the imagination of those, including soldiers, who have not shared them'[5]—but it does not compare in terms of horror to many other examples of man's inhumanity to man. Compared with Hitler's killing of six million Jews, or the hideous slaughter at the time of India's gaining of independence in 1947, or the fire storm created by the bombing of Hamburg in 1944, or Stalin's starving of recalcitrant peasants in the nineteen-twenties, or compared with endless other examples of barbarity and savagery in other centuries, the First World War was quite a clean affair. To start with, those who took part were grown men in full possession of their faculties who fought, willingly in most cases, to uphold causes they believed in. Civilian casualties were small: women, children, and old people were not killed or maimed in any great number. Furthermore, the damage to cities, towns, and farms and all the other marks of human endeavour over the centuries, was limited to very small areas. The destruction was tiny compared with the Second World War. These points seem to me to be overlooked by so many people who nowadays use the First World War as the prime example of the evil of war. What makes me shudder is the thought of children being killed violently, or of the unarmed and defenceless being treated brutally. Wars which are fought solely between armed formations of grown men can never to my mind be put in the same category as those which directly involve civilian populations as well.

My next point is that war* is a part of life. As long as any man or woman in this world is ready to use violence to achieve any aim, however worthy, the seeds of war will continue to exist. I am not going to write at length of the rights and wrongs of war; all I want to say is that to me it seems to be an unavoidable fact of human existence. Mankind can no more escape from war than from any other of its fundamental activities. What I want to show in this book, among other things, is that out of the stupidity and cruelty which leads him into war, man is often able to find again his truest virtues. To me the terrible slaughter of 1914–1918 was to some extent compensated for by the courage, unselfishness, and patience of the officers and men who fought in the front-line trenches. The 'glory' of war lies here. The danger is that those who see the falseness of many outmoded concepts of 'glory' may persuade themselves and others to believe that courage is no longer a virtue. In fact courage in the face of adversity remains the supreme human quality. Nothing will ever be built, or last, without it. A society that loses its courage can only fade and crumble away. I believe this to be a very real danger in comfortable, prosperous societies in the Western world today. We forget too easily how harsh and savage life can be, and how easily powerful forces could shatter our apparently safe and comfortable existence. The qualities of character which sustained those who fought in the First World War may not seem of great importance in the Britain of over fifty years later, but they may be needed again at any moment. This is a truth which we forget at our peril.

Finally, I believe it is essential to study the actions of those who lived in the past with a sympathetic mind. To jeer at those who have gone before us is a game fraught with pitfalls. After all, it will only be a fraction of time before we ourselves are the stuff of history. Most of us try to make a decent job of our lives, and though we make many mistakes, we feel entitled to a certain understanding of our difficulties and

* *I do not necessarily mean the type of action seen in the First or Second World Wars, but refer to conflict attended by any degree of violence—what the late Lord King-Hall called 'werre', or 'confusion, discord or strife'* (Defence in the Nuclear Age, p. 22).

problems before judgement is passed upon us. The least we can do is examine the actions of our own forbears with generosity, and attempt to see clearly all the influences which affected them. It is our duty, as Edmund Blunden wrote in his poem 'Victorians', to:

> . . . read first, and fully shape
> The diagram of life which governed them.[6]

The 2nd Scottish Rifles
in 1914

*Since England's anti-militarist tradition ran strong and deep,
it was still composed of volunteers, without a conscript to its
name. In size, therefore, it could not match the massive arrays
of divisions and corps which several European countries were
preparing to mobilize. But in quality, as it was soon to prove,
it was unrivalled in Europe, or the world.*

John Connell's description of the Regular Army in 1914.
From WAVELL, SCHOLAR AND SOLDIER[1]

THE 2ND BATTALION The Cameronians (Scottish Rifles) had
been given this official title in 1881 when a considerable
reorganization of the British Army took place under the
influence of Edward Cardwell, Secretary of State for War.
One of the major parts of Cardwell's reform of the service was
to group infantry regiments into pairs, each pair thus combined forming a new single regiment of two battalions based
on a territorial area in which it would have its depot and from
which it would find its recruits. It was also arranged that in
time of peace the battalions would be so posted that one was
stationed in Great Britain or Ireland and the other overseas.
The Home Service battalion was given the responsibility
of keeping the overseas battalion up to full strength by sending
it periodic drafts of men, and it was accepted that in doing
so its own strength might often be low. This system lasted,
apart from the disruption caused by the First World War, up
to 1939, and proved very adequate for its primary purpose of
providing garrisons abroad to guard the British Empire.

[15]

Before Cardwell's reforms the two battalions which were brought together to form The Cameronians (Scottish Rifles) had been known as the 26th (Cameronian) Regiment and the 90th (Perthshire) Light Infantry. The 26th became the 1st Battalion of the new Regiment, the 90th became the 2nd Battalion. More or less from the outset the battalions called themselves respectively the 1st Cameronians and 2nd Scottish Rifles, only using their full titles on rare occasions.

The 90th was very proud of a number of its traditions. The first of these was the story of its raising, which is a romantic one. It was raised by Thomas Graham of Balgowan, a Perthshire landowner who achieved fame as one of Wellington's generals and was eventually created Lord Lynedoch. Graham married in 1774 the Honourable Mary Cathcart, who was one of the great beauties of her day. She was painted four times by Gainsborough, and the most famous portrait of her hangs in the Scottish National Gallery. She unfortunately suffered from her family's hereditary consumption, and in 1791 Graham took her to the South of France to see if the climate there would help to cure her. There was no improvement in her condition, however, and in June 1792 she died. While her coffin was being taken back through France for burial in the United Kingdom an incident took place at Toulouse which:

. . . was to fill Graham with an unrelenting hatred of revolutionary France and to change the whole course of his life. An unruly mob of 'half drunk rascals' insisted on opening the coffin, which they suspected of containing contraband, and did so with brutal violence. Graham was horrified at this sacrilege.[2]

The combination of this outrage and other scenes he witnessed of the French Revolution convinced him that war with France was not only inevitable but fully justified. Gradually the determination grew in him to raise a regiment to fight the French, and in 1794 Graham was issued a letter of service to raise 'the Ninetieth Regiment of Foot, or the Perthshire Volunteers'.

The distinction of being 'formed into a Light Infantry corps' did not come to the 90th until 1815, and then it was due more to the fame earned personally by Graham, now

Lord Lynedoch, than its own record during the Napoleonic Wars, which had not been particularly noteworthy. In those days the Light Infantry were almost on the same social footing as the Guards and the Green Jackets (60th Rifles and Rifle Brigade), and so the members of the 90th were delighted at this honour.

During the nineteenth century the 90th was involved in the main campaigns of the British Army. It fought in the Crimea, and in the Indian Mutiny, when it took part in the relief of Lucknow. It also took part in the Zulu Wars, and was at the battle of Ulundi in 1877 as part of a column commanded by one of its own officers, Colonel Evelyn Wood, later to become a Field-Marshal. Two other officers of the 90th also rose to this rank; one was Rowland Hill, one of Thomas Graham's original officers when the Regiment was first formed, and the other Garnet Wolseley, perhaps the most famous of the three.

After the amalgamation in 1881 the 2nd Scottish Rifles, as they were now known, served for a time in India, and then took part in the Boer War. In the early stages they were brigaded under the command of a distinguished Green Jacket General with battalions of the 60th Rifles, the Rifle Brigade, and the Durham Light Infantry. They fought extremely well at Spion Kop on 24 January 1900, and after the battle were warmly congratulated by this same General who told them that although they had only recently been converted into Rifles 'we of the old Rifle regiments are proud of the part they had taken in the battle and warmly welcome them into our comradeship'[3]—a signal honour even though phrased slightly pompously.

From South Africa the battalion returned to Maryhill Barracks, Glasgow, in 1904, and thence in 1906 to Aldershot. It remained there until 1910, when it moved to Colchester. In 1911 it was posted overseas, allowing the 1st Cameronians to return home to take up the Home Service role in accordance with the Cardwell system. The overseas station it went to was Malta, and it is with the battalion on that island that this study really begins.

At the beginning of 1914 the 2nd Scottish Rifles were in

St. Andrew's Barracks, a few miles from Valetta. These, the third barracks they had occupied since arriving in 1911, were much the best. Well-built and spacious, they were ideally situated, with the sea only a half a mile away and good rifle ranges close at hand.

The battalion numbered about a thousand officers and men. The structure, numbers, and equipment of a battalion have changed since 1914, but it remains in principle much the same today as it was then. The best way to describe it might be as self-sufficient. It contained all the elements to enable it to operate independently, and yet it was commanded by an officer who might be expected to know every man in it. It was therefore a large and powerful body of men, but at the same time small enough for leadership to be intimate and for most of its members to know each other well. In 1914 four battalions were normally grouped into an infantry brigade commanded by a Brigadier-General, who deployed them and passed orders to them, but did not interfere in their method of carrying out his instructions. In some overseas stations the grouping might not be into a brigade, but into a 'garrison', with more or fewer than four battalions, depending on local conditions.

Although for operational purposes it formed a part of an infantry brigade, a battalion was also part of another larger formation, the Regiment. Thus in 1914 the 2nd Scottish Rifles were in Malta as part of the Malta Garrison of five battalions, under the command of a Brigadier-General. At the same time they were part of the Regiment, whose origins have just been described, known as The Cameronians (Scottish Rifles). The Regimental area was Glasgow and the county of Lanarkshire. The complete Regiment was a big affair, and consisted just before the outbreak of the War of the following:

1st Bn (known as the 1st Cameronians) on home service in Mary-
        hill Barracks, Glasgow
2nd Bn (known as the 2nd Scottish Rifles) in Malta
3rd Bn Special Reserve, based on Hamilton, Lanarkshire
4th Bn Special Reserve, based on Hamilton
5th Bn Territorial Bn, based on Glasgow
6th Bn Territorial Bn, based on Hamilton
7th Bn Territorial Bn, based on Glasgow

8th Bn Territorial Bn, based on Glasgow
The Regimental Depot in Hamilton, where Regular recruits were
trained.

Special Reserve battalions existed to hold civilians who
agreed to join up in time of war, but did not do any training in
peace-time other than attend a yearly camp. They were thus
largely 'paper' formations. When the First World War started
they trained the reservists on their strength and sent them
as required to join other battalions of the Regiment. The
Territorial battalions, on the other hand, were viable oganiza-
tions of part-time soldiers who not only went to camp each
year, but trained on two evenings a week and at weekends.
They went to war as formed bodies under their own titles,
and required only a month or two's training after being
embodied before being ready for active service.

Although members of the 2nd Scottish Rifles were conscious
of belonging to the two larger groupings—that is the Regiment
and the Malta Garrison—their main concern was for their
own battalion.

Command of the battalion was vested in a Lieutenant-
Colonel. To help him carry out his numerous duties he had
his Battalion Headquarters. The officer element consisted of
his Second-in-Command, a Major, and two principal staff
officers, the Adjutant and the Quartermaster. The Adjutant's
responsibilities were to organize the daily running of the
battalion, to produce written orders for mobilization and
operations, and to ensure that the drill and turn-out of the
junior officers and men were of a high standard. The Quartermaster, always promoted from the ranks, dealt with the stores
and supplies. Also a part of the battalion headquarters were
the Regimental Sergeant-Major, the clerical staff who worked
in the Orderly Room (the battalion's 'head office'), and the
Regimental Police. The latter ran the Guard Room, where
prisoners were confined, and maintained order and discipline
throughout the barracks.

The rest of the men were divided into four companies, each
commanded by a Major or senior Captain. Various members of
each company were detached on numerous duties such as,
to name only a few, working in the Officers' or Sergeants'

Mess, cooking, looking after the transport, or playing in the Pipe or Bugle bands. Until 1913 battalions had been divided into eight companies, but all Regular battalions were reorganized in that year into four. Each company had four platoons, and each platoon four sections. Counting out those of its members employed on the sort of tasks mentioned above, the fighting strength of a company was roughly two hundred. Platoons were therefore about fifty strong, and sections ten or so. As pointed out earlier, overseas battalions such as the 2nd Scottish Rifles were kept right up to strength, sometimes to the detriment of the other Regular battalion on home service. However, this latter battalion could always rely on men of the Regular Army Reserve to join it on the outbreak of War. The Regular Reserve was made up of men who had served their time in an active battalion—known as 'colour' service—and had then gone into the reserve. Reserve service was an obligatory part of a soldier's engagement, which was normally seven years with the colours and five on the reserve.

Before describing the personalities and life of the 2nd Scottish Rifles in more detail it would be best to explain at this stage the tension between them and the 1st Cameronians. Although both formed part of the same Regiment there was a good deal of animosity between the two battalions, which was not really killed until the 1930s. The trouble sprang from the fact that the 90th considered themselves in every way vastly superior to the 26th.* The officers were conscious of social superiority, and the men of the distinction of being in the Light Infantry. For all ranks the amalgamation with a rather dull, heavy-footed, 'marching' Regiment like the 26th was most distressing. Unfortunately the 26th thought rather a lot of themselves as well; they were a hundred years older than the 90th, had been raised by the Earl of Angus, a member

---

* Garnet Wolseley, joining the 90th in 1854, recorded; 'Amongst the officers of my regiment, nice fellows as they were, only a few cared much for the Army as a profession. All were proud of belonging to a splendidly drilled Light Infantry Battalion—drilled according to the practice of war in the Peninsula, before the introduction of the rifled musket. They thought themselves socially superior to the ordinary regiments of the Line, which were always spoken of as "grabbies". Many of them were well connected, and some were well off. It was in every respect a home for gentlemen, and in that respect much above the great bulk of line regiments.'[4]

[20]

of the Duke of Hamilton's family, and they had one of the finest fighting records of any infantry regiment in the British Army. The 26th were quite unprepared to bend the knee to the 90th, and a state of undeclared war was quickly established between the two battalions. Over the years those who had served in one of the two original Regiments faded from the scene, and by 1914 to a stranger's eye little difference between the 1st and 2nd Battalions would have been discernible. But in a rather silly way the old rivalry between them was kept up. It was slightly forced, and did not go very deep with the more sensible members of either battalion, but it was there, and could at times cause bitterness and unhappiness.

One of the people who suffered to some extent from this animosity in the early part of 1914 was the new Commanding Officer, Lieutenant-Colonel W. M. Bliss. Bliss came to take over the 2nd Scottish Rifles from being a Company Commander in the 1st Cameronians in March 1913. There was some resentment at the arrival of a '1st Battalion man', and this aggravated an already uncomfortable situation. Bliss's predecessor had left Malta in November 1913. For the four months that elapsed the Second-in-Command, Major George Carter-Campbell, had taken command. Among the officers Carter-Campbell had been popular; by all ranks he was well respected. Bliss found himself arriving to displace a well-trusted figure. If these two difficulties were not enough, his arrival was also viewed with distrust because he was unmarried. A Commanding Officer who lives in the Officers' Mess is always in a rather difficult position. His relationships cannot be completely relaxed with his subordinates, because he has such considerable powers over them, and however easy conversation may seem to be in a Mess when he is present, there will always be a slight tension beneath the surface. Bliss, moreover, was a rather shy and retiring man, with an austere manner. His strength lay in his integrity and uprightness of character, but these qualities take time to be appreciated. Having no obvious appeal to the loyalty and support of his officers, his early days with the 2nd Scottish Rifles cannot have been easy.

For Major Carter-Campbell the early days of 1914 cannot

have been easy either. He had been very active when in command of the battalion for some months after Bliss's predecessor left in 1913. To quote an officer serving in the battalion at the time: 'Characteristically Carter-Campbell commanded as if he was the permanent C.O. and not just a locum tenens for a C.O. on leave, with most beneficial results especially as regards morale and confidence.' When the new Commanding Officer arrived it must have been difficult for him to give up the reins and drop back into second place again. It is a measure of his character that he was able to do so with no outward show of resentment, and was able to serve loyally under Bliss.

Carter-Campbell was a very fine type of Regular officer of his day. During the War he was to rise eventually to the command of the famous 51st Highland Division. Everyone who knew him speaks very highly of him, and he obviously had the gift of inspiring great confidence in his subordinates. The same officer just quoted continues:

George Carter-Campbell was an outstanding officer, small and neat in appearance with a rather dry, incisive manner. Good, though not exceptional brains were allied to shrewd practical ability and a capacity for putting his finger on essentials. A strong, resolute character whose judgement of people and their abilities was remarkably good. In this connection the regiment had to thank him for several instances of accelerated promotion of Warrant Officers and N.C.O.s, which in those days was most unusual and caused considerable heart burning, but whose future results unquestionably endorsed his judgement. Both morally and physically he was fearless. He was a martinet but by no means unapproachable, and although he may not have enjoyed much affection there is no doubt that he inspired respect and confidence. On active service he was imperturbable under any conditions however bad, as witness his leadership at Neuve Chapelle.

The other officers in the Headquarters were the Adjutant and the Quartermaster. The Adjutant acted as the Commanding Officer's staff officer on all matters connected with the organization, discipline and routine work of the battalion, and in these matters had considerable latitude for imposing his own ideas on the detail of the unit's daily life. For the young officers and all the other ranks the Adjutant was the person who had most influence on standards of bearing, turn-out, and behaviour. The Adjutant was a most important figure in any battalion. The 2nd Scottish Rifles were lucky to have two extremely good officers in this position in succession. Lieutenant J. C. Stormonth Darling was Adjutant from 1910 to 1912, when he was posted to the 1st Cameronians on promotion to Captain. He was a big man physically, and a powerful heavyweight horseman. He was strict with junior officers and other ranks alike, and demanded very high standards. He was not particularly clever, but full of common sense, and blunt and forthright in his speech. There was a definite type like him found in the Services in those days; possibly Field-Marshal Allenby is the finest example. They tended to have great influence on those around them, and certainly Stormonth Darling did much to impress the importance of meticulous attention to duty into the minds of the officers and N.C.O.s of the 2nd Scottish Rifles.*

Stormonth Darling was succeeded as Adjutant by Captain W. I. Maunsell. Maunsell was a Roman Catholic, and very religious. He was a much more intellectual type of man than his predecessor, and held his position successfully by quiet and unspectacular hard work rather than any obvious facet of personality. When working as Adjutant to Carter-Campbell the two of them have been described as a 'masterly combination'.

To round off a strong team at Battalion Headquarters was the Quartermaster, Captain Tommy Finn. Finn had started his service in 1880 with the 90th as a Band-boy, and was eventually to finish in 1919 as a Lieutenant-Colonel Quartermaster. He was a short, stout, Glasgow-Irishman, with a jovial personality and an unrivalled knowledge of his job. Stories abounded of his ability to score off other units and Headquarters in obtaining extras for his own battalion. Added to his ability to get what he wanted, he was extremely good at dealing with the rougher elements among the men,

---

* *Having won a D.S.O., Stormonth Darling was killed in 1916 in the late stages of the Battle of the Somme when in command of a Territorial Battalion of the Highland Light Infantry.*

and never had any trouble from even the most unruly.

The other officers in the battalion were divided among the four companies. The Company Commanders were: 'A' Company—Major E. de L. Hayes; 'B' Company—Captain E. B. Ferrers; 'C' Company—Major H. C. Ellis; 'D' Company —Major H. D. W. Lloyd. They were all devoted to their companies, and to the battalion as a whole, and all were bachelors. The advantage to the battalion of having these unmarried Company Commanders was enormous. They had no distractions, especially overseas, other than their own sports and hobbies, to take them away from the care of their men. This was undoubtedly the major interest of their life. Perhaps to the modern eye this 'care' might seem a little peculiar, being much concerned with control and punishment, and not exercised with much sympathy for human weakness. But care it was in the true sense of the word. More than anything else in the world these Company Commanders wanted their men to do well and be a credit to the battalion. Some of them were commanding companies for many years, and they could not have carried on with unflagging interest had they not been devoted to the training and well-being of their men.

One of the longest connections with a particular company was that of Captain E. B. Ferrers. Not only was he command- ing 'B' Company* for some time before the First World War, but after many vicissitudes he was to do so again in 1919. Ferrers was a very remarkable character. Known always as 'Uncle' in his later years, he had joined the regiment from Cambridge, where his father was at one time Master of Gonville and Caius College. He was always eccentric, and had a most ready wit. At the same time he was the kindest of men, and had the very highest code of personal honour and integrity. I had the good fortune to meet him once or twice as a boy, and he stands out remarkably clearly in my mind. He was very good with children, and took a great interest in their doings.

His approach to soldiering was rather old-fashioned.

* For some odd reason he often referred to it himself as 'B' Troop.

Smartness, fitness, and marksmanship were the things he concentrated on, and of course regimental tradition. His tactical and general military knowledge was not great, but when he eventually came to command a battalion in the 1920s his ability to gain the devotion of the officers and men alike made him extremely successful.

Although quite unlike anyone else in many respects, and, in some of his more peculiar ways, entirely original, 'Uncle' Ferrers typified many of the virtues and failings of officers of his day. He looked on war as a sort of personal test, and longed to prove himself. He attached great importance to his sword, and is reputed to have slept with it in his bed. It would be wrong to think of others going to such lengths, but there was certainly an element of his almost medieval approach to war in many of his contemporaries. Another aspect was his contempt for higher authority, which he was always ready to express at a suitable moment. This is illustrated by his reaction, when a battalion commander, to a letter from his divisional commander complaining about the poor standard of saluting by his officers at the march past after an Aldershot Garrison Church Parade. Having been handed the letter by his Adjutant, he threw it into his wastepaper basket, and said: 'I and my men go to Church to worship God, not the divisional commander.'

In examining the officers of the 2nd Scottish Rifles, the picture that appears is one of a generally high-level of ability and keenness. It is always tempting to draw attention to weakness and shortcomings, but most people would admit that when one knows others well one finds mostly good in them, and would agree that the majority of people they meet and deal with in their daily round are pleasant and competent. It is always at second-hand that one hears of whole groups of nasty or useless people. Certainly the more I discover about the officers of the 2nd Scottish Rifles the more I believe them to have been a good collection. As well as having good senior officers, there were many young ones of great promise. From time to time thoroughly idle and irresponsible ones turned up, but normally they were not tolerated for very long. The usual method of getting rid of them was quietly to ask them 'to send in their papers'. This meant writing to the War Office for permission to retire from the active list onto the Reserve of Officers. When they did this they were able to leave without fuss or bitterness, and with the opportunity to save face outside the Regiment by declaring truthfully that they had retired of their own accord. Usually the grounds on which an officer was asked to retire were incompetence or stupidity. Rarely was it for any moral failing; when it was, heavy drinking was the most common reason.

Two of the outstanding younger officers in the battalion in early 1914 were Lieutenants A. C. L. Stanley Clarke and R. N. O'Connor. Stanley Clarke came to the regiment from Winchester and Oxford, where he had captained the University Soccer XI. In turn he captained the battalion team, and under his captaincy it won several competitions. From this he gained considerable standing with the men, since soccer, either playing or watching it, was one of their main interests. In the War he eventually commanded a New Army battalion, and one of his officers of those later days, who describes himself as 'essentially civilian', has written:

Where we were exceptionally lucky was to have Chris Stanley Clarke as C.O. for two years—a great leader and a strong personality, steeped in regimental tradition. Drafts of officers and men from any regiment were personally welcomed into the battalion. Temporary and regular officers were all the same to him. I am sure that he could have welded into a first-class fighting unit any mixed battalion of infantry.

Lieutenant R. N. O'Connor was to have a very remarkable career. His greatest achievement came in the Second World War at the end of 1940 and in early 1941 when, as a Lieutenant-General, he commanded the Western Desert Corps and inflicted a crushing defeat on the Italians in Cyrenaica. Shortly afterwards he was captured by the Germans, and although he later escaped he had become, as Correlli Barnett describes him in *The Desert Generals*, 'the fogotten victor'. Today his name is well known in purely military circles, but he is perhaps less well known in the world outside than he deserves to be. As a subaltern in 1914, he already showed the unmistakable signs of greatness. His main quality throughout his life has been complete integrity. He is now, as he always was, absolutely honest, direct and without pretence. He is a very simple person, always kind, quiet and courteous, and yet there is such strength of will and mind obvious in his every word and action that none would dare take advantage of his gentleness. As Barnett says: 'There was little here of the façade of greatness, yet no one could talk a quarter of an hour with him without being aware of unusual qualities of character and personality.'[5] Within the small world of the 2nd Scottish Rifles he was an important figure even as a subaltern. The influence of such a person, even when young and junior in rank, can be extraordinarily powerful. It was a great loss to the 2nd Scottish Rifles when in August 1914 O'Connor was posted home to the staff of the 22nd Infantry Brigade, part of the 7th Division in the B.E.F.

Other young officers who deserve special mention are Lieutenants W. B. Gray-Buchanan and W. J. Kerr. Neither survived the War, and so one cannot show how their early promise developed, but they are considered by their contemporaries to have been the equals of Stanley Clarke and O'Connor. Another in the same category was 2/Lieutenant J. F. Evetts, who was to rise to be a Lieutenant-General in the Second World War. 2/Lieutenant C. R. H. Stirling was another unusually gifted young officer. In the summer of 1917 he was in command of the 2nd Scottish Rifles at the age of twenty-five, having won the D.S.O. and M.C. In July 1917 he was wounded by shell fire near Ypres, from which he never recovered, dying the following year.

Although the occasional one drank too much, in general the officers of the 2nd Scottish Rifles were an abstemious lot. Their life centred around the Officers' Mess, which was run as much as possible like a comfortable country house of the times. Food was good, and officers paid about 4*s*. a day to supplement their rations. This sum would be equivalent to four or five times as much half a century later, and it enabled the Mess to buy the best foodstuffs available and to employ a good chef. This messing charge and other subscriptions meant that an officer was bound to have a Mess bill at the end of each month of about £10. Anything he drank came over and above this sum, and few of the junior officers could afford to drink more than an occasional whisky and soda before dinner and a glass of port after it.

The Mess was run on strict lines, and there were many rules. Only Turkish cigarettes were allowed to be smoked in the ante-room, and no smoking at all was permitted between 7.30 p.m. and the start of dinner. After dinner smoking was only permitted after the port had been circulated twice. Officers changed into Mess kit for dinner four nights a week, and on the other three—Wednesday, Saturday and Sunday—they changed into dinner jackets for supper. Supper was little different to dinner, but slightly less elaborate. Each officer had his own servant, who not only looked after his kit and equipment, but also did a share of waiting in the Mess. The term 'batman' was used for soldiers who looked after Warrant Officers, not, as in later days, for those who looked after commissioned officers. The job of officers' servant was much sought after, as it combined a fairly comfortable life with a chance to make extra money in the form of extra duty pay and the occasional tip.

The general atmosphere in the Mess was free and easy, with certain accepted rules on the conduct of junior officers. For example, a subaltern on joining spent six months during which time he was not expected to address a senior officer without being spoken to first. After this period had elapsed he had to wait until he had three years' service before he could stand on the hearth-rug in front of the ante-room fire. The Colonel and Field Officers (Majors) were always addressed as 'Sir', and all officers junior to them stood up when they entered the Mess. Today such courtesies are reserved for the Commanding Officer only, but the position of Majors has changed greatly. A Major in 1914 would normally be over forty. He might well be like Lloyd in the 2nd Scottish Rifles who had returned in 1913 from a ten-year tour of duty in Egypt where he had been Military Governor of a province the size of Great Britain.

Other rules worth mentioning were those affecting topics of conversation. A woman's name might never be mentioned, nor could 'shop' be discussed. The embargo on mentioning female names probably went back to the days, about a century before, when duelling was prevalent. The ban on talking 'shop' has died away rather in the modern Army, which may or may not be a good thing. Certainly in 1914 it served an essential purpose. Officers' lives were so centred on service life, and they lived for so long in the same environment, that had they not banned 'shop' in the Mess they would have become impossibly introverted bores. Another good reason existed for not discussing military business in a Mess. However well trained the Mess waiters and batmen might be about not discussing anything they overheard, there was always the danger that some of them would be tempted to pass on things they had picked up, while, say, waiting at table, to their friends. Such information travelled very fast on the 'grapevine'. The result might be wild rumours circulating in the battalion which could have had a most unsettling effect.

This rather carefully controlled life, with its numerous minor rules and customs, was not at all strange to young officers of the day. They were used to similar controls in their homes, at their school, and at Sandhurst, or to a lesser extent, at the University. On arrival in a regiment it was simple for them to adapt themselves to the customs of the regiment. The background of the officers of the 2nd Scottish Rifles was very similar. They came from about ten public schools— Eton, Harrow, Winchester, and Wellington predominating. Their fathers were in the Army, the Church, or the Law, or were what one might call lesser landed gentry. One or two might have been connected with business in various ways, but would have been successful enough to avoid being directly concerned with 'trade'. Trying to find an understandable classification one would probably get nearest by describing them as 'upper-middle class with upward connections'.

It would be wrong, however, to assume that they were very well off. One or two had a lot of money, but The Cameronians (Scottish Rifles) was not an expensive Regiment as things went before the First World War. The average officer in the 2nd Scottish Rifles had a private income of about £250 a year.

The Regiment itself only insisted on £100 a year though £200 was recommended. This needs to be seen in perspective. The Coldstream Guards at the time considered £400 a year to be the minimum for an ensign on joining, while some of the cavalry regiments expected an officer to have £1,000 a year.* One must remember that an officer's pay as a 2/Lieutenant was 5s. 3d. a day, which is only £95 16s. 0d. a year. So even a relatively inexpensive regiment expected a young man to produce more from his own resources than he could earn. Set against the general level of incomes of the country the young officer of the 2nd Scottish Rifles was very well off; in comparison with members of some of the richer Regiments he was relatively poor. Certain Regiments which were not expensive were sometimes referred to before 1914 as 'younger sons' Regiments', and The Cameronians (Scottish Rifles) could well be put into that bracket.

Taking our young officer with £250 a year of his own, it is interesting to see what he could do with his money. With his pay added, his total income less tax was about £330 a year. The minimum possible Mess bill was £10 a month which accounted for at least £120 a year. A certain amount to drink, some tobacco, clothes and upkeep of uniform would have taken another £80 or so. The £130 left would be available for his own amusements. This might cover local travel, if stationed abroad, or possibly keeping a hunter if at home. Certainly it was not enough to allow of any great extravagance, and for this reason officers of the 2nd Scottish Rifles lived generally abstemious lives and spent most of their energies on their profession and regiment.

In very general terms Regular Army officers before the First World War had a very high status in Great Britain. Within the Army itself different regiments had their own positions on what might be called the 'status ladder'. To understand properly the ramifications of this side of army life

---

* *Cavalry Regiments were the most expensive of all in those days because officers had to provide at least one charger themselves, and could hardly serve in England with less than two hunters and three polo ponies as well. Although officers of the Foot Guards were normally just as well off, they were not bound to incur such big expenses as cavalry officers.*

is almost impossible to anyone not reared in a military environment. However, it is worthy going into the matter, because nearly all human beings are strongly affected by these questions of social degree, often to a much greater extent than they would care to admit.

As I have said the various Regiments demanded certain minimum levels of private income from the officers joining them. These levels were fairly well known, and the Regiments fell into order of status very much in accordance with them. It would be wrong, however, to imagine that things were worked out on an entirely mercenary scale. There were always a number of poorer officers in the most expensive Regiments, who had been accepted on grounds of exceptional promise, or unusual skill at games, or, most likely, ability as horsemen. On the other hand, a young man might be very well off but find himself unable to get into a much sought after Regiment due to other better qualified candidates blocking his way, or because he had not done particularly well at Sandhurst. This man would then find a vacancy in a less popular Regiment. Although to modern eyes this obsession with private incomes looks rather strange, it had a good deal to recommend it. All officers in the Regular Army came from a small section of the population, and even in a quite ordinary Regiment like The Cameronians (Scottish Rifles) they mostly came from a handful of the best schools in the country. All officers had very much the same interests, and the system of regulating entry to Regiments by personal wealth—remembering the many exceptions—ensured that an officer served with others who could do things on the same scale as himself. Thereby the situations were generally avoided where a very rich man could unsettle his fellows by living at a rate they could not afford, or where a poor officer was made to feel out of things by living among people much better off than himself. All this looks more sensible if one thinks of the pre-1914 Army as a way of life that people were prepared to pay to share, rather than as the profession from which thay hoped to earn their livelihood. In that context it is reasonable that an officer should pay the price he could afford.

On the 'status-ladder' the 2nd Scottish Rifles would come

about half-way in the Army. Above them in popular reckoning would be the Household Brigade, the cavalry Regiments, the Green Jackets and the Highland Brigade. Below them would be the bulk of the English county Regiments, artillery other than Horse or Field, engineers, and the few corps and services which then existed. On roughly the same level in general estimation would be the Light Infantry,* the R.H.A. and the Field Artillery, and the best English County Regiments. Before leaving this subject it is best to point out that in the days I am writing about things like class and status were never discussed. At a certain level in society everyone knew the nuances and ramifications of the system, but they were never spoken about directly.

On joining his Regiment, an officer before the First World War provided all his own uniform. Thereafter he was responsible for its upkeep, and replacement when necessary. Today the same system applies, but the officer is given a large grant for the initial purchase. In the 2nd Scottish Rifles an officer had to be in possession of full dress, worn on occasional ceremonial parades and at a Royal levée on first commissioning; patrol dress, consisting of a very heavily frogged jacket with a mass of heavy black braid on the collar and sleeves; undress patrol, similar in cut but without accoutrements; Mess dress, for wear at dinner and at military balls; service dress, khaki, for daily wear; and field service dress. With all, except the last, Douglas tartan trews were worn. In the field breeches for mounted officers, or khaki knickerbockers and long puttees for the others, took the place of the tartan.

Matters of dress tended to take up a great deal of time and attention. A good-looking officer who was always smart could certainly go quite a long way on these qualities alone. Although not openly admitted, the possession of a 'good leg for a boot' could be a definite advantage to an aspiring officer. All this of course reflected similar preoccupations in civilian life at the top of the social scale. The world before 1914

---

* *By the early 20th century the Light Infantry had descended a little, in the 'pecking order' of Regiments, from the position they held at the beginning of the previous century.*

was an easy, civilized place for the rich, and they had ample leisure and wealth to spend much time and money on their clothes and their personal appearance.

In addition to his uniform, and suitable plain clothes for all social activities met with in the civilian world, an officer needed the correct clothes and equipment for different sports and games. Looking at sports first, the horse provided numerous forms. At home hunting, polo, steeplechasing, and point-to-point racing filled the whole year between them. An infantry battalion such as the 2nd Scottish Rifles might not follow these sports in quite the same style as the cavalry, but they usually had their own Regimental race included in the local hunt's point-to-point near whatever barracks they found themselves in the United Kingdom. This was customary for many Regiments. At Colchester in 1910 at the Essex and Suffolk meeting eleven officers had started in the Regimental race. Overseas, polo and racing could be indulged in practically everywhere, the same ponies usually being used for both. The battalion was able to raise teams for polo tournaments in Malta, and a number of officers were interested in racing. One or two bought special racing ponies. These sports were strongly encouraged, as was participation in the other field-sports such as shooting, stalking, and fishing. Abroad, every effort was made to find similar sports to those enjoyed at home.

All these sports were ones the officers indulged in on their own. Just as important were the different games which were played with the men. The main ones were football, hockey, cross-country running, and boxing. Rugger and cricket were also played, but to a limited extent. The great point about hockey was that it could be played almost anywhere, and the British Army used its drill squares as much for hockey as for their obvious purpose. One of the things that pleased the 2nd Scottish Rifles most on moving to St. Andrew's Barracks in Malta was the fact that both the two squares were suitable for hockey, whereas their previous barracks had not been able to provide this particular amenity at all. Unlike hockey, football could only be played on softer surfaces, though anyone used to green pitches in England might think some of the Army's Eastern grounds quite hard enough. Officers were rarely good or keen enough to play in battalion football matches—Stanley Clarke was an exception—but a proportion would always be found playing in company games. Boxing, which has always been popular in the Army, was very much so in the 2nd Scottish Rifles. If an officer happened to be a really good boxer, capable of boxing for the battalion or in local individual championships, he could earn great respect from the men under his command. This still applies today, but fifty years ago, when prize-fighters were still remembered vividly, the ability to use one's fists was an even surer cause of admiration.

Having brought the officers and men together on the games field, it might be a good moment to leave the former and concentrate on the soldiers they commanded. And at the start I want to make the point, as clearly as possible, that the Regular soldier of pre-First World War days was not a drunken wastrel fit only to be described as 'the scum of the earth'. There is a picture in many people's minds of the pre-1914 Army as a mass of brutal savages under the control of bored, foppish officers who hardly ever had any contact with them at all. If I can succeed in this book in dispelling any misconceptions about officers I shall be glad, but I shall be happier still to dispose of lingering and ridiculous misjudgements of their soldiers.

The background of the other ranks—a generic term used until recently to describe all those in the British Army not holding a commission—in the 2nd Scottish Rifles was varied. The majority came from industrial Lanarkshire and Glasgow, and were unskilled labourers before joining up. A good proportion came from other parts of the country, particularly London and the Newcastle area. There were also a number of countrymen from the Western Lowlands of Scotland, and quite a few miners from the mining villages of Lanarkshire. Though many of these men were illiterate, the ranks contained a good leavening of better-educated men. This element was largely composed of men of the middle classes who had fallen out with their families, or had decided to join the Army in search of adventure and travel. A good number of these men became in due course Warrant Officers and senior Non-Commissioned Officers, and were eventually commissioned as Quartermasters.

A good example of the better-educated category was Lieutenant J. Graham, who came out to Malta in late 1914 to take over as Quartermaster from the redoubtable Tommy Finn. He had previously been Regimental Sergeant-Major (R.S.M.) of the battalion, before being given his commission. He was an intelligent and well-educated man, with a quiet and dignified manner. He exercised most effective control without any fuss, and was much admired and respected throughout the battalion.

An example of a different type of man who also had a successful career in the ranks was the man who succeeded Graham as R.S.M., before in his turn earning his commission as a Quartermaster. This was R.S.M. 'Tubby' Wood, whose figure was admirably described by his nickname. He was much more the conventional stage figure of a Regimental Sergeant-Major. His naturally loud and powerful voice was fully employed, sometimes a little more than necessary. However, there was less venom in his tongue than might appear, and his loyalty and long service to the Regiment excused most faults. He had a good sense of humour, and was able to produce the flow of quick repartee which enabled a Warrant Officer to get the best out of men he drilled.

The position of a Regimental Sergeant-Major in the British Army has always been unique. He is the senior member of a unit not holding a commission, and is responsible to the Commanding Officer for the daily routine of unit life. If he is good at his job the unit will reflect his personality in the efficiency with which all simple duties and procedures are carried out. Often the little things, which individually in themselves are not particularly important, add up to be the most important factor of all. This is the same with any corporate body. Where small duties can be carried out in a slipshod way it will eventually be found that bigger matters are allowed to slide. The 2nd Scottish Rifles were lucky during the years preceding 1914 to have Graham and Wood as Regimental Sergeant-Majors, but these two were followed by an even better man in September 1914, just before the battalion left Malta.

R.S.M. J. Chalmers was a great man. He had been awarded the Distinguished Conduct Medal (D.C.M.) in South Africa as a young soldier. In the First World War he was to win the Military Cross, and the Russian Order of St. George for his bravery, as well as being mentioned in despatches. He was also to be recommended for a commission, an honour which he always refused on the grounds that he could do more good for the battalion in his position as Regimental Sergeant-Major than as a junior officer. Throughout his service he was the epitome of the good soldier. He possessed the dignity and quality of character which enabled him to meet his seniors and his subordinates on equal footing, and to play his part in the military scheme of things without fear or favour. His complete integrity, coupled with the highest standards, which he invariably lived up to himself, made him the perfect leader. The force of his personality and example was particularly felt in the Sergeants' Mess.

The Sergeants' Mess in a British battalion is used by Warrant Officers, Colour-Sergeants and Sergeants. Before 1914 the only Warrant Officers were the Regimental Sergeant-Major and the Bandmaster. Each company had a Colour-Sergeant who looked after the discipline of the men as well as their pay, clothing and accommodation. When the number of companies in a battalion was reduced from eight to four, the Colour-Sergeant's duties were split among two men. A Company Sergeant-Major (C.S.M.) was appointed to look after discipline, drill, and documentation, while a Company Quarter-Master-Sergeant (C.Q.M.S.) was allotted to each company to handle pay, clothing, accommodation, etc. Company Sergeant-Majors were made Warrant Officers, Class II, and from the same date Bandmasters and Regimental Sergeant-Majors were referred to as Warrant Officers, Class I. The changes did not, however, alter the way in which life carried on in the Sergeants' Mess.

The Mess was used for feeding and recreation, but usually only a few senior members lived in the Mess building, the remainder having 'bunks', or small private rooms, in the same buildings as the rest of the men in their companies. It has often been said that the Sergeants' Mess is the back-bone of a unit, and there is a great deal of truth in this. Certainly no battalion can run well with a bad one. In the Mess the Regimental Sergeant-Major is absolute master, and the members take their lead from him not only in matters of etiquette and behaviour, but in the whole pattern of their lives. A man of the calibre of Chalmers could gather around him a group of men whose loyalty to him was absolute, and on whom his example, constantly refreshed by daily contact, was stronger than any other influence.

The Warrant Officers and Sergeants of the 2nd Scottish Rifles were of a very high standard indeed. Among them were C.S.M. Docherty of 'D' Company and C.S.M. Culley of 'A' Company. Docherty was small, neat, and quiet, but a very strong character, and possessed of a clear mind and excellent judgement. He had won the Distinguished Conduct Medal in the South African War. Culley was an impressive figure, being very strongly built, with black hair and a big black moustache. He was a kindly man, and balanced firmness with tolerance to just the right degree. Two other first-class C.S.M.s were Conway and McBeath, both of whom were commissioned in late 1914. (Conway returned to 'B' Company as an officer in early 1915, and was badly wounded at Neuve Chapelle.)

In any Scottish battalion an important figure is the Pipe-Major, who can in fact hold any rank from Sergeant to Warrant Officer, Class II. The Pipe-Major of the 2nd Scottish Rifles was quite junior, having transferred from being a Corporal in the Cameron Highlanders to take up the appointment when the battalion was in Colchester. His name, suitably enough, was Cameron. Although quite young for his position in those days, he was a great success. A fine looking man, he was not only a good piper himself but an excellent teacher of young pipers. When the War came he insisted on leaving the Pipes and Drums and joining a company as a platoon Sergeant. As such he was killed at Neuve Chapelle.

One of the strong Cockney element in the Sergeants' Mess was Sergeant Bryant, whom Captain M. D. Kennedy remembers vividly. He recalls Bryant drilling him as a newly arrived subaltern in Malta, and very sharply ticking him off for stamping his feet in the manner taught at Sandhurst by Guards Sergeant-Majors instead of doing the quick turns of a Rifleman. 'None of your Guards tricks 'ere, Sir,' the shocked voice of Bryant had reminded him.

The Sergeants' Mess was run on roughly similar lines to the Officers' Mess, except that the food was less varied, and the evening meal was tea at 6 p.m. and not dinner. The R.S.M. was treated in the Mess in the same way as the Commanding Officer in the Officers' Mess, and the same rules applied about not talking 'shop'. Entertainment consisted of social evenings and games nights, to which officers were invited. There were also occasional dances, and the big event of the year was the Christmas Draw. Drinking could be heavy in a Sergeants' Mess, and it required a strong R.S.M. to ensure that it did not get out of hand. On an ordinary evening there would be many games of dominoes, whist and euchre* going on in the Mess, and the general atmosphere would be similar to that in a good country pub at home. A higher percentage of Warrant Officers and Sergeants were married than officers, but even so the majority were single men, and the Mess would normally be fairly full.

All the men below the rank of Sergeant were described by the general term of 'rank and file'. This referred to the fact that they were all in the ranks together when formed up on parade by companies. The officers stood in front of each company, the C.S.M. on the right flank, the C.Q.M.S. on the left flank, and the Sergeants behind. Corporals, Lance-corporals, and Privates were all together in the ranks in fours. It should not be assumed from this, however, that the rank of Corporal did not carry any weight. The average length of time from joining it took a man to reach the different rungs on the promotion ladder was four years to Lance-corporal, eight years to Corporal and twelve to Sergeant. A full Corporal was therefore likely to be a mature man with wide experience, and he would not allow his authority to be taken lightly. This

* *An American card game for two, three or four persons.*

[38]

authority was backed by official rules which set him very much apart from the rest of the men. Although the junior N.C.O.s lived in barrack-rooms with the Privates they were forbidden to walk out together in the evenings. Also, a Private always had to address a Corporal by his rank, and outside the barrack-room stood to attention when speaking to him. The importance attached to these rules in all Regular battalions is brought out in Robert Graves' *Goodbye to All That*. He describes how his Commanding Officer in the 1st Battalion The Royal Welch Fusiliers in 1916 called all his officers together, and after issuing a general 'rocket' to them went on:

I have come here principally to tell you of a very disagreeable occurrence. As I left my orderly-room this morning, I came upon a group of soldiers; I will not particularize their company. One of these soldiers was in conversation with a lance-corporal. You may not believe me, but it is a fact that he addressed the corporal by his Christian name: HE CALLED HIM JACK! And the corporal made no protest! To think that the First Battalion has sunk to a level where it is possible for such familiarity to exist between N.C.O.s and the men under their command! Naturally, I put the corporal under arrest, and he appeared before me at once on the charge of 'conduct unbecoming an N.C.O.' I reduced him to the ranks, and awarded the man Field punishment for using insubordinate language to an N.C.O. . . .[6]

The rights and wrongs of such insistence on minor matters are arguable, but this story indicates how important the old Regular Army thought them.

Life for the rank and file was very much a matter of restrictions. The day was controlled from reveille at 6 a.m. to lights-out at 10 p.m. A man had little free time when he could do exactly as he liked, and Sunday mornings were filled with the different phases of Church parade—company inspection, battalion inspection, march to Church, the service, and then possibly a march past a senior officer afterwards. When men were completely free they often indulged in military training of their own accord, and it was quite normal for them to go to the range on Saturday afternoons. This was partly due to an interest in shooting for its own sake, and partly because of the cash value of being a good shot. Each year all Sergeants and below in the infantry had to qualify on the range. Proficiency pay of 6d. a day was awarded to Marksmen and 1st Class shots. For a Private being paid 1s. a day skill with his rifle could earn a 50 per cent rise in pay, which was something very worth while.

The social life of the soldier was entirely wrapped up in the battalion. To give an idea of it, I can hardly do better than quote from a fascinating article which appeared in *The Covenanter*, the magazine of The Cameronians (Scottish Rifles), in February 1963. It was written by ex-C.S.M. Robert Leggat, and in fact refers to the years after the First World War. However, the conditions he describes are almost exactly the same as they were overseas before 1914. Having described how he joined up straight from school, Leggat continues:

In those days the army carried its own life with it wherever it went, and you lived pretty much the same, whether you were in India or China or any other place. You lived between the barrack-room and the wet canteen, without any social life at all. For all the years I was in India before the war, I was never in a house. Never. If you were up on the Frontier in a place like Razmak you lived inside barbed wire, but even where the folk weren't in the habit of taking pot-shots at you there was nothing to go out for. You'd maybe buy a few things in the bazaar, but that was all. . . .

It's strange to look back on some of it now.

There was a ritual every evening. The men would make themselves absolutely spotless—uniform pressed, boots polished, hair plastered down, bonnet on just so—as if every one of them had a girl-friend waiting at the gate. But they had no girl-friends, and they were never out of the gate. They went straight down to the wet canteen and got drunk. That was what they got dressed up for.

It didn't matter what continent you were in, it was always the same. Everything was organized inside the battalion—football, rugby, hockey, boxing. You got the odd leave in a rest camp, but that was just the Army again without the parades. On $3\frac{1}{2}d$. a day ration money you couldn't spend a leave anywhere else, without going broke as soon as you started. You got a paid leave home once in six years before you left.[7]

What of the men who lived this life? It is not easy to generalize—the rank and file form less of a pattern than their seniors, all of whom were gathered together by much tighter processes of selection and into smaller groups. Fortunately Kennedy has provided pen-portraits which bring to life some of the men serving at the lower levels in the Scottish Rifles.

One who at first did not impress Kennedy was Private McHugh from Glasgow:

As a peacetime soldier he had struck me as a rather dour, surly sort of fellow, who disliked being ordered about. The War showed him up in a very different light. There was no more dependable man in the platoon and no one more ready to do his full share of work and over. The smart peacetime soldier is not always the best in the trenches, whereas men like McHugh, who have shown no very great promise before, prove themselves to be possessed of wonderfully fine qualities, totally unsuspected in the quiet times of peace.

McHugh I would say represented quite a strong element in the battalion. The Scottish character inclines towards this sort of man, and anyone who has served in a Scottish Regiment will easily recognize the type.

Of course there were many who were both smart in the days of peace and good soldiers in action. Kennedy had two excellent Corporals of this type called Forster and Harrison. These were the kind of men who in course of time would have become senior N.C.O.s, being as much at home in barracks as in the trenches. Much of the efficiency of the Army depended on junior leaders of this sort. Unfortunately Harrison never had a chance of fulfilling his early promise, being, like so many others, killed at Neuve Chapelle.

Another type often met in the ranks before 1914 was the man who had the ability to become a junior N.C.O. but could not resist the temptation of drink. Kennedy describes one:

Then there was Private Murray, who also hailed from Clydeside. A typical 'old soldier', with 17 or 18 years colour service to his credit, he too was the kind of man who could be trusted to do his best when things were at their worst. His one failing was a liking for strong drink. He had been promoted more than once to the rank of Lance-corporal, but he had never been able to retain that rank for more than a day or two, as he invariably celebrated his promotion by 'throwing a drunk'. His prompt demotion then followed as a matter of course.

Of the same breed as Murray was Private Plank. He was invalided out of the Army during the War as a result of wounds, and while in hospital wrote to his Company Commander, Ferrers. Recalling the long years they had served together he ended: 'I know, Sir, that I sometimes went on the wallaby, but thank God I never did anything to disgrace the Regiment!'

Drunkenness was the main crime in the Army. In a Scottish Regiment it was more prevalent than in an English, largely because heavy drinking was the main outlet of the civil population in Scotland, and particularly in and around Glasgow. When one considers what the existence of the poorest classes was like in a Scottish industrial city before 1914 it is not suprising. Life was hard and rough, and the cold, grey streets and prevailing ugliness on every side must have been daunting to even the bravest spirits. Drink, mainly cheap wine and whisky, provided a way of escape. When they drank it was to gain oblivion. The cheery, social drinking common in an English country pub was unknown in Scotland; a man went to a bar to get drunk and forget for an hour or two the miseries of his daily round. Scottish soldiers brought the same outlook into the Army with them.

This hard life outside the Army must be borne very much in mind when one is looking at the life of the Regular soldier in 1914. Conditions in the poor quarters of Glasgow and other big cities do not make a pretty story. If one feels that Army life was rather hard and dreary, as it certainly was by modern standards, one must remember that in comparison with what a man may have faced at home it could prove a haven. The order, the discipline, the cleanliness, the security could mean much to a man reared in a slum tenement. Food was ample, if sometimes not particularly appetizing, and the pay was regular although small. Because of these things the Regular soldier before the First World War was generally a happy man.

Apart from the material conditions of his life being in many ways superior to the harsh existence outside the service, the soldier found happiness in two other things—comradeship and loyalty to his Regiment. These again meant more to many of the men than it is easy to imagine. Along with the hunger and greyness of life outside there often went loneliness and a sense of being unwanted. Lord Moran shows how much it could mean to a man from a slum to find that he was a member of a worth-while organization where he was really wanted:

I do not doubt that many unpromising specimens were transformed by training; in particular by that part of training which consists in inculcating *esprit de corps*. I remember men recruited at the street corner by starvation who came to act on the principle that if the Regiment lived it did not matter if they died, though they did not put it that way.[8]

Whether the rank and file of pre-1914 were different from men of other generations is difficult to judge. Ferrers told Kennedy in 1924, when the two were discussing this very problem, that he felt that the soldier of before the First World War was a tougher man, but in many ways easier to manage than those he found himself commanding ten years later. He found the post-war soldier 'rather puerile' in comparison; less drunken, but more inclined to petty dishonesty; less rough, but more apt to look for help in time of difficulty, rather than standing square on his own two feet. My own suspicion is that the men of the British Army in pre-1914 days were just a little better than soldiers of any other time. Their generally hard early lives had taught them both to fend for themselves and to endure privation and discomfort, while the simple, disciplined life of the Army gradually developed their latent qualities. One should think of the Privates of the 2nd Scottish Rifles in Malta, therefore, as men of many varied types, with numerous different facets to their characters, but held together by toughness of spirit, strong discipline, and most important of all, fierce loyalty to the Regiment. This last quality cannot be over-emphasized—it is essential to realize that it was the strongest single influence on the lives of everyone in the battalion.

The course of these lives, in peacetime at least, was straight-forward and untroubled. For the men the day started with reveille at 6 a.m. (The modern military habit of using the twenty-four hour clock and talking about '0600 hours' was unknown.) Reveille was sounded by a bugler, and as the last notes died away a piper at his side struck up *Johnnie Cope*.* Throughout the rest of the day bugle calls controlled the barracks. Every man had to know all the calls, and an essential part of his training was to learn them. Certain of the calls were sounded at set times, such as Reveille, meal calls, Retreat, Last Post and Lights Out. At all these a piper followed the bugler, playing such tunes as *Brose and Butter* after each meal call, and *Soldier, lie down on your wee pickle straw* at Lights Out. For others, the bugler played on his own. These were the calls which normally summonsed members of the battalion to report to important people. If, for example, the R.S.M. wanted to see the C.S.M. of 'A' Company he told the bugler to call him. The bugler then played 'A' Company's special call, followed by the number of 'G's' used to signify C.S.M. It was a very simple and efficient system, and in the days when few soldiers had watches it had the added advan-tage of letting them know the time by reference to the set calls.

At reveille a mug of tea was usually available, known throughout the Army as 'gun-fire'. At 6.30 a.m. on normal days physical training (P.T.) took place for about half an hour. Junior officers had to be on parade, and either did exercises in the ranks with the men or acted as instructors. Some mornings a company might go for a short run. On occasions during the summer an early-morning drill parade might take place, usually on Saturdays at 7 a.m. This would be either an Adjutant's parade, with all officers junior to the Adjutant present, or a Regimental Sergeant-Major's parade, on which no officers would appear.

After breakfast Company orders were held at about 9 a.m. The main purpose was not so much to give out orders, as to

---

* Johnnie Cope *is a traditional reveille tune played in most Scottish Regiments. It is the tune of a comic song which starts 'Hey! Johnnie Cope! are ye wakened yet?' The reference is to General Cope who was defeated by the dawn attack at Preston-pans in 1745 when he and his men were all surprised asleep in their camp.*

[44]

administer discipline, and to interview men who wished to to see their Company Commander about some personal problem. The Company Commander sat at his desk in his office with the junior officers of the Company standing behind him. Men were marched in by the C.S.M., those who had charges against them for trial being hatless and escorted by two other men of equal or senior rank. Most minor offences were dealt with by the Company Commander either by a ticking off, award of extra fatigues, or confinement to barracks. A more serious case would be remanded for trial by the Commanding Officer, who held his orders each day at about 10 a.m. If the Company Commander had a member of his company due to appear in front of the Commanding Officer he would go to the Orderly Room to be present when the man was marched in. This was so that he could answer questions about the soldier's character and general standard of behaviour if the Commanding Officer wanted to hear about these things.

At some time after the Company orders the Company Commander, if not at Battalion Orderly Room, or one of the other officers would inspect the junior ranks of the company and their living accommodation. Great attention was paid to the care and cleanliness of equipment and clothing, and in the barrack-rooms every detail had to be right. Blankets had to be folded on beds to an exact size, and all kit not in use had to be folded and stored in exactly the same way by every man in the company. The private soldier had to get used to standing for long periods either being inspected, or waiting to be. His officers and N.C.O.s in their turn were expected to examine every item with minutest care.

The accent placed in the Army life on cleanliness and 'spit-and-polish', or to use a modern expression 'bull', needs to be seen in its correct light. Much of it was overdone, and there was always the tendency for the outward display to be brought into such prominence that it completely wrecked the purpose for which an inspection was carried out. For example, many old soldiers kept a complete set of spotlessly clean kit which was neatly folded and ready at all times to be laid out for inspection. They actually wore, on the other hand, various items such as socks and shirts which were never shown, and whose cleanliness and state of repair might be far from perfect. It was also known for washing-rooms and lavatories (ablutions and latrines in Army terminology) to be kept spotless, while the men actually used old buckets to wash in and the bushes behind their barrack-blocks as lavatories. But these abuses were rare; certainly in a battalion like the 2nd Scottish Rifles, where the officers were close to the men, such things could not occur.

There are two reasons why the frequent inspections were most important. In part it was due to the fact that many of the soldiers had simply never been brought up to observe normal rules of personal hygiene. A man who had started life in a slum tenement with one cold tap and one lavatory for six families, numbering possibly fifty people, took a long time to learn the importance of cleanliness. For these men the constant inspections were essential; for the others who had been lucky enough to be brought up better it was no doubt a nuisance, but obviously there could be no discrimination between one man and another in such matters. Furthermore, the tendency in corporate bodies is often for the lowest to drag down the others, and many men brought up to tidiness and cleanliness might have slipped back if not watched. The other reason why insistence on a high standard in these matters was so important was the danger of disease caused by dirt in so many of the Army's stations overseas. The war was always on against skin complaints in particular, and a man who failed to keep himself and his clothes clean could easily render himself unfit for service.

After Company office and the morning inspections were completed, the day's training would start. For the private not employed on some specialist task, training fell under three main headings—drill, weapon training and shooting, and route marches. Field tactics were also taught, but the essential qualities expected of the soldier were to be smart and steady on parade, to shoot well, and to be able to march. Because of these relatively simple requirements, training normally ended at midday, and the afternoons were devoted to games. The most important specialists in the battalion were the signallers and the members of the Animal Transport section. Signalling was carried out by four main methods, all of which were visual. These were small flag morse, lamp using morse, semaphore, and heliograph. Telephones had just been introduced in the form of field sets, but were not widely distributed. Wireless had passed through various trial stages, but was only used between divisional and higher headquarters. Regimental signallers had not yet been introduced to it at all. The transport in the battalion was all horse drawn, and consisted of waggons and field kitchens. The latter was a useful vehicle which enabled meals to be prepared on the line of march. Also in the care of the transport section were the officers' chargers, of which there were nine. These were allotted to the Commanding Officer, Second-in-Command, Company Commanders, Adjutant, Signal Officer, and naturally the Transport Officer himself. For those who worked with the transport there was not much time off. The proper care of horses was looked upon as supremely important throughout the whole Army. Not only had all the horses to be well fed and shod, but they had to be groomed so that every speck of dirt was removed and their coats shone. Also all the 'tack', the harness and saddlery, had to be kept spotless. In spite of the hard work the transport section was a popular place, and men vied with each other to be selected for it. Partly this was caused by a desire to get away from drill and parades into the more homely atmosphere of the stables, and partly from a genuine fondness for animals found in many of the men. Often a soldier would become absolutely devoted to the horses in his care, and would spend much of his small pay on buying sugar and titbits for them.

Just as the course of each day followed a set pattern, the year was divided into recognized training phases. In the United Kingdom from October each year until the following February was known as the 'individual' training period. During this time officers and men concentrated on learning those skills which affected them personally as individuals. For example, it was during these months that new signallers would be trained, or that the R.S.M. would hold courses (known as 'Cadres') for junior N.C.O.s to teach them the way he wanted them to carry out their duties. Leave was taken during the months of individual training so that all ranks would be available for the more important phases in the spring and summer.

In March, again in the United Kingdom, company training began, with simple tactical exercises and marching predominating. After this came battalion training in the summer, and eventually manœuvres in the early autumn. The scope of this later training depended on the station. A battalion in the south of England would find itself taking part in large-scale manœuvres on Salisbury Plain with up to five divisions engaged; for the 2nd Scottish Rifles in Malta the culmination of the year would be an exercise against another battalion.

Because of this shortage of space for field training in Malta, and also because of the heat in the summer, the training year there was different from the normal pattern at home. Little could be done at any time beyond individual training and small exercises, and so the winter became the more important training period, and the summer was used for leave. From May to October therefore saw little activity in Malta other than the simplest training, and of course the endless fatigues which occupied so much of the private soldier's time in any station.

One of the results of the pattern of training in Malta, affected as it was by geography and climate, was to highlight an important aspect of the training of the British infantry before 1914. I refer to its much higher standards of marksmanship and fitness than of tactics. In any theatre there was a tendency for tactical training to be sketchy; in Malta it was almost completely ignored. Tactical doctrine in the Army was based on *Field Service Regulations, Part I (Operations)*. This excellent handbook was known to officers, and was studied carefully for examination purposes. On the other hand there is little evidence of the lessons contained in it percolating down to the private soldier. One cannot avoid gaining the impression that tactics were something of an academic study for officers rather than a vital part of the military knowledge of all ranks.

[48]

The official teaching on the assault of an enemy position was the use of fire and movement in combination. While one part of a formation fired at the enemy to keep their heads down, all the time supported by artillery, the other would rush forward. Then the two parts would reverse their roles, and in this way the attacking force would get near to the enemy position.

The object became the building-up of a heavy line roughly 200 yards short of the hostile front. If this line could first beat down resistance by sheer fire-power it would postpone its advance until it had done so. If that were not completely achieved but the prospects of a charge looked good, the signal would be given by whistles and by hand, and the whole line would dash forward.[9]

Whether many members of the 2nd Scottish Rifles thought much about theories of this nature I do not know, but I think it is doubtful.

What is certain is that those things they did concern them-selves with were done with great enthusiasm. Their approach to their training might be limited, but they were keen. To quote again the officer whose comments I have used earlier in this chapter: 'Amongst a large majority of all ranks there was a strong urge, almost ambition, towards professional excellence.' The question of 'professionalism' will appear again later, but the impression I want to leave before follow-ing the battalion to France and Neuve Chapelle is that of a well organized, well trained, and proud body of men. There existed a remarkable degree of mutual confidence between the officers; amongst the Warrant Officers and Sergeants; and between these two bodies and the ranks below. For all pride in being members of the battalion and pride in their profes-sional ability were driving forces which overshadowed all other considerations. It is not suggested that they were unique in this respect, but that the attitude and example of some out-standing officers and Warrant Officers was cumulative in effect and permeated the whole unit. As the battalion marched out of St. Andrew's Barracks for the last time on 15 September

1914, with the Pipes and Drums at the head of the companies formed in column of route, it was typical of the best of the 'contemptible little Army' which was to prove itself before long, whatever its limitations, one of the staunchest the world has ever known.

The Battle of
Neuve Chapelle

I do not believe that a better battalion landed in France.[1]

From GENERAL JACK'S DIARY 1914–1918. Written
on 31 August 1915, shortly after he joined the
2nd Scottish Rifles

REMEMBERING THE EXTRAORDINARY optimism of the
British Army in 1914, and the feeling that the War would be
over by Christmas, one can imagine how delighted the 2nd
Scottish Rifles must have been to sail out of Valetta harbour
on 15 September. At last they would feel themselves a part of
the great conflict which so stirred men's imaginations in those
early days. At last, after years of training for war, they were
to face the reality which must often have seemed so remote
when carrying out peacetime manœuvres; as regular soldiers
they were now going to be used for the purpose for which they
had so long prepared.

The troopship arrived a week later at Southampton, and the
battalion marched to a tented camp on Baddesley Common,
near Romsey. It became part of the 23rd Infantry Brigade
along with the 2nd Bn The Devonshire Regiment, 2nd Bn The
West Yorkshire Regiment and 2nd Bn The Middlesex Regiment. A few days later it moved to Hursley Park, near
Winchester, where a large draft of men joined from the 4th
(Special Reserve) Bn of the Regiment. An element of these
men is described in the official Regimental History:

Many of them wore ribbons of Boer War medals and a few of them
were perhaps past their prime. There was one man at least who had

completed twelve years' colour service before the outbreak of the
South African Campaign. He had re-enlisted in 'the old Regiment'
for the Boer War and again for this one. He thought this would
have to be the last time he joined up 'as his age was beginning to
tell on him'.[2]

The return of these reservists to the battalion was very welcome. On the whole they found little difficulty in settling down
again into a military life. The biggest snag that most of them
found in their process of readjustment was getting used to
wearing army boots again, and to marching long distances.
The older ones were quickly fitted into jobs where their
experience and maturity outweighed any physical weakness.
Even an active service battalion had to employ many men as
cooks, storemen, clerks, etc., and many of the elderly reservists
were put into these sort of jobs.

On 4 November 1914 the battalion embarked on the troopship *Cornishman,* and the next day arrived at Le Havre,
where it spent a few days at a Rest Camp before moving up
into the line on 8 November. On 14 November the battalion
went into the trenches for the first time. The War had now
settled down into the static pattern of trench warfare which
was to change little until 1918. They took over from a
French Regiment, the 156th, south-west of Messines. Later in
the War men were to learn how to make themselves as comfortable as possible in the trenches, but at this stage the most
extraordinary rules were in force. No smoking was allowed, nor
was it permitted to have braziers for warmth or fires for
boiling water. Presumably these rules went back to the Boer
War, when a flame or a puff of smoke had given away a position
to the enemy watching across the veldt. The result was that
all food had to be eaten cold, and the only drink was cold
water. The Regimental History quotes one of the officers:

Nothing to see but bare mud walls of a narrow muddy trench;
nowhere to sit but on a wet muddy ledge; no shelter of any kind
against the weather except the clothes you are wearing; no
exercise that you can take in order to warm yourself and set up
circulation, and not even a pipe or a cigarette, or a book or a
paper. . . .[3]

The 2nd Scottish Rifles had arrived in the War with a vengeance.

For the next four months there was to be little change from the pattern of trench warfare at its dullest and most uncomfortable. Periods of three or four days in the line alternated with similar periods in reserve in billets two or three miles to the rear. In spite of the lack of activity, however, there was a steadily mounting roll of casualties, mainly caused by German snipers and by stray shots. At this stage shelling was fairly light, and when it did start everyone took cover. Machine-guns were not great killers at this time, because again when a burst was fired all heads were kept low. The sniper, however, was a different danger altogether. The Germans kept their snipers for long periods in the same areas, and they came to know every yard of the British trenches. To start with the sentries of the 2nd Scottish Rifles watched through loopholes in the parapet of the trenches. One by one they were shot through the head, as the enemy snipers with telescopic sights on their rifles dealt with the loopholes in rotation. The battalion was forced to fill in the holes and rely on periscopes for observation. These periscopes did not become an official issue until 1915, and were purchased privately to begin with. Due to their limited field of view they were not very satisfactory, particularly for officers, who needed to study the enemy lines constantly and in detail. The Regimental History describes what happened:

Officers found it necessary to examine the opposing trenches through field glasses, and infinite care had to be taken when this was done. The least exposure drew a sniper's bullet. The black glengarry drew fire at once, so a brown woolly cap was worn; that was much less conspicuous. The head was then raised very slowly into a niche in the sandbags on top of the trench and lowered just as slowly when the examination was completed; an apprehensive operation.[4]

In spite of the care taken the battalion lost seven officers killed and five wounded between November 1914 and March 1915, with losses among the N.C.O.s and men in the same proportion. Some of these losses had been sustained in minor

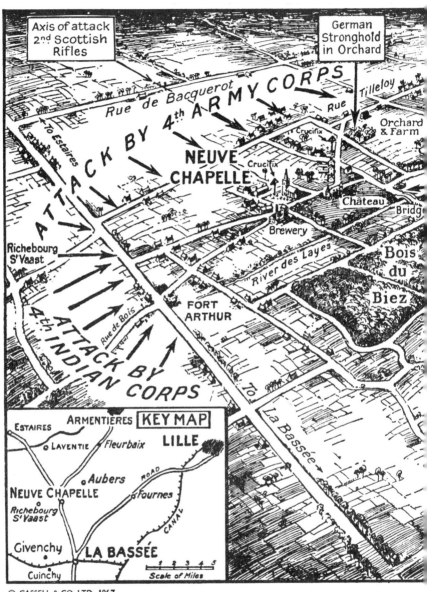

Axis of attack
2nd Scottish
Rifles

German
Stronghold
in Orchard

Rue de Bacquerot

ATTACK BY 4th ARMY CORPS

To Estaires

Tilleloy

Rue

Crucifix

Orchard
& Farm

NEUVE
CHAPELLE

Crucifix

Château

Bridge

Brewery

Richebourg
S'Vaast

River des Layes

Bois
du
Biez

ATTACK BY
4th INDIAN CORPS

Rue de Bois

FORT
ARTHUR

To

La Bassée

KEY MAP

ARMENTIÈRES

ESTAIRES

LAVENTIE   Fleurbaix

LILLE

ROAD

Aubers

Fournes

NEUVE CHAPELLE

Richebourg
S'Vaast

CANAL

Givenchy

LA BASSÉE

Cuinchy

1 2 3 4 5
Scale of Miles

© CASSELL & CO. LTD. 1967

*A view of the battle-field of Neuve Chapelle based on a contemporary
picture map published by the* Daily Mail.

actions and raids, but the majority had been picked off by snipers. It was an unnerving business to live with this constant unseen danger; and when taken in conjunction with the excessively uncomfortable conditions in the trenches produced a most dispiriting effect on all ranks.

Just how uncomfortable the conditions were is brought out in the following passages from Captain Malcolm Kennedy's manuscript. From the time the battalion arrived in France until he was wounded at Neuve Chapelle, Kennedy, then a Lieutenant, was in 'B' Company under 'Uncle' Ferrers. Describing the winter 1914–1915 he has written:

As the time wore on, the weather conditions grew steadily worse. Trenches became waterlogged; in some instances they were abandoned in favour of hastily constructed sand-bag defences. To attempt to dig new trenches was useless, as water was struck after digging down only a few inches. Wherever possible, however, the old trenches remained occupied, as they provided better cover than a mere wall of sand-bags. Defence works of the latter kind offered too tempting a mark for the enemy gunners. They would, in fact, have been entirely useless, had it not been that their closeness to the German trenches gave them a certain amount of immunity from shell fire, as the German gunners were afraid of hitting their own people.

Thanks to the issue of gum boots which was made after a time, it was possible to wade about in most of the trenches without getting soaked through. In some parts, however, even this form of protection was of no avail, as the boots came only to the knees whereas the water came over them. One of my most vivid recollections is the sight of our C.O., making his daily tour of inspection of the trenches with the water-mark high up his riding breeches—a clear indication of the depth of water through which he had been forced to wade in some of the worst sections of the trench.

This constant immersion in icy cold water played havoc with the feet, and made them swell to such an extent that at times it was agony to keep on one's boots. To take them off, however, to gain relief would have been fatal, as it would have been impossible to pull them on again. . . .

No one who was not there can fully appreciate the excruciating agonies and misery through which the men had to go in those days before anti-'trench-feet' measures were taken, and other similar measures adopted, to make trench life more endurable. Paddling about by day, sometimes with water above the knees; standing at night, hour after hour on sentry duty, while the drenched boots, puttees and breeches became stiff like cardboard with ice from the freezing cold air. Rain, snow, sleet, wind, mud and general discomfort all added their bit to the misery of trench life. There was the constant danger to oneself and one's friends from enemy action, which took a steady and ever increasing toll of lives that could ill be spared; the terrible monotony of the daily and nightly routine; manual labour and sentry duty night and day with insufficient sleep; never warm, never dry; dog-tired and weary in body and mind.

Among men living a life like this a breakdown in morale would have been understandable. I am assured, however, that there was none. Kennedy remembers one case of a man shooting himself in the hand in another company, and some speculation that it may have been intentional rather than the accident the man himself claimed it to be. But on the whole, while most officers and men were tired and rather dispirited, there was a complete determination to 'stick it out' whatever the conditions.

As February 1915, a particularly foul month in terms of weather, drew to a close rumours were circulating that a spring offensive was to be expected. The 2nd Scottish Rifles looked forward to any sort of activity that would break the dreadful monotony of life in the trenches. Everyone longed for something to happen that would liven up the course of the War, and above all would enable them to move freely and have a chance of closing with the enemy. On 2 March 1915 came the word that all had been waiting for.

The previous evening the battalion had come out of the line and had moved into billets in a village called Pont Richon. In the morning all officers were assembled at Battalion Headquarters and sentries were posted around the building to ensure that there should be no eavesdroppers. Colonel Bliss then told them that the 8th Division, of which the 23rd Infantry Brigade was part, was to be withdrawn to Merville for a short rest. After this rest it was to prepare for an attack on the German-held village of Neuve Chapelle. The attack at Neuve Chapelle was to be the break-out of a big offensive by the British First Army towards Lille. The First Army now numbered six divisions and was commanded by General Sir Douglas Haig. As the officers listened to Colonel Bliss their excitement mounted. It seemed that this was to be the start of a great move to sweep the Germans out of their trenches and to open the War up again after the long period of static operations. (To clarify all the different formations and commanders the Diagram on page 239 has been produced.)

Kennedy describes what happened after the Colonel's talk on 2 March:

Marching to Merville later that same day, the Battalion spent the next few days in an arduous programme of physical training, bayonet fighting, bombing practice, route marches, attack schemes and other forms of activity—hardly a rest in the strict sense of the term, but a badly needed change after the prolonged inertia of trench life. News of the coming assault was still confined to officers only and the need for strict secrecy about it was stressed, but it was clear to all that something unusual was brewing and spirits rose accordingly.

On 7 March orders for the coming attack were given to the officers. As these were operation orders they came down the channel of command in the normal way, and were given first by the Commanding Officer to Company Commanders, and by them in their turn to Platoon Commanders. At each level the officer giving out the orders explained the general plan, and then fitted in his own instructions for his particular body of men. The general plan is shown on the Picture Map, and this was explained to start with. They were then told that in the 4th Corps sector the attack on Neuve Chapelle would be carried out by the whole of the 8th Division, with a Brigade of the 7th in support. The fire of over two hundred guns would be concentrated on to the divisional front. Within the 8th Division, the 23rd Infantry Brigade would be on the left, with the 25th on its right. The first objective of the 8th Division was the German front line, and support trenches. The second objective was the village of Neuve Chapelle, and the farm known as the Moated Grange. This second objective was to be attacked at the same time as the 4th Indian Corps assaulted

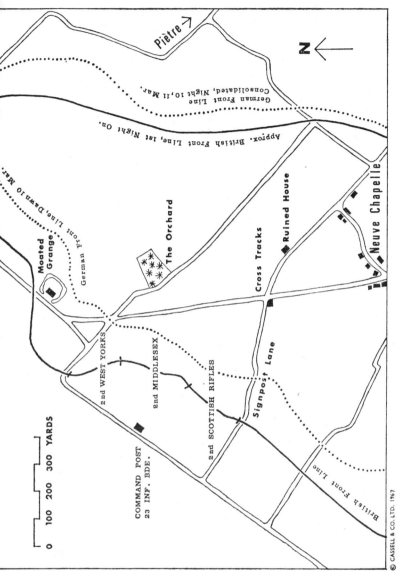

Piètre →

N ←

German Front Line Consolidated, Night 10, 11 Mar.

Approx. British Front Line, 1st Night On.

German Front Line, Dawn 10 Mar.

Moated Grange

The Orchard

Ruined House

Cross Tracks

Neuve Chapelle

2nd WEST YORKS

2nd MIDDLESEX

Signpost Lane

2nd SCOTTISH RIFLES

British Front Line

COMMAND POST
23 INF. BDE.

0   100   200   300   YARDS

Sketch Map

© CASSELL & CO. LTD. 1967

it from the South. The Sketch Map can be referred to from this stage.

Within the 2nd Scottish Rifles, which was detailed as the right assault battalion of the 23rd Brigade with the Middlesex on its left, the two forward companies were to be 'A' and 'B'. Because of the narrow frontage allotted to a company only two platoons could go over the top together. The other two platoons in each company had therefore to follow these leading ones a moment or two later. 'C' and 'D' Companies were nominated to be in support, and to move forward in the same formations as 'A' and 'B' but two hundred yards behind them. The junior officers were tremendously elated to get definite orders at last, and visions arose of a crushing defeat of the enemy and the start of a triumphal progress to Berlin. This elation was not dampened by the warning that those members of the leading platoons who came through the battle alive should think themselves lucky, nor by the warning that heavy casualties were also be be expected in the preliminary bombardment. The German trenches were so close to those from which the battalion was to launch its attack that any shells falling short would almost inevitably land on the men waiting to go into the attack. After each Company Commander had finished giving his orders he passed round aerial photographs for the junior officers to study and copy in the form of sketch maps to use on the day of the battle.

The Company Commanders had been left to decide for themselves whether they and the officers in their companies would carry swords in the attack. 'Uncle' Ferrers in 'B' Company had no hesitation at all in ordering swords to be carried in his company, and so it happened for probably the last time in any battle in the War that a proportion of the officers of the 2nd Scottish Rifles led their men into action with swords in hand.

While the troops who were going to make the attack were getting themselves ready, other preparations were going on all around them. The artillery were given elaborate timed plans of fire to be put down in support of the infantry. Batteries were given specific tasks, and these included cutting the enemy wire in front of his trenches, pulverizing his actual positions with a violent burst of concentrated fire just before the British infantry advanced, and finally lifting as the advance started and firing to the rear of his front line into his support and communication trenches. Most of the guns supporting the 8th Division were moved into position several days before the operation, and they were anchored down to platforms of heavy timber. They then 'registered' on the targets allotted to them for the attack, firing at them under the control of an observation officer so that the exact range to each target could be noted. Unfortunately two six-inch howitzer batteries did not arrive out from England until the eve of the battle. It happened that these were the guns allotted to the area to be fought over by the 2nd Scottish Rifles and the 2nd Middlesex, but because of their late arrival neither battery was able to register its targets before the attack, nor to get its guns bedded down into really firm firing positions.

Other preparations that were going on are described in the Regimental History:

Owing to the difficulty of finding adequate cover for the troops immediately prior to the assault, it was found necessary to construct additional trenches and lines of breastworks in or behind which the assaulting troops would 'form up' before attacking. Ladders were made and steps cut in the front parapets to enable the assault troops to get out more quickly. Communication trenches were reconditioned and improved. Portable bridges were built to facilitate crossing flooded trenches; others were provided to assist our troops to cross the German trenches.

The supply and delivery of stores and ammunition for the attack was helped greatly by the laying of wooden tramlines to within a few hundred yards of the front line. Extra lengths of rail were stacked well forward. During the night of the first day of the battle, the 8th Division actually pushed its tramlines into Neuve Chapelle. Roads leading up to the front of the First Army were also improved. Over one thousand men were detailed in readiness for repairing the roads into Neuve Chapelle.[5]

After operation orders had been given out on the morning of 7 March, the 2nd Scottish Rifles left Merville along with most other units of the 8th Division to start their gradual move towards the front line. In pouring rain they marched to billets near Estaires. The next day, 8 March, was bitterly cold, with showers of rain and snow and a stormy wind. From Estaires officers went forward to reconnoitre the route the battalion would take up to the front, and to visit the trenches from which they would make the assault. One of these was Lieutenant Kennedy. All along the roads and tracks he followed were batteries of artillery working on their gun emplacements, and every building he passed was packed with troops. As he plodded back having made his reconnaissance he spoke to a gunner officer who told him 'that the German trenches had been registered at 1,700 yards. He was very sanguine about the chances of success; the infantry he said would meet with little opposition, as there would be nothing left of the German front line after the guns had plastered it for the thirty minutes that the preliminary bombardment was to last. His optimism was pleasantly reassuring, but proved to be sadly misplaced when the great day came.'

On the evening of 8 March the men were given their orders for the attack. It was also at this time that everyone was told that it was to take place on 10 March.

Lance-Corporal Smith (9175), an N.C.O. of the Military Band, was employed as a stretcher-bearer with 'C' Company. He has written of the briefing he received before the battle:

We stretcher-bearers were quartered in a cowshed, and on the afternoon of the 9th, the Regimental Medical Officer, Captain McCreedy, R.A.M.C.,* briefed us for the coming battle.

Captain McCreedy was the ideal officer; conscientious, sympathetic and courageous. We bearers had great respect for him. In briefing us he pulled no punches as to the hectic work that lay before us; as the following will show as far as my memory can recall.

'You all realize,' he said, 'that sooner or later, either side will attempt a breakaway from trench warfare. It is what we all expect and look for, and with the weather improving the sooner the better. We have decided to make the first move, and the 8th Division is chosen for the job. This is the set-up. Our brigade, the 23rd, will spearhead the attack to be launched tomorrow at dawn. The initial objective is the village of Neuve Chapelle, used as a German

---

* *Stands for Royal Army Medical Corps. All doctors joined this Corps, and were attached to battalions, often for many years.*

advanced supply headquarters; and the immediate objective of the Scottish Rifles is a local brewery on the outskirts of the village.

(How we laughed as we heard this. It sounded so appropriate an objective for 'the old Mob'!)

'To-night,' he went on, 'the battalion will move up into the line; with "A" and "B" Companies in the front trench, and "C" and "D" supporting in assembly trenches behind. You must be prepared for a slogging day, for there will be casualties—perhaps many. I therefore look to each of you bearers to give his best, as I am confident you will. I must warn you that an intense bombardment of the German positions will precede the attack, by far the biggest concentration of artillery ever attempted, so be prepared for a really big noise; which you may find tolerable when one considers the devastating effect it will have on the enemy, and minimizing opposition. Finally, remember clearly—your first-aid dressing is the commencement of a wounded man's recovery. You will find me at hand at most times. That's all—and good luck.'

Just that! But it effectively prepared us for whatever lay ahead.

The weather remained cold and wet with a piercing wind throughout the next day. Now that everyone knew what was happening the general feeling among all ranks was a longing to get on with the battle. This urge is always strong when people have to face something they are frightened or apprehensive about. Anyone who has waited to go into the boxing ring, or run a race, or play in an important football match will know the feeling; even more so anyone who has waited to go into action. The cold and discomfort of their billets also made the men of the battalion anxious to get moving, and conversation largely consisted of remarks about getting on with the battle quickly.

Finally, in the late evening of 9 March, the battalion set off, with the rest of the 23rd Infantry Brigade, to march the six miles or so to the positions from which they were going to attack. The march was slow and uncomfortable, and the men were heavily loaded. The official history of the 8th Division describes the way they were equipped:

The men had the rest of the day's ration and one iron ration in their haversacks, and carried two extra bandoliers of ammunition and two empty sandbags. They were without packs, but wore great-coats, the skirts in front fastened back in French fashion.[6]

Many writers about the First World War have described the discomfort and frustration of these long night marches—long usually in time rather than in distance—but nowhere have I found a better description than A. P. Herbert's:

Yet that night's march to the trenches was an experience that made full compensation. It was already dusk when we moved out of the rest-camp, and the moon was not up. As usual in new units, the leading platoons went off at a reckless canter, and stumbling after them in the gathering shadows over rocky, precipitous slopes, and in and out of the clumps of bush, falling in dark holes on to indig-nant sleepers, or maddeningly entangled in hidden strands of wire, the rear companies were speedily out of touch. To a heavily laden infantryman there are few things more exasperating than a night march into the line conducted too fast. If the country be broken and strewn with obstacles, at which each man must wait while another climbs or drops or wrestles or wades in front of him, and must then laboriously scamper after him in the shadows lest he, and thereby all those behind him, be lost; if the country be unknown to him, so that, apart from purely military considerations, the fear of being lost is no small thing, for a man knows that he may wander all night alone in the dark, surrounded by unknown dangers, cut off from sleep, and rations, and the friendly voices of companions, a jest among them when he discovers them: then such a march becomes a nightmare. . . .

No war correspondent has ever described such a march; it is not included in the official 'horrors of war': but this is the kind of thing which, more than battle and blood, harasses the spirit of the infantryman, and composes his life.[7]

The march was broken about half-way at the village of Pont du Hem, which the battalion reached at 1 a.m. on 10 March. Here Lieutenant Graham, the Quartermaster, was waiting with a meal of hot stew.

After about an hour the column moved on again. The battalion arrived at 4 a.m. at the trenches occupied by the 2nd Bn The Northamptonshire Regiment, from which it was to make its assault. During the night the Northamptons had sent out parties to cut passages through their own protective wire entanglements to make way for the attacking troops in the morning.

They had also done a lot of work on putting up ladders and cutting steps in the parapet of their forward trench to make it easy for the attackers to get out. After the Northamptons had filed back out of their positions the 2nd Scottish Rifles had to sort themselves out into the correct formation for the attack. For the two forward companies the frontage was little more than 200 yards, and each had two platoons of forty men apiece to line up in its own half of this distance. As a result there was almost a man to every yard, and it can be imagined how difficult it was to get everyone in the right place in the darkness. To make things worse the night was bitterly cold and the trenches were more than usually slippery with ice underfoot. As daylight approached the Platoon Commanders of the platoons which were to lead the assault climbed on to the parapet to note where the Northamptons had made passages through the wire, and to study the lie of the ground they would have to cross. One of these was Malcolm Kennedy:

The German position facing 'B' Company seemed to be not more than 50 or 60 yards away—unpleasantly close if shells fell short during the preliminary bombardment, but a blessing for the short time this would mean for the men to be under fire during the actual assault. The wire in front of the German trenches, however, looked thick, and running along the crest of their parapet was a sturdy hedge. One could but hope that the gunner officer's prediction of the German trenches, wire, and everything else being blown to bits would prove correct!

The weather was misty, and bitterly cold, at dawn. By this time, about 6.30 a.m. the 2nd Scottish Rifles were fully deployed for the attack. Battalion Headquarters was between the leading platoons of 'A' and 'B' Companies, packed in the front-line trench. Close behind were the remaining platoons of these leading companies in recently constructed shelter trenches, and behind them, also in shelter trenches, were 'C' and 'D' Companies. About a hundred members of the battalion were well back and out of the battle. These were the

Quartermaster's men, the transport section, and various odd men left behind through unfitness or to do some special job.

After dawn the weather showed signs of improvement, but it was still too misty for aerial reconnaissance or good artillery observation. The men waiting in the trenches shivered in the cold, but they were lucky not to have to put up with much greater discomfort. During the night a German officer had noticed unusual movement in the British lines, and that the trenches were packed with men. He had guessed that an attack was coming, and had sent a message to his supporting artillery for fire to be brought down. The reply was that fire could only be opened by permission of the Corps Commander, and it seems that nobody was prepared to find or wake this illustrious man. As a result, the British trenches escaped a shelling which would have devastated the men packed in them so tightly.

The German strength in their forward position opposite the 23rd Brigade was quite small, being only two companies. Light manning was a feature of German trench tactics at this time. They relied on their wire to hold up an attack, and on their machine-guns to destroy the attackers on the wire. Reserves were held well back, but ready to be used for counter-attacks as required. Along their front opposite the battalion the wire entanglement varied from six to fifteen yards in width. On the outside it consisted of wired knife-rests and, closer to their trenches, of wire strands strung low on wooden posts.

Just before the British artillery was due to start its shelling of the German wire, printed slips were handed to every officer and man in the trenches. This came from the Commander of the 4th Corps, of which the 8th Division was part. It finished by saying: 'The Army and the Nation are watching the result and Sir John French is confident that every individual in the 4th Corps will do his duty and inflict a crushing defeat on the German 7th Corps which is opposed to us.' This message had been preceded by a Special Order of the day to all officers issued before moving up on 9 March. It had painted a very rosy picture of the conditions under which the attack was to take place. Presumably the Staff felt it was right to give the brightest possible picture of the situation, but some of the difficulties were treated too lightly. The superiority of the

British in guns and man-power certainly gave cause for optimism, but it was unwise to be too confident. War is a chancy and hazardous affair in which success is rarely achieved easily, particularly against such an enemy as the German Army.

The bombardment which started at 7.30 a.m. was quite small in comparison with some of the colossal barrages fired later in the War, but it was something much greater than those who waited to attack at Neuve Chapelle had ever heard before. The noise was deafening, but curiously exhilarating. A man had to shout in the ear of his neighbour to be heard above the din:

After the first few shells had plunged screaming amid clouds of earth and dust into the German defences, a dense pall of smoke enveloped the enemy lines. The sickening fumes of lyddite blew back into the British trenches. Great masses of earth and huge jagged chunks of metal (shell fragments) hurtled through the air. In places, the waiting troops were covered with soil and dust. The whole ground quivered as in an earthquake.[8]

The effect of this tremendous noise was to make the waiting soldiers feel more and more elated. The excitement caused by the roar of the guns was mixed with the feeling that no Germans could possibly be left alive after the shelling had finished. When the initial concentrated firing was finished the bombardment was carried on at a steadier rate. Men started to talk and crack jokes, and the officers went round from time to time to see how they were getting on. In 'B' Company 'Uncle' Ferrers was in particularly good form, and grinning happily at everyone. In Kennedy's platoon many of the Riflemen laughingly shook hands with him in case they were not to meet again. The odd casualty was incurred, but fortunately there were far fewer than had been expected. Among them was the Second-in-Command of 'B' Company, Captain Peter Kennedy (no relation of M. D.) who was killed outright by a flying fragment of shell. The men who were lightly wounded refused to be left out of the attack, and one at least went over the top with a handkerchief round his head and the blood trickling down his face.

The great moment for which everyone was waiting was 8.5 a.m. The officers stared at their watches, and almost before the correct second arrived the 2nd Scottish Rifles started to surge up out of the trenches. Ferrers was first out from 'B' Company, his monocle in his eye and his sword on his hand. As the guns stopped firing there was a moment of silence. Then the guns started again, firing behind the German lines on to the village of Neuve Chapelle. Almost at the same moment came another noise; the whip and crack of the enemy machine-guns opening up with deadly effect. From the intensity of their fire, and its accuracy, it was clear that the shelling had not been as effective as expected. Worse than its lack of effect on the enemy was the fact that it had scarcely touched the wire. Instead of being broken up, the wire and the thick hedge looked just the same as they had before the bombardment.

Only a minute elapsed before the leading men of the battalion reached the wire, but in that time terrible execution was done to 'A' Company on the left. The Company Commander, Major Hayes, and C.S.M. Culley were both killed on reaching the hedge. Many of the men never got that far, and eventually the company was brought to a halt. The wounded either lay where they were among the dead, or crawled back towards the trench they had come from. Those lucky enough not to be hit had little choice but to either lie in what cover they could find near the hedge, or drop back to the trench-line in much the same way as the wounded. Sergeant Noble of 2 Platoon, 'A' Company, has described what happened to him:

I received a ricochet bullet into the left hip at the first line of trench. I rushed the barbed wire and dropped near where a portion of the German trench was blown in and when I came to, I saw Germans rushing past the opening. I shot three, head, neck and face. I blacked out and later when I came to saw our wounded crawling the opposite way I was looking. I dragged myself back to our trench and was dressed by L/C Collins (Band).

'B' Company on the right was luckier, and managed to get up to the wire with fewer losses than 'A'. Ferrers story of his own adventures was related in a letter he wrote to Kennedy about a week later from hospital:

I got through the wire and over their parapet just to the right of where your hedges ended. When I got there the cupboard was bare, and someone shot me, as I thought in the right ankle, as I started for the next trench. This was really rather a relief as no one else was up and I was feeling exceedingly lonely. I couldn't walk so I lent up against the parapet and waved my sword and generally marked the distant point. I could see the lads all hung up in wire and I fancy some were firing half and quarter right but before I could appreciate the situation I took it again in the right thigh. As it came out very low down right in the middle of the stomach I accepted that as final and being fallen on my back partly on sand-bags and partly in a puddle I concluded to stay as long as I was and take stock of my worldly affairs. I doubted that I'd live very long but as I'd had all I'd ever wished for I didn't worry much over that. I calculated the lads would have finished with the wire and be coming over the parapet soon and I thought if I saw them started for the next trench that would do me very well. I made out that I had a bit of a chance if I could only keep absolutely still. Never did I feel the least doubt, but it was very lonely on my side of the parapet. I could see down towards the hedge for a few yards and by screwing round my head I could see toward the Bosches 2nd trench but that was about all. Presently someone I knew quite well but I got so mixed up I cannot remember who, tumbled through the fence, looked very lost for a moment but bucked up no end when he saw me. He started to Holla the rest on like a good 'un and when that produced no immediate result said to me, 'It's no good Sir they won't come'. I said 'Don't you worry about the lads they'll come all right.' There was some sort of frightful battle going on behind my head for he ran off there, and then Cpl Kennedy came over my gap and was hit and Harris and Plank and a few others cropped up and all got into action to the right. They were frightfully pleased about something I think they'd got some Bosches round a corner and were killing them; but I couldn't twist my head round to make sure. C Coy began to come up and built up a sort of a firing line about fifteen or twenty yards beyond me. Dodd was with them and presently I was told he was badly hit in the shoulder. Then I heard Snowden's voice. . . .

[The letter goes no further because Ferrers fainted at that point and the letter was posted from the hospital without being completed.]

Of how he got to the German trenches Kennedy later had

little idea. He had a vague recollection of tearing at the wire with his bare hands, and with the help of Corporal Forster dragging away the remains of one of the knife-rests which held up the enemy wire. A German soldier fired from four or five yards while they were doing this, and missed them both. He must have then bolted, as they were able to struggle through the remaining strands of wire and reached the hedge, which ran right along the parapet of the German front-line trench. Looking through the hedge, Kennedy saw what appeared to be a small orchard, with another thick hedge on the other side some sixty yards away. Running back from the point where he found himself was a communication trench set at right angles to the front-line trench. Not more than twenty yards up this was a group of Germans, struggling to get past each other in their haste to reach their support trench in the rear. 'It was', he has written, 'too good a chance to miss.' Resting his elbow on the parapet, he fired all six rounds of his revolver into the struggling mass. Having quickly reloaded, he tried to break his way through the hedge. This proved, however, to be thick and prickly. It took a considerable effort for him and Corporal Forster to get through, but eventually they struggled out to the other side. The German front-line trench, immediately at their feet, was empty except for a number of dead and wounded. Groups of Germans were still falling back through the orchard or up the communication trench, while others were firing from the support trench, which was now seen to run along the hedge on the other side of the orchard. Except for the small groups of Germans, and one or two riflemen of 'B' Company who had also struggled through the hedge, Kennedy could see nobody. He shouted to Forster to follow him, and was on the point of jumping across the trench at his feet when a bullet hit him with a blow that sent him reeling backwards. Before he had time to recover his balance he was hit a second time, and pitched back off the parapet, through the hedge and on to the ground on the other side. In his own words: 'The return passage through the hedge, involuntary though it was, was far more rapidly and easily made than the original breakthrough a minute or two earlier.' A good number did, however, get through the wire and the hedge, and the gap they made was to become increasingly important as the battle went on.

While 'B' Company were making their assault and break-through 'C' and 'D' Companies had moved into the trench from which the attack had been launched. 'C' Company on the left had now been joined in the trench by many of the survivors of 'A' Company, who had dropped back after the failure of their first assault. The moment had arrived for the Commanding Officer to take action and change plans. He decided to direct the whole of the second wave into the right half of his small battalion front with the aim of exploiting the success of 'B' Company, rather than allowing anyone to follow in the bloody footsteps of 'A'. Hurried orders were issued for this change of plan, and then the second wave clambered out of the trenches and charged forward. As they came into the open they were fired on heavily from over on their left flank. This fire came from strong positions in front of the 2nd Middlesex. Once again the 2nd Scottish Rifles suffered heavy casualties. Almost the first to be killed were Colonel Bliss, and beside him his Adjutant, Captain W. B. Gray-Buchanan, who had recently taken over from Maunsell after the latter had been killed.

The reason why the German positions in front of the 2nd Middlesex and 2nd Scottish Rifles were able to inflict such losses on the two battalions was the absence, already mentioned, of two six-inch howitzer batteries until the eve of the battle. Alan Clark, in *The Donkeys*, describes the background to this unfortunate absence. Having explained how it was noticed during the planning stage of the battle, he goes on:

. . . inconceivable though it seems, no alternative arrangements were made to cover the gap. The two missing batteries finally appeared on the evening of the 9th—the day before the assault— and had not sufficient time to build up gun platforms or lay their telephone lines to the forward observing officers, much less to range on their allotted targets. For these reasons they played no part in the bombardment of the following day: an omission that was to far-reaching consequences.[9]

The German positions which did the most damage were two machine-gun posts in front of the Middlesex. Not only did they virtually wipe out the 2nd Middlesex with frontal fire, but they caused many of the losses in the 2nd Scottish Rifles with deadly enfilade, or flanking fire.

In spite of this enfilade fire, and the death of the Commanding Officer, the second wave of the 2nd Scottish Rifles kept going. A large number of men managed to reach the point where 'B' Company had made their breakthrough into the German trenches. As they came up to this point they found Ferrers, as described just before his letter comes to an end. He was now smoking a cigar, and was waving everyone on. With the 2nd Scottish Rifles at this stage were the leading platoons of the 2nd Bn The Devonshire Regiment. The Devons had been in support behind the Scottish Rifles, and had come forward to join the second wave of the attack. Picking up various members of 'B' Company as they went, this body now forced on steadily until they were in the position shown on the Sketch Map as 'Cross-tracks'. At the deepest the penetration of the German lines was about 400 yards. It is possible for someone writing today to make this all sound fairly clear. It is essential, however, for anyone wishing to understand the battle to realize how far from clear it was to those taking part.

To start with, nobody had seen the ground over which they were advancing. A few officers had seen the short stretch up to the first hedge, but none had seen farther than that. The officers had seen air photographs and made sketch-maps before the attack, and had undoubtedly briefed their men as well as they could. But by 9.30 a.m. practically every officer had been killed or wounded, and the N.C.O.s who took their places had to go on memory. No doubt some were given maps by their wounded officers, or took them from the dead, but most of these N.C.O.s had to find their way forward with little to guide them. Added to this difficulty was that of not knowing what had happened to other members of the battalion, nor to the flanking battalions. It must have become clear quite soon that the Middlesex on the left had been held up, but just how badly was probably not known for a long time. The general noise, the constant sound of rifle and machine-gun fire from all sides, and the sudden bursts of shells, were all upsetting to those trying to struggle across the slippery, icy fields. Worse than all this was the shock of seeing so many others killed and wounded, particularly after being led to believe that all would go smoothly. Last, but by no means least in the list of confusing factors, was knowing who was left in charge at each level—company, platoon and section. Of all the moments when soldiers want guidance from their leaders, a difficult stage in an attack is the most vital. Now, just as they needed directions and encouragement more than ever before these men of the 2nd Scottish Rifles did not know where to turn. Time and time again the pattern of command changed as officers and N.C.O.s were killed. The extraordinary thing is that in spite of all these elements of chaos the attack continued and retained a certain cohesion.

The situation at 9.30 a.m. in terms of losses in the battalion was grim. Only two officers were not dead, or wounded so badly as to be out of the battle. One of these was Carter-Campbell, the Second-in-Command. He had remained behind when the attack first started, waiting for the moment when he might be called forward to take over from the Commanding Officer, in accordance with normal military custom. Kennedy, lying wounded by the hedge, saw him come forward after Bliss had been killed. He has described him walking up looking 'calm and collected; he was taking in everything he saw. He seemed oblivious of the fact that he was in full view of the Germans, who were sweeping the ground he was crossing with rifle and machine-gun fire. Had it not been for the signs of carnage all round, it might have been imagined that he was summing up the situation on a peace-time training scheme.' The other officer left in action was 2/Lieutenant W. F. Somervail, recently joined from the Special Reserve.*

Casualties among the Warrant Officers and Sergeants had been heavy. C.S.M. Culley of 'A' Company had been killed, and so had the C.S.M. of 'B' Company. Probably thirty out of a total of fifty in the battalion would be a fair estimate of the number of senior N.C.O.s killed or wounded at this stage. Of

---

* *Somervail had only been in the Army for about eight months at this stage. He was killed later in the War as a Captain, having won the D.S.O. and M.C.*

the rank and file the figure is impossible to estimate accurately, but about three hundred and fifty would be fairly near, of whom one in three was killed. Overall, it might be said that a casualty had been incurred for every yard of the ground the battalion had taken. Although many more were to be killed or wounded before the battle was finished, the worst slaughter was over by 9.30 a.m.

Casualties referred to in this way seem almost commonplace and unremarkable. But four hundred human beings lying dead or wounded in a space little more than 200 yards by 100 is almost too terrible to consider. It requires a great effort of imagination to picture the hideous carnage—the often grotesque shapes of the dead and the broken, shattered bodies of the wounded. Some idea can be gained from the picture following page 170, though the bodies are hard to distinguish.

After 9.30 a.m. a slight pause ensued, during which time Carter-Campbell sorted out those members of the battalion who had managed to keep up with the advance. Stragglers kept on coming in, and little groups which had strayed off to the flanks were collected and redeployed in the right places. A certain degree of order was established again, and the companies gathered their own members. At 10.10 a.m. heavy guns started to fire on the wire and trenches of the German position which had held up the Middlesex so badly, and from which so much execution had been done to the Scottish Rifles, particularly 'A' Company. This position was now to the left of the battalion, and some 350 yards behind it. The fire was put down by 18-pounders, and 4·5-inch and 6-inch howitzers. It was accurate and effective, unlike the first bombardment, and the Middlesex were able to move forward as soon as it was completed. The concentrated fire of so many guns on a small area had been enough to cut the wire to pieces, and also kill most of the Germans in the trench behind it.

By 11.30 a.m. the Middlesex had taken the enemy front-line trench and were pushing on steadily beyond it. Before long, meeting little opposition, they reached The Orchard, shown on the Sketch Map. As the Middlesex advanced, so did the Scottish Rifles. They were lucky after covering about 200 yards to avoid being badly shot up by the British artillery.

They were just reaching the point on the Map marked 'Ruined House' when the British gunners started to shell this area. A quick withdrawal was made, and little damage was done, though at this point Carter-Campbell was wounded in the head. It was not a bad wound, and after having it bound up he was able to carry on in command of what was left of the battalion.

This episode highlights another of what one might call 'confusion factors' of battles in the First World War, namely the difficulty of co-ordinating artillery fire with infantry movement. In modern days, with every known method of communication passing constant messages between the men on the ground and the guns, it is easy for mistakes to be made. In 1915 it was dangerous to fire on any targets which had not been included in a carefully prepared fire-plan. I have been unable to discover quite why the guns opened up at this stage on the area of 'Ruined House', or whether the battalion had any warning that shelling might start. Having fallen back out of the area under fire, the Scottish Rifles settled down in a rough position astride Signpost Lane from which they were not to move until much later in the day.

This is a good moment at which to go back to the ground near the start of the attack, where the heaviest casualties had occurred, to see what was happening to the wounded. Kennedy, having been hit twice, lay beside his hedge for five hours before the battalion stretcher-bearers reached him. Throughout this time, from about 8.10 a.m. until well after 1 p.m., a member of his platoon had stayed beside him, refusing adamantly to leave him. Once the stretcher-bearers had arrived this man carefully picked up his rifle and trudged off to find the rest of the battalion.

Of the stretcher-bearers, Kennedy writes: 'It was impossible to speak too highly. Hour after hour they had worked under heavy fire, bringing in the dead and wounded, till they themselves were near the point of exhaustion.' A stretcher is an awkward, clumsy thing to handle, particularly with a heavy man to move. During 10 March the sixteen stretcher-bearers in the battalion must have carried into the Regimental Aid Post any number up to thirty casualties per pair. Considering that for the first two hours they were under fire it was a remarkable effort.

Many of the casualties carried back with such care died before they were able to receive treatment for their wounds. One of these was Major Lloyd, 'D' Company Commander, who came in to the Aid Post just after Kennedy. He was in great pain, and asked for morphia. An injection gave him slight relief, but he died very soon. The irrepressible Ferrers survived his three wounds, and a long period in hospital after he eventually got back to England. The Regimental History at a much later date records: 'Major E. B. Ferrers, D.S.O., who had been severely wounded at Neuve Chapelle on 10th March 1915, rejoined the 2nd Battalion for duty on the 21st February 1917.'[10]

At the front, the battalion remained astride Signpost Lane until about 6 p.m. on 10 March. Just behind them were elements of the 24th Infantry Brigade, which had been waiting since 3.30 p.m. to push through and carry on the attack towards Piètre. This attack could not start on time because another brigade which was expected to have appeared on the left was not there. It was then discovered that this brigade had in fact carried on with its own advance earlier in the afternoon against little opposition, and was now well ahead of where it was thought to be. While this problem was being sorted out the 2nd Scottish Rifles lay where they were and waited. Lying and waiting is a much bigger part of war than doing and dying. Here was a battalion which had taken part in one of the bloodiest assaults of its history and in the first ten hours it had been almost inactive for about eight. Unless one understands that this is the way things go in war one cannot appreciate what it is really like. It has rightly been said that war is 10 per cent terror and 90 per cent boredom.

When the 24th Brigade did get moving at last darkness was near. It managed to force its way forward to a position some 300 yards ahead of 'Ruined House', but by this time the Germans had got a second line of defence established in the general area of Piètre, and this was well reinforced with machine-guns. As night fell the 24th Brigade could advance no farther, and they settled down to consolidate their position in the dark. The Scottish Rifles followed them a short way and then established themselves in the 'Ruined House' and an old British trench on its left.

The night passed peacefully, though not without activity. One of the highlights of the evening was the arrival of the Quartermaster, Graham. He brought a hot meal right up to the position, and also ample rations for the following day. Carter-Campbell moved constantly round the men, who were in remarkably good shape. The strength of those with him is hard to assess, but it must have been about three hundred all ranks. Sergeants had settled down quickly in command of companies, and the battalion was in every way a viable military unit, in spite of being low in strength.

The night of 10/11 March was passed in feverish activity on the German side. Along the line shown on the Sketch Map as German Front Line, Night 10/11 March the amount achieved was remarkable. Rough breast-works were constructed which amounted to little more than a low continuous mound thrown up in front of a shallow trench, but this was sited between already existing strong-points. Extra machine-guns were put into the strong-points, and extensive new wire entanglements were erected. Reserves were brought up to man the new line, while a strong force equivalent to a British division was held ready for a counter-offensive.

At the British higher headquarters plans were made during the night to carry on with the offensive at first light next morning. The result of the first day's attack had been the capture of the enemy's front-line defences on a front of 4,000 yards, and a penetration to a maximum depth of 1,200 yards, though in most places the depth was nearer 800 yards. The village of Neuve Chapelle and the farm Moated Grange had also been captured. For an attack carried out against well prepared positions it had been a definite success by any standard. It certainly was enough of a success to warrant further effort the following day. When orders for operations on 11 March reached the 2nd Scottish Rifles the battalion discovered that it was to be held in reserve, with the rest of the 23rd Brigade, for an attack in the 8th Division sector. The attack was to start at 7 a.m. following a fifteen-minute bombardment of the known German strong-points opposite the British breakthrough. The short length of time for which the bombardment was scheduled was due to the fact that shells had already become scarce, and many batteries had little ammunition left after the heavy firing the previous day.

The assault which started at 7 a.m. was a complete disaster. The artillery fire from 6.45 a.m. had been directed only against strong-points known before the start of the battle, and had not been heavy enough really to damage them. No fire at all landed on the breast-works and trenches constructed during the night. The British advance was met with a tremendous volume of machine-gun and rifle fire, and was stopped dead almost as it started. Also, the German artillery was ready, and put down heavy fire for a period of nearly three hours. This was largely directed just behind the British front line, much of it on to Neuve Chapelle and Moated Grange. The Scottish Rifles were quite heavily shelled, and suffered a number of casualties. Later in the day further attempts were made to advance, but failed everywhere along the front. The 23rd Brigade was not called on to move from its reserve positions, and when night fell the 2nd Scottish Rifles were still in and around 'Ruined House'.

The men in a reserve position should not be thought of as enjoying a danger-free and idle existence, particularly when only a few hundred yards from the enemy. They were likely to be shelled at any moment, possibly more heavily than troops in closer contact with the Germans, as happened on the morning of 11 March. The amount of work done on improving defences was certainly far greater in a reserve or support position than in the front line. At the same time sentry and watch-keeping duties were just as heavy. It is fair to say that by the night of 11/12 March the Scottish Rifles were becoming thoroughly exhausted. The small size of the battalion, whittled down a little more during 11 March, allowed little relief for anyone. This weariness which was such a feature of the First World War is well described in C. E. Montague's *Disenchantment*.

For most of his time the average private was tired. Fairly often he was so tired as no man at home ever is in the common run of his work.

If a company's trench strength was low and sentry-posts abounded more than usual in its sector a man might, for eight days running, get no more than one hour off duty at any one time, day or night. If enemy guns were active many of these hours off guard duty might have to be spent on trench repair. . . . So most of the privates were tired the whole of the time; sometimes to the point of torment, sometimes much less, but always more or less tired.[11]

It is worth quickly considering what had happened to a member of the Scottish Rifles, standing on sentry duty at 1 a.m. on 12 March, since the battle began. Two full days, forty-eight hours before, he had stopped at this time for a meal on his way up to the line. At that moment he had already been on the march with a heavy load for some hours. After that halt he had marched on again until reaching the Northampton's trenches at 4 a.m. When he went over the top at 8.5 a.m. on 10 March he had already spent one night without sleep. The exertions of the first day of the battle had certainly allowed no time for rest, even though the worst of the fighting was over in quite a short time. The night of 10/11 March had been one of great activity, and probably the first chance of an hour or two's rest came during the day on 11 March, though this was interrupted by the shelling during the morning. Before coming on duty our sentry might have been employed during the hours of darkness up to midnight 11/12 March on a working party reinforcing some part of the trench system. So now, at 1 a.m. on 12 March, he was likely to have had no more than four hours sleep in the past forty-eight hours, and he had been far from fresh when this period began. For a young man such a strain could indeed be 'torment'.

The British plan for 12 March was to make another attack at 10.30 a.m. in an attempt to break out from the bridge-head around Neuve Chapelle. However, the enemy took the initiative, and made a counter-attack at dawn. This was completely repulsed, with much slaughter, and many prisoners were taken. Unfortunately this repulse was not followed up, and the Germans were given time to recover. In fact they were not only given time to recover but, due to the confusion of reports about the action, the British attack was postponed until 12.30 p.m. Everything was made even slower and more muddled by thick mist which covered the whole battlefield. When the attack did start at 12.30 p.m. it was not very successful, though slight advances were made.

By this time the strain of the action must have been beginning to tell at all levels. Everyone was getting tired, and the more tired they became the longer things took to organize. As far as one can make out back at First Army Headquarters confused reports percolated to General Haig, which made it appear that the repulse of the German counter-attack at dawn was part of the same action as the attack at 12.30 p.m. Anyway, he was given the impression that a major breakthrough had been achieved, and that an opportune situation had arisen for a full-scale follow up. At 3.6 p.m. on 12 March he issued orders to his Corps Commanders to 'push through regardless of loss, using reserves if required'.[12] For this message to be passed to battalions in the 8th Division took over three hours. It was not until 6.15 p.m. that the Commanding Officers of all battalions in the division were gathered together in the Headquarters of the 23rd Infantry Brigade to be given their orders. The Commanding Officer of the 2nd Scottish Rifles was by this time 2/Lieutenant Somervail, who was also the only officer left. Carter-Campbell had been wounded a second time, on this occasion severely, at 4 p.m., and had been evacuated.

When the orders had been given out, the Commanding Officers of the battalions involved had numerous duties to attend to. The basic procedure at this stage in an attack is for the Commanding Officer to send a warning order to his battalion, and then to make a reconnaissance of the approach to the start line for his assault, and as far as possible of the enemy positions. While he is reconnoitring, his subordinates move forward as a result of the warning order, and meet him at a suitable place to be given their instructions. In due course they carry out the same simple routine with their juniors, until finally everyone is clear at all levels on what to do. To cut this short in broad daylight with fresh troops would be risking disaster; to cut it out altogether in a combination of falling night and mist, with spent men, was unbelievable. From here the story of the battle becomes a sorry tale, except for the courage, willingness, and effort of the soldiers who tried to do the impossible. All 2/Lieutenant Somervail had time to do was to hurry off to join his small force, briefly explain to them what to do, and then lead them to a point on the road between

'Cross-tracks' and Neuve Chapelle village from which they were to lead the rest of the 23rd Infantry Brigade up to the assault position. Fortunately he had at his right hand throughout this phase the magnificent, imperturbable figure of R.S.M. Chalmers. Somehow the exhausted men were assembled in the dark, and they moved to their positions on the road in time. At about 8 p.m. they set off. They followed the road south into Neuve Chapelle village, and then turned left up the eastern side of the road triangle. At 9 p.m. they had covered a distance of some 600 yards and were in position for their attack. This little march sounds a trivial thing, but was in reality a remarkable tribute to the battalion and its young commander. Often enough on a peacetime exercise a far more experienced officer than Somervail has bungled a night move made under infinitely easier conditions. He had managed to get his tired men into the right place at the right time in the most difficult circumstances, and this is one of the main tests of an infantry officer.

The 2nd Devons arrived in position on the left of the Scottish Rifles at about 9.30 p.m. Confusion among other units behind was so great, however, that the attack was postponed until 11.30 p.m. and then again for another two hours. Even with these delays, only half the correct number of battalions were ready on the 8th Division's front at 1.30 a.m. on 13 March. However, no further orders to wait had reached the Devons and the Scottish Rifles, and so at this moment they advanced towards the German positions, which were about 200 yards ahead of them. Luckily a message reached them, just after they had started, cancelling the attack. What would have happened if they had gone on is anyone's guess. They might have been lucky, and have taken the enemy by surprise, particularly as he was exhausted as well. But the most likely outcome would have been that they would have blundered on to his position in the darkness and been badly shot up by his machine-guns firing down the wire on fixed lines, and by defensive fire from his artillery. The attack was doomed to failure, and it is fortunate it was never pressed home.

With the attack called off, the Scottish Rifles dropped back and occupied the trenches just behind them, from which the

assault had started. They remained in these trenches throughout 13 March and 14 March, and were relieved on the night of
14/15 March. They marched back during the night along much
the same route that they had travelled on their way into
action six full days before. Billets were found for them on the
La Bassée–Estaires road near Rouge-Croix, and here they had
their first proper sleep for nearly a week.

The party that paraded next day to be checked and sorted
out was, not counting 2/Lieutenant Somervail and R.S.M.
Chalmers, one hundred and forty-three strong. Quickly steps
were taken to start building up the battalion again. From the
1st Cameronians, at the time part of the 19th Brigade serving
farther north, came Major R. Oakley as Commanding Officer
and Captain R. C. Money, M.C., as Adjutant. General Money, as
he is now, has told how extraordinarily undaunted he found the
handful of survivors.[13] Much of this he puts down to the influence of Chalmers, whose example had a great effect. Much of it
he also attributes to the plain toughness of the Lowland 'Jock'.

Reinforcements also poured out from home from the 3rd
and 4th (Special Reserve) battalions of the Regiment. General
Money reckons that about 800 men joined between 17 March
and 9 May 1915, when the 2nd Scottish Rifles went into action
again at Aubers Ridge—and, incidentally, once again suffered
heavy casualties, though not quite as bad as at Neuve Chapelle.

Many of the men who had been wounded at Neuve Chapelle
returned in due course to the 2nd Scottish Rifles. General
Jack records his pleasure at seeing a 'smart draft' of Scottish
Riflemen arriving at a base camp in July 1915, and notes that
they were mainly made up of those who had recovered from
wounds received at Neuve Chapelle.[14]

In spite of these parties of survivors returning, the 2nd
Scottish Rifles was never again the same battalion that it had
been before Neuve Chapelle. It lived on in name, and certainly
in spirit, but those men who had gone over the top on 10 March
were always in the minority in the years after the battle.
Sadness at this fact is only lightened by remembering that, in
spite of everything, nothing had been able to break the morale
of such men. They were probably as near unconquerable as
any soldiers in the history of the world.

An Assessment of
the Battle

Why are they dead? Is Adam's seed so strong
That these bold lives cut down mean nothing lost?
Indeed, they would have died; ourselves ere long
Will take our turn. That cheque is signed and crossed.
But, though this dying business still concerns
The lot of us, there seems something amiss
When twenty million sudden funeral urns
Are called for. Have you no hypothesis?[1]

From WAR CEMETERY, by Edmund Blunden

As 2/LIEUTENANT SOMERVAIL and his weary, tattered
men trudged back to billets on the night of 14/15 March 1915
it is reasonable to suppose that their thoughts were confined
to simple issues. There would be worry in their minds about
dead or wounded friends, and no doubt a certain feeling of
satisfaction at times at the thought that they had done their
duty well throughout the battle and had never broken. Their
main concern, however, would be with rest and food, and how
long they would be out of the line. It is not likely that their
thoughts would have strayed much on to questions of what
the battle had achieved, and whether the sacrifices made had
been worth while. For us, however, who look at their exploits
fifty years later, and try to learn what we can from them, this
aspect is important. Before trying to find out why these men
fought so well, it is essential to make at least an attempt to
measure the value of their efforts. We must face the fact that
it may have been all rather unnecessary: indeed little more

[83]

than a waste, a flinging away of human life for no real gain. We must, I believe, have some hypothesis, even though I am going to concern myself at this stage with a few hundred 'sudden funeral urns' at Neuve Chapelle rather than try to comment on the whole War and its twenty million.

The first thing to do is to establish what the casualties were. In the course of the battle the total British losses were 583 officers and 12,309 other ranks killed, wounded and missing. German losses were about 12,000, including 30 officers and 1,657 other ranks taken prisoner.

In the 2nd Scottish Rifles, the casualty roll needs to be examined carefully. To get the right answer is more difficult than one might think. The story has always been told in the Regiment that the battalion went into action 900 strong, and only 150 came out. If this were the case casualties would have been 750, but the known total of killed, wounded, and missing, all ranks included, was 469. What happened to the other 281? The explanation is probably this: the strength was 900 when the battalion landed in France in 1914. By March 1915 this had dropped through battle casualties and sickness to about 800. When it went into action at Neuve Chapelle about 100 men were out of the line, as was explained in Chapter 2. So about 700 went over the top on 10 March. When they came out of the line on the night 14/15 March the 700 had been reduced to around 200. Of these many were suffering from slight wounds or sickness, and reported for treatment as soon as possible. Thus only 143 were fit and able to parade for the first roll-call after the battle was over, and these have become the 150 survivors of the Regimental legend. I have laboured this point because it is to my mind important to understand the reality of the casualty figures so often quoted about First World War battles. It almost lessens the true magnitude of the losses to exaggerate them. One comes nearer to feeling the real sorrow of Neuve Chapelle in knowing that 13 officers and 112 other ranks were killed during the battle, and 344 of all ranks were wounded and missing, than to airily say that 750 were 'lost'.

The next thing is to see what, in terms of tactics, the British attack achieved. The bald facts are that the British captured and held a salient approximately 4,000 yards wide and 1,000 yards deep, which included their first objectives of Neuve Chapelle and Moated Grange, but that they failed in their aim of making a large scale break-out towards Lille. The battle was therefore a tactical victory if measured purely in terms of ground taken, or a defeat if judged against the aim with which it was launched.

Another requirement is to look at the result of the battle from a strategic point of view. Two achievements on this score can be recorded. First, the relationship of the British Army with the French was much improved after Neuve Chapelle. Before the battle the French had been of the opinion that the British were not doing their fair share of the fighting; after the battle Haig's Chief Intelligence Officer, Brigadier-General Charteris, wrote: 'Neuve Chapelle has had unexpected results. It has made the French think highly of our Army. Joffre is sending his Corps Commanders to see D.H. and learn how we succeeded in attacking and ousting the Germans from an entrenched position.'[2] Second, by attacking at Neuve Chapelle, the British drew German reserves away from the Champagne area, where the French were having a bad time. That this was largely fortuitous does not prevent it from being an achievement.

From this brief profit and loss account of the battle one can possibly produce a verdict along these lines. Since the losses on both sides were roughly the same, neither the British nor the Germans could claim to have scored a victory in terms of destroying more of the other side's man-power. Because they contrived to gain quite a substantial area of ground, by First World War standards, and also to relieve pressure on their French allies to the south, the British could claim to have won a small victory. At the same time the Germans, because they had prevented the British achieving their real aim of breaking out towards Lille, could certainly claim that they had not been defeated. It might therefore be said that the battle of Neuve Chapelle was drawn, with the advantage slightly to the British.

If this was all that there was to it, one would have to say that the lives of the men who were killed in the battle had been wasted. There are, however, further factors which must be taken into consideration before making any decision. First, one must remember that Neuve Chapelle was the first offensive of the B.E.F. Having been involved almost on arrival in France in 1914 in the retreat from Mons, the B.E.F. had played a somewhat inglorious part in the battle of the Marne. It had then, at considerable cost, held the German attack at the battle known as 'First Ypres' in October. After that it had taken most of the winter to reorganize, and had been, as John Terraine puts it, 'incapable of *any* offensive effort. . . .' Therefore this first offensive should be seen as something of an experiment, and an opportunity to learn important lessons.

In connection with these lessons I will turn to Liddell Hart's *A History of the World War 1914–1918*. Having said that save as a pure experiment the attack at Neuve Chapelle stood self-condemned, he goes on to write:

In design, however, the attack, entrusted to Haig's First Army, was both original and well thought out. After an intense bombardment of thirty-five minutes' duration on a two thousand yards' frontage, the artillery lengthened their range and dropped a curtain of fire to prevent reinforcements reaching the enemy's battered trenches, which were rapidly overrun by the British infantry.*

Complete surprise was attained, and most of the first positions captured; but when, in the second phase, the frontage was extended the artillery support proved inadequate. Further, owing to scanty information and to the two Corps commanders waiting upon each other, a long pause occurred which gave the Germans five clear hours to organize fresh resistance. Then, too late and mistakenly, Haig ordered the attack to be pressed 'regardless of loss'. And loss proved the only result. An underlying factor was that the narrowness of the attack sector made the breach more easy for the defenders to close, although this defect was unavoidable owing to the general shortage of munitions, especially heavy guns and high explosive shell for them.[3]

In showing how the correct deductions were not made from what happened, Liddell Hart writes:

* *Except, of course, opposite 2nd Middlesex and 2nd Scottish Rifles.*

It was clear that the small-scale experiment had only missed success by a narrow margin, and that there was scope for its development. But the Entente Commands missed the true lesson, which was the surprise attainable by a short bombardment that compensated its brevity by its intensity. And only partially did they appreciate the fact that the sector attacked must be sufficiently wide to prevent the defender's artillery commanding, or his reserves closing, the breach. Instead they drew the superficial deduction that mere volume of shell-fire was the key to success. Not until 1917 did they revert to the Neuve Chapelle method. [4]

If the lesson of the surprise value of an intense bombardment was missed, another one was not. It finally became only too clear at Neuve Chapelle how important communications had become in modern war. But whereas lesson number one was a question of having the equipment but not knowing how to use it, lesson number two was more a matter of realizing what was needed but not having the tools for the job. The following passage from John Terraine's *Douglas Haig: the educated soldier*, brings this out very clearly. Although referring to First Ypres it is entirely valid for Neuve Chapelle. He explains the difficulty Haig had to face as confused, delayed and inaccurate reports reached him, and he had to make his plans from them.

'Reports reached him': all through the battle—and the remainder of the War—the whole question of reporting was to prove a terrible stumbling block. Time after time, at Ypres, one learns of every runner being 'killed almost immediately after leaving the headquarters trench', 'none of the messengers reached brigade headquarters', etc. Vision was restricted, telephone lines were continuously cut; it is almost impossible, in this age of highly developed communcations, to imagine what the 'fog of war' was like at that time. Every *known* device was tried to overcome this problem, at one time or another during the War; devices which required another twenty or thirty years to be invented and produced could not, of course, be used. And the answer to the often repeated question, 'Why didn't General X do this or General Y do that?' is all too often, 'Because he had no information; he simply did not know what was happening'. Nor was this a matter of 'going up to have a look'; very often the men in front saw least of all. [5]

One should remember too that there was not only the need for good communications to bring the information to the higher commanders, but also to take their orders forward once they were issued. Communications being a two-way business, delays were normally doubled.

Finally, in trying to gauge whether Neuve Chapelle was a waste of lives or not one must consider the attitude of the men who actually fought in the battle. They were the ones who actually lost their lives, and it is presumptuous to discuss their sacrifice without endeavouring to picture what they themselves felt.

Kennedy has written about the longing of all ranks of the 2nd Scottish Rifles for some sort of action during the long gloomy winter in the trenches. Here are his words to describe the way that the officers received the news of the impending attack on Neuve Chapelle: 'To say that this information was welcome would be a gross under-statement. Nothing that has happened since our departure from England has cheered us up more than the news just imparted to us.' Of course the fact that the battalion looked forward to the battle does not necessarily mean that it was not wasteful. But to realize how much they looked forward to it is to start to see it in perspective.

The front-line soldier in a good infantry battalion in 1915 was primarily concerned with getting on with his job of defeating the Germans, and had little time to indulge in reflections on the ultimate value of what he was doing. In his mind the Germans were going to be defeated by his own battalion; whether Devons, Middlesex, Scottish Rifles, or what you will. Some of the officers might discuss occasionally the competence or otherwise of higher formations and Generals, but all their real interest was centred on the battalion. The biggest thing of all was that the battalion should do well; this bound all ranks together as nothing else could. For a member of the Scottish Rifles there was one overriding fear, and that was that he should let the battalion and his company down when the great moment came. Obviously there were a few who did not feel like this, but the vast majority were conscious of this need to play their part as being important above all else. Welded together in this way, the 2nd Scottish Rifles welcomed the coming of the battle, and were not, I believe, put óut by its outcome. There was no bitterness afterwards, and the survivors were again ready for anything after a few days' rest.

It would also be wrong to think of any of these men being 'thrown into battle'. There has been a great deal of nonsense written and spoken ever since the War on this theme. Field-Marshal Haig is always being attacked for throwing men to their deaths; the less experience of warfare a commentator has the more angry he gets on this score. Of course the men who died at Neuve Chapelle were not 'thrown' in—they went of their own accord. Could a man like 'Uncle' Ferrers be 'pushed' into battle? In all probability he never thought for one second of following the directions of a General. As far as he was concerned the Scottish Rifles were fighting for King and Country, and to uphold their own honour as a Regiment. When they came to the moment to close with the enemy a General or two might have to co-ordinate arrangements, but beyond that the 'brass-hats' meant nothing. A current saying among Regimental officers of those days was: 'Generals! Generals! I hate bloody Generals!' Whatever the student of history may find out about the influence of higher commanders on the course of the war, he can be sure that it was not a factor of much interest at the lower end of the chain of command. Members of good battalions went into action to fight for the 'old battalion' because they wanted to. Sir Arthur Bryant has written in *English Saga* of the later years of the First World War:

Yet there was no surrender, for on both sides of the line congregated all that was most heroic and constant in the manhood of the most virile nations of the old world. These fighters, hidden from one another in the slime, subjected day and night to a ceaseless tornado of screeching death out of the darkened sky, tortured by every foul breath and sight that can appal the sensitive mind, were in that place and hour because they had chosen to be there.[6]

Although this passage refers to 1917, it was even truer of 1915 that 'they had chosen to be there'.

Naturally attitudes towards the battle changed during its course. As the day approached, it is fair to imagine that the average man was gripped with that strange fear which has been discussed already and is perhaps best described as butterflies in the stomach. No doubt a number of individuals started to wish themselves out of the fight, though they would be unlikely to air such thoughts. When the bombardment started all these fears of anticipation fled, and everyone obviously enjoyed the half an hour during which it lasted. The peak of their elation must have come at the first moment of breaking out 'over the top' in the few seconds before the German machine-guns started. From then on the picture changed. Those who were lucky enough not to be killed or wounded in the first hour faced, as we have seen, six days of frustration and cold and a dreadful weariness. For the wounded there was pain, often unbearable, and terrible discomfort. Many of them were taken back and patched up, but then lived on as shattered wrecks for long miserable years. These latter wounded were perhaps worse off than the dead. But in spite of this gloomy picture, I am firmly convinced that if some magic power had been able to show everyone in the battalion what was to happen to him, and had then given him the option of going away or staying to see the battle through, that only a handful would have left. I am sure, also, that those who did survive the battle, even the badly wounded who never recovered, felt when it was over that they had done the right thing. Indeed, there was nothing else they could have done if they were to be true to themselves, their friends and the battalion. It seems to me that any verdict one comes to when trying to assess Neuve Chapelle must take full account of this aspect.

My final verdict on Neuve Chapelle is, for what it is worth, that it was a failure, but not a waste. I would sum it up in two sentences like this. The British Army had to take the offensive, and they very nearly succeeded in achieving victory. Although they did not learn the lessons they should have done from their narrow defeat, it was proved beyond doubt that the B.E.F. was a magnificent fighting force. Whether this comment has any value I do not know.

What I do know is that the 2nd Scottish Rifles, a Regular infantry battalion of the British Army, gave an example during the course of the battle of all the qualities which make up high morale in a military sense. The determination of the first hour and the complete disregard for personal safety were followed by the ability to endure and carry on regardless of weariness and discomfort shown in the long days afterwards.

Morale Defined

. . . it has always been a military axiom, that a man's will to fight is the ultimate arbiter of battles and that this is governed by the thoughts however elementary which pass through his head.

It is not the number of soldiers, but their will to win which decides battles.[1]

        Lord Moran, THE ANATOMY OF COURAGE

IN THE BROADEST terms, morale is concerned with the way in which people react to the conditions of their existence. It is usually applied to those aspects of life which are difficult and dangerous, and often has military undertones. The *Concise Oxford Dictionary* defines it as: 'Moral condition, especially (of troops) as regards discipline and confidence.'[2]

The maintenance of morale is recognized in military circles as the most important single factor in war: outside these circles there is sometimes difficulty in appreciating why this is so. Military historians who have not themselves experienced command in war make the mistake of attributing too much importance to tactics. In his famous lectures on 'Generals and Generalship' Field-Marshal Lord Wavell showed how tactics ought to be valued. Having quoted Socrates on the qualities necessary in a General, with a passage starting 'The general must know how to get his men their rations. . . .' Wavell said:

Now the first point which attracts me about that definition is the order in which it is arranged. It begins with the matter of administration, which is the real crux of generalship, to my mind;

[92]

and places tactics, the handling of troops in battle, at the end of his qualifications instead of at the beginning, where most people place it.[3]

Tactics are relatively less important than most other aspects of war because tactical manœuvre depends on the action of men, and the first requirement is to get the men concerned to execute the plan correctly and keenly. The truth is that a brilliant plan of battle in the tactical sense can be a complete failure if morale is bad, while a poor plan can be made to work well if morale is good. The more academic one's approach to military affairs, the greater one's divorce from this truth. Historians can so easily read appreciations, plans, and orders for battles and miss the two vital points that first of all the plan may never reach the troops who are meant to carry it out, and second that the troops may not do what they are told when they get their orders. As shown in the closing stages of the battle of Neuve Chapelle, war is a desperately muddled, confusing, and chaotic business. The fact that an order to attack is given does not mean that an attack will take place. Due to a whole series of disasters the orders may never reach the troops. Telephone lines may get cut, wireless sets may be out of action, staff officers may cause excessive delays in getting clarification of obscure points, and runners may get lost. Worse still, even if the order does finally arrive the troops may be too demoralized to take much notice. All these things can happen in a war; the best insurance against their happening is high morale at all levels. Take the feat of 2/Lieutenant Somervail and R.S.M. Chalmers in getting the 2nd Scottish Rifles up to the start line in time for that final abortive attack on the night of 14 March. The thing to realize is how easily such a move might never have been made at all. Suppose the men had been really demoralized, and had refused to move? A strong leader would probably have got them going in the end, but suppose there had been a weak man in charge? Nothing would have happened. It is obvious that in some units on that night nothing did happen. Nobody will ever know the whole story, but there must have been some battalions who had come to the stage of virtually refusing to move. These failures are not worth labouring, however. What is worth stressing is that where morale remains high, as in the 2nd Scottish Rifles, something can always be achieved. The plan can be bad, the conditions appalling, the task hopeless: a good battalion will make something of it. As Napoleon said in his famous, but often misquoted, pronouncement: 'À la guerre, les trois quarts sont des affaires morales, la balance des forces réelles n'est que pour un autre quart.'[4]

If we accept that morale is all important, the next thing to do is to describe some of its aspects. Morale in a military formation at any time has as its hall-mark a quality of cheerfulness. This does not mean that everyone must wear a perpetual grin, but the impression of men with good morale is one of good cheer. Sulky faces, either in barracks or in action, are the best single guide to low morale. The awful expression of a dispirited soldier should cause his commander more worry than anything apart from the actuality of defeat in battle.

Cheerfulness apart, the manifestations of good morale tend to divide themselves fairly neatly into those which apply to peacetime or active service out of the line, and those which are found when actually in battle.

In peacetime, or out of the line, one of the best guides is saluting. To walk into a barracks or camp where morale is high is obvious to any experienced officer in the first two minutes. About three smart, cheerful salutes give the clue. Where soldiers have good officers, whom they trust, they are happy. Having good officers, they salute them well and their salutes are properly returned. It is as simple as that. Turn-out and bearing are also guides to morale, but not quite so obvious. There are some units and sections where the men take a great pride in their work, but are not well turned out. In First World War days the Animal Transport section of an infantry battalion had a lot of rather untidy men, but they were some of the stoutest of all; in a modern army drivers and mechanics can be the same. In fact a sort of pride in being grimy can be built up—in being the men who do the hard, dirty jobs—and most effective it can be. Furthermore, very smart turn-out can occasionally be the cover for poor performance. The ultra-

smart shirker is a definite military type, just as is the desperately untidy man who always carries on and gives of his best
in all circumstances.

On the whole though, in spite of these exceptions, turn-out
is a good guide to morale. The important thing is that it must
be the second stage. The first is that the man must be good
at his job and proud of himself; from this he will naturally
become clean and tidy. General Jack described the draft of
men who had been wounded at Neuve Chapelle, and were
returning to the Scottish Rifles, as a 'smart draft'. A group of
good soldiers will always be a smart group.

Behaviour is the next guide to morale, though it has to be
seen in perspective. Certainly no unit with good morale has
continual cases of bad discipline. On the other hand, some of
the soldiers in a first-class battalion may from time to time
cause annoyance by becoming troublesome in their local town.
The experienced officer knows almost by instinct whether the
trouble is due to poor morale or high spirits. Good soldiers
must have a bit of devilment in them, and it is no good
becoming alarmed at occasional outbursts of misbehaviour.

Another guide to morale is the treatment accorded to
visitors. This applies mainly at the Officers' and Sergeants'
Mess level. In a battalion with good morale people are well
received. Walking into the Mess of a good battalion should be
a thoroughly pleasant experience for a visitor, while rude or
casual treatment will quickly give him the measure of the
people he is visiting.

Points such as these provide a guide to morale out of
battle. In action cheerfulness remains pre-eminent, closely
followed by health. Health must be looked at under two
headings—hygiene, and numbers of men reporting sick.

Attention to hygiene is a sure criterion of morale. A good
battalion can be quickly noted by the care taken over building
lavatories and burying refuse. In the First World War this
matter of keeping trenches clean was enormously important.
Everything was foul enough as it was with mud, dead bodies,
rats, flies and all the unavoidable filth everywhere; to make
things worse by carelessness was inexcusable. A battalion
which could care so little about the fate of its successors that

it could leave its trenches unnecessarily filthy was one which had sunk towards really low morale. To do so was a mixture of apathy and selfishness, which are sure signs of bad morale. In relation to both groups of men and individuals it is always indicative of low spirits when people are selfish and inconsiderate.

The second aspect of health, namely reporting sick, is well summed up in this extract from *General Jack's Diary* for 19 February 1916 when he was Second-in-Command of the 2nd Scottish Rifles: 'The Medical Officer . . . says he has never seen such small battalion "sick parades" as ours. Our daily average of men reporting sick is about 6, and he has been accustomed to 20 to 30. The size of the sick parade is one of the guides in assessing the value and morale of troops.'[5] In a good battalion men feel that they are of value, and wish to give of their best. Because of this they do not go sick, but struggle on through minor ailments to the point where they can either recover or are really ill. Everyone knows how much or how little can be made of most illness; it is the will of the man which decides whether he will go sick or carry on. Lord Moran quotes from his diary written in the trenches: 'This morning a man came with an abscess in his hand and some fever. Last night there were ten degrees of frost and his hand must have given him hell, throbbing throughout his cold watch, but he would not hear of hospital, he would not even hear of rest. He meant to go back and when I had cut it, back he went.'[6]

Another sure guide to infantry morale, which applied particularly to the First World War, is the attitude to patrolling. In the trenches a good battalion prided itself on dominating 'No Man's Land'. Every night patrols would move out from the sector occupied by such a battalion; from a poor one there would be no activity. This should not be confused with foolhardiness. It was in fact a form of insurance, and resulted in fewer casualties than occurred where patrolling was infrequent. In the latter case the enemy would soon realize that they were faced by a poor unit, and would become very active themselves. The lazy battalion would find itself constantly harried by night, and would suffer a steady drain of casualties.

Suffering unnecessary casualties is itself another pointer to low morale. As Robert Graves puts it: 'In battalions where morale was low, one-in-fifty risks were often taken in laziness or despair.'[7] He reckoned that even one-in-two-hundred risks ought only to be taken when in a hurry. I must stress that this applies only to unnecessary risks. There are times when big risks have to be run, as when in an attack or some phase of actual combat with the enemy. The cynical way to put it might be that the soldier's duty is to preserve his life by being careful at unimportant moments so that it is ready to be sacrificed when the right time comes.

But to be cynical about sacrifice is dangerous. There are more ways in which morale can be recognized—one being the readiness of men at all levels to accept responsibility—but the final test is preparedness to sacrifice oneself. Joost A. M. Meerloo, a great expert on the psychology of people under stress and danger, has written:

Somewhere along the line, good morale means solving that mythological anxiety about death being something dark and obscure; and it means the willingness to accept fate. Accepting fate and duty and responsibility is living in a different way: it is living with the moral courage to stand for moral principles that you have gathered in your life and without which life is not worth living.[8]

This leads me on from showing how morale can be gauged to the study of some various, unrelated factors which affect it. The first is a theory of my own, based on Meerloo's description of the two opposite types of person who can resist 'brainwashing'.[9] These he describes as those 'with a history of lifelong rebellion against all authority', and those with a background, stretching back into infancy, of love and affection.[10]

It is my contention that high morale can spring from two sources, which I would call 'nobility of spirit' and 'bloody-mindedness'. These phrases are not wholly the ones I am looking for, but I can find no better. Nobility of spirit, found in the person with a background of love and affection, gives rise to the characteristics usually quoted in connection with good morale. They include love of a cause, love of one's country, loyalty, *esprit de corps,* and unselfishness. All are of great importance, and more will be said of them. What I want to look at first, however, is 'bloody-mindedness': its influence is less obvious, but should not be underrated.

A big part of the British soldier's ability to bear hardship well has always been due to an element of 'bloody-mindedness'. It is without doubt the case as far as the Scottish soldier is concerned. When using the term I do not mean a surly refusal to do what is ordered but a refusal to give way to conditions which might be expected to make a man sour. It has an element of rebellion in it, of course, but the rebelling is not so much against authority as against difficult circumstances. As things get worse the man with this quality becomes more determined to stick them out. It is as though the spirit says: 'I can take it—nothing can break me.' When the battle is at its worst the 'bloody-minded' man proves his staunchness. Private McHugh was a good example of this type of soldier. Kennedy found him at first 'a rather dour, surly sort of fellow', but in action discovered him 'to be possessed of wonderfully fine qualities'.

In attending to the needs of junior soldiers, care must be taken not to forget the morale of the leader, which is as important as that of the men he leads but is often overlooked. It is easy to forget that the leader must have his own morale nurtured if he is to meet the demands of his subordinates. These demands are heavy:

We are becoming more and more aware of how important leadership is in boosting morale. The leader is the embodiment of the valued human relationships for which we are willing to offer our energy and even, when needed, our lives. Through identification with him we borrow his fortitude. . . . The leader must be both a scapegoat and a giant. Our own inner strength will grow, depending on the leader's guiding personality.[11]

Anyone who is going to be these things to other men must be helped in his task.

Of course responsibility, and the very fact of being a leader, helps. The leader knows that other men look to him, and he is supported by their concern in his doings. Having to set an example brings out the best in most of us. Further, the officer or N.C.O. has less opportunity for introspection and less time to think of himself than his men. There are other men's affairs to arrange, and even a Corporal with a small section is taken out of himself and his own worries in looking after his subordinates. What the leader needs more than anything is information. He must be told what is going on so that he can make his own plans and can tell his men what is happening. Only slightly less important to him than information is encouragement. If the leader is not properly looked after himself he may crack, and that is disastrous.

Very few men are staunch enough to go on if their leader breaks. To quote Meerloo again: 'His doubts may become our doubts; his loss of confidence makes us lose our self-confidence.'[12] Although it was unlikely, but not unknown, for an officer in the British Army in 1914–1918 physically to run away, there were always some who did so in the sense of giving up the effort to play their part as leaders and inspirers of their men. They ran away from their duty, and their effect could be very harmful.

Connected to some extent with the morale of the leader is the question of belief in a cause. It always seems to me that the writer or speaker about war has more faith in causes than men who actually fight. Of fighting soldiers who have the time to believe in causes the majority are likely to be found in the ranks of the leaders. In 1914 many private soldiers were caught up in the national wave of emotion about the War, but it cannot have lasted long. In a vague way a number probably went on believing that they were fighting for freedom; anyway to avoid being ordered about by Germans. But probably only a handful felt deeply that they were fighting to preserve a way of life, or to destroy a tyranny, or for any great and lasting good. Perhaps to say 'felt deeply' is wrong, and it would be more correct to say 'were conscious of the fact'. To feel deeply about things, so that feelings become a strong influence on action, is unusual. A man who can translate his beliefs into deeds is rare, and normally to be found in a position of responsibility. As Meerloo puts it in discussing the type of person with a high resistance factor:

People in whom a religious faith or a political conviction is a deeply rooted, living thing have this same sense of belonging, of being needed, of being loved. Their allegiance is to a whole group or to a set of ideals rather than to individuals. To such people, beliefs are real and concrete, as real and concrete as people or objects. They provide a bulwark against loneliness, terror, fantasies conjured up by the unconscious, and the' unleashing of deep-seated conflicts, a bulwark that is as strong as the memory of love. Yet, such mentally strong people form a minority in our conflict-ridden society.[13]

Wherever the mentally strong person is found, whether an officer, N.C.O. or private, his faith becomes of great importance to all those around him. The sort of person who does believe in causes tends to have both enthusiasm and energy, which qualities will evolve into inspired leadership or great devotion to duty. Montague describes a touching example of the latter case:

There was the pallid and bent London clerk, faintly disguised in khaki but too blind to fight, now working furiously fifteen hours each day of his seven-day week in the orderly-room—no Sunday here, no Saturday afternoon—for pure love of international right.[14]

Looking at causes in the sense of believing in them brings me to the other sort of cause—the one linked with effect. The best cause of high morale in this sense is victory. No attention to all the well-tried methods of keeping soldiers in good heart can compare for effectiveness with giving them success. History provides many examples. Napoleon in Italy in 1796, Allenby in Palestine in 1917, Montgomery in North Africa in 1942, and Slim in Burma in 1943 and 1944, show how armies which have started to lose faith in themselves can be turned into invincible forces by the tonic of victory. On the other hand, the First World War demonstrated how morale can continue to be high in defeat, or at least without conclusive victory. There are, I believe, two reasons for this. One was the quality of 'bloody-mindedness' already discussed; the other was the fact that such big losses were sustained.

To give loss of life as a cause of high morale may seem odd, and perhaps a little callous. However, a soldier gets less and less eager to fight the longer he stays in the battle area. A few men thrive on war, but most get progressively more unwilling to face danger as time goes on. A certain doggedness will keep them at their place of duty, but they become increasingly unwilling to face danger. No man can go on for ever; he is, as Lord Moran has shown, eating into his capital of courage all the time. Men become tired of war, and armies which are always in action tire as well. The only way they avoid this process is by being replenished with new men. The unpleasant truth is that heavy losses lead to big reinforcements of fresh men. The British armies in 1914–1918 were constantly receiving transfusions of new blood. Keen, eager young men kept pouring out to replace the killed and wounded, and in this way morale was constantly renewed. Had there been less loss of life it is possible that morale might not have remained so high.

The standard causes of good morale are good food, adequate rest, mail, proper medical care, efficient equipment, and good welfare services, particularly to help families at home, and all are immensely important. Armies can fight well for periods without any of these things, but never for very long. An effort such as was sustained over the four years of the First World War would not have been possible had the administrative requirements for maintaining morale not been adequately met.

A further aspect of morale is the difference between those qualities which are inherent in a soldier and those which are inculcated by training after he joins the Army. Inherent strength comes from the way a man is brought up, particularly in his early years. 'Mental backbone and moral courage go deeper than the intellect. Fortitude is not a physical or intellectual quality; it is something we get from the cradle, from the consistency of our parents' behaviour, and from their beliefs and faith.'[15] I do not believe that the man of normal physical and mental development who has been properly reared in a good home with real love, affection, and interest is likely to break down under the normal strain of war. Naturally if he is physically or mentally handicapped he cannot be expected to face the same difficulties, though there are those who have. The man who cannot survive is the one who is overfaced by abnormal demands, or the one who has never had a proper start in life. On the other hand, one can show that many men who had an appalling childhood were able to react with just as much courage in 1914–1918 as those who had the good fortune to be well brought-up. What is the explanation?

My feeling is that much of it was due to military training and, to repeat a quotation, 'in particular by that part of training which consists in inculcating *esprit de corps*'.[16] In many ways of course this aspect of military training was filling some of the gaps left by a poor upbringing. Above all it was the fact of being wanted, of belonging, which mattered so much. To be a member of a platoon, and also of the larger world of a Regiment was a tremendous thing to the boy from an unhappy home environment.

Along with this factor of belonging must be judged the effects of discipline. So important is discipline in a study of morale that a whole chapter is devoted to it,* but here I turn once again to Meerloo:

Nevertheless, there is usually an inner relation between discipline and morale. Only when a certain amount of initial disciplinary training is given to youngsters or soldiers are they well conditioned for that personal inner strength which is based on self-confidence and trust in the group as a whole, together with confidence in the authorities.[17]

Trust in the group is an essential part of the soldier's development. At the lowest levels the individual is dependent on his immediate fellows to an extraordinary degree. A private soldier in action finds that his section becomes the centre of his life. He finds his platoon and company important as well, and as far as reputation is concerned he thinks occasionally about the battalion and division he is in. But the small groups are the vital ones. In the First World War, especially in its early stages, men were rarely conscious of more than their own companies. Operations were on a relatively small scale, and life revolved within the company. Everything had a

* *Chapter 7.*

'family' flavour: for battalions like the 2nd Scottish Rifles, which hardly changed, apart from a number of casualties, from arriving in France until Neuve Chapelle, this was the natural way of things to soldiers of a long-service army.

One or two general ideas on group morale seem worth adding. It is obviously one of the things that affect us all deeply throughout life. From the earliest age we have to learn to live with other people, starting with our own families. Very soon we meet a formally constituted group for the first time when we go to school. From that moment on life is a continuous pattern of adjusting to groups of all kinds. In our reactions to groups our personalities are expressed. Some want to lead and organize the group, others to serve it; some want simply to belong, and there are those who try to disrupt it. The soldier finds in the groups he belongs to—section, platoon, company, battalion—the interests and affections which the civilian finds in societies, clubs, churches, firms or what you will. Perhaps the soldier's group loyalty is stronger than the civilian's: if this be true there are two reasons for it. First, because in a good unit it is being actively encouraged all the time. Second, because on active service at least all the members of a group rely on each other for their very existence. In war it does not take long for the soldier to discover how dependent he is on his comrades.

Another interesting side of group morale is the degree of influence required to improve or lower it. Taking a company of soldiers as an example it is amazing what influence small numbers can have. Obviously the man at the top, the company commander, has the strongest opportunity of influencing the group. A really good leader can get results with almost any collection of human beings. At the same time a small number of bad soldiers with strong characters—even a single man at times—can have a most disruptive effect. The only thing one can say is that most human beings are fairly easily led in one direction or another. The extent of one man's influence depends on two factors; the first is his position in the group, and the second is the resistance to him from other strong personalities. A determined man in a position of responsibility can always master difficult subordinates because of the advantages he starts with. On the other hand these advantages can be nullified by unwillingness to use them fully. When this happens, and the leader is lazy or lacking in confidence, the way is open for a troublesome subordinate to get a much greater measure of control than is healthy. At moments of great stress in battle one man who breaks down, or deliberately tries to undermine his fellows, can cause a whole company to run away if not resisted. A story told me by someone who was a young Medical Officer in France in 1914–1918 shows how such a lead in the wrong direction had to be broken. On one occasion in the battalion to which this M.O.'s Field Ambulance was attached, a soldier suddenly started screaming out as a German attack was being launched: 'Get out! Get out! We're all going to be killed.' The rest of the men in his trench started to break. There was only one thing to do, and a Sergeant did it. He picked up a spade and hit out with it as hard as he could, splitting the man's head in half and killing him instantly. The rot was stopped, and the German attack was repulsed. As an example of how one man nearly caused a disaster and how the day was saved this story seems to me of great interest. The way it was dealt with may sound excessively brutal, but it was the only answer at the time.

The way a disruptive personality usually works on a group is not quite so dramatic as the case just quoted. His normal way of working is through constant complaint. Traditionally the British soldier has always been allowed to grumble fairly freely, and in men coming from a country where freedom of speech has long been established one understands the need for it. After all, much of war is horrible, and the free man wants to express his feelings about the fact. In doing so he gets rid of a lot of his frustrations, and becomes the sounder soldier because of it. There is, however, a limit to the amount of grumbling that is tolerable. It is not really difficult to judge where the limit comes; it is around the point where the grumble can still be turned into a joke. Once he gets past that point the grumbler can only be ignored with dangerous consequences. If not resisted his discontent will fester and eventually undermine his fellows. At bottom the vicious grumbler is the man who has broken, and whose morale is beginning to slip. Lord Moran says: 'It came to me quite suddenly that the complaining man was the man who was not wearing well, that boredom was a symptom and not a cause of unrest. It was the man himself and not the life he led that was at fault.'[18]

Vicious grumbling should not be confused with what John Brophy calls 'Plain-speaking about war, the cold eye and the literal tongue turned upon what lies beyond the flag-waving and speech-making. . . .'[19] A certain amount of coarse and mocking comment from the men in the ranks about their lot was an important part of the ability of the First World War Army to survive the worst conditions it met.

> . . . when the romantic conception of war proved false, out of date, useless, the man in the line was helped in his daily endurances if he could ridicule all heroics and sing, with apparent shamelessness, *I don't want to be a Soldier*, or *Far Far from Ypres I want to Be*. The songs satirized more than war: they poked fun at the soldier's own desire for peace and rest, and so prevented it from overwhelming his will to go on doing his duty. They were not symptoms of defeatism, but strong bulwarks against it.[20]

One of the most interesting things about human behaviour in war is the enormous difference between two apparently similar men in their reactions to danger and suffering. In normal living such differences do not appear so great. The habitual criminal and the saint are not often met; one usually sees a mass of people who make much the same sort of effort as each other and lead lives of roughly the same quality. In war everything is exaggerated. The good man, who goes on uncomplainingly doing his duty to the end, is divided by an enormous gulf from the shirker, the selfish man, and the coward. It is not necessarily a difference in potential, indeed the good soldier and the coward can change roles, but in performance. Either a soldier is at his place of duty, or he has found some way of getting away from it. There are no half-measures.

It was the knowledge that this is true that led men to go back to the trenches in the First World War even when the chance of avoiding a return was offered in the most tempting form. Frequently a man could not return whatever happened. The damage done to him precluded any chance of his going back, and to do so was pointless, as his physical condition was not good enough.* But frequently a man was offered the opportunity of avoiding going back to the front line when he knew that he was still just able to stand the strain, however much he might hate it. In such a case a man had only his own conscience to guide him. Resisting the temptation to stay in London was part of 'the secret battle' of A. P. Herbert's hero Harry Penrose. When the chance came to him to get a job at the War Office in Intelligence he nearly accepted it. In discussing whether to take the post he said: 'But sometimes . . . when I think of some of the bogus people who've been out, perhaps once, and come home after three months with a nice blighty in the shoulder, and got a job, and stayed in it ever since . . . I feel I can't do that either, and run the risk of being taken for one of them. . . .'[22] Eventually he refused the post, and went back to France, though not for this reason alone. This fear of joining the ranks of those who were 'dodging the column' forced many a weary man to extend himself to the limit.

Most men I am sure returned to battle because they had realized the extent of the gulf between the shirker and the good soldier. They wanted to be on the side of the angels at all costs, and however deeply they hated the War they could not stay away from the battlefields as long as it lasted. Many writers have gone back to Shakespeare's lines from *Henry V* to help them describe this compulsion to stay at the front however great the individual's longing to get away from it. They have quoted:

> And gentleman in England now a-bed,
> Shall think themselves accursed they were not here;
> And hold their manhoods cheap, whiles any speaks
> That fought with us upon St. Crispin's day.[23]

* *Ferrers' return to the 2nd Scottish Rifles in 1917[21] was an example of a pointless return, however admirable in intention. He badgered everyone he knew to let him go back to the front, and eventually got his own way. But he was not really fit enough, and after a month or two was invalided home again. The spirit was willing, but the flesh was still too weak to survive the trenches in winter.*

and in doing so have rightly highlighted one of the greatest factors in good morale.

It is for consideration whether the influences which lead to good morale are unchanging or not. One's first reaction is to say that morale is one of the many aspects of human nature which are little different in the twentieth century from what they were in Roman times. Further, the significant aspects of it—the importance of leadership, of victory, of unselfishness, of willingness to sacrifice oneself, of cheerfulness—are all much the same as they always have been. On the other hand, comparing 1915 with fifty years later one cannot help thinking that soldiers of the earlier days needed less sympathy, comfort, and interest than their modern counterparts, and perhaps most important of all, less explanation of why they should carry out certain actions. On this line, one can go back to 1815 where one sees that Wellington's soldiers needed less of all these attentions than the men of 1915. So perhaps the natural first reaction needs qualifying. One can, perhaps, say that morale is an unchanging quality, and that the ways of sustaining it are in principle unchanging as well, but that where the change comes in is in the methods of applying these principles. As men get more used to comfort, more sophisticated and more intelligent it becomes essential to take more trouble over their morale. The problem is not to discover what keeps the soldier in good heart, but how to apply lessons learnt throughout history to the pattern of modern life in its increasing complexity.

My second point on the nature of morale is to assess the influence of national characteristics. These characteristics stem mainly from geography. The climate, type of soil, and general position of a country dictate the sort of life that is led there. From the type of life spring certain ways of doing things, which in turn harden into unmistakable characteristics. Taking the Lowland Scots as a race one observes that they come from a fairly cold and rather barren area with sea coasts on both sides. The people are therefore outward looking and used to moving away from their own land to find their fortunes. At the same time, within their own boundaries they have the dour attitude of those who live in a hard land with little luxury. Springing from this environment, the Lowland soldier carries easily recognizable traits of character. He refuses to be much impressed by anyone or anything, which comes from his country's long seafaring and wandering tradition. He has a rather serious outlook, and his affections are not easily touched. This comes from the harshness of the land he derives from. Quite a good case could be made for the staunchness of Lowland Scots soldiers being attributable to national characteristics, but at the same time the point should be made that in the 2nd Scottish Rifles there were men from many different parts of the country, and even if the Lowlanders made up the largest single element in the battalion they were by no means an overall majority. It would be wrong to attach too much significance to national characteristics in connection with this study.

To close this chapter, here is a definition of military morale.

High morale is the most important quality of a soldier. It is a quality of mind and spirit which combines courage, self-discipline, and endurance. It springs from infinitely varying and sometimes contradictory sources, but is easily recognizable, having as its hall-marks cheerfulness and unselfishness. In time of peace good morale is developed by sound training and the fostering of *esprit de corps*. In time of war it manifests itself in the soldier's absolute determination to do his duty to the best of his ability in any circumstances. At its highest peak it is seen as an individual's readiness to accept his fate willingly even to the point of death, and to refuse all roads that lead to safety at the price of conscience.*

* *For comparison, here is a definition from Webster's Dictionary:*
Morale
2a: a confident, resolute, willing, often self-sacrificing and courageous attitude of an individual to the functions or tasks demanded or expected of him by a group of which he is a part that is based upon such factors as pride in the achievements and aims of the group, faith in its leadership and ultimate success, a sense of fruitful personal participation in its work, and a devotion and loyalty to the other members of the group.

Officers

But since there are no bad soldiers but only bad officers, the merits of the officers of the army which went to France in 1914 cannot go unrecognized. There was no 'officer corps' in the old British Army. These were in no sense a caste, set apart from civilians; they made no claim to be a social, political or intellectual élite: they were neither arrogant nor exhibitionist. Their principal failing was a cheerful, larky amateurishness—a survival of the Cavalier strain in the English blood—but there were enough natural Cromwellians amongst them to prevent it from getting out of hand. Their virtues were the essential complement of the Army's virtues; and the unifying force was not an army tradition but a regimental tradition, which the N.C.O.s and private soldiers shared to the full with the officers.

John Connell, WAVELL, SCHOLAR AND SOLDIER[1]

OF ALL THE truisms of the military profession, and it has more than its fair share, the truest is the one at the start of the passage quoted above. To the young officer the importance of his own influence is often not obvious, but experience continually brings home the lesson that in any military formation the quality of the men in charge is the most important single factor towards efficiency. The same applies to most other walks of life, but in none so much as in the services. The reason is simple to explain. Military affairs are regulated by orders, and people are taught at all levels to obey these orders. Below commissioned rank obedience becomes one of the main military qualities. It follows therefore that the soldier, or other rank, is influenced at every turn of his daily life by orders from his officers. If these orders are sensible, and passed to him in a manner which he can understand readily, then the soldier's performance and reactions will be entirely different from what they will be when orders are stupid and come to him in a muddled or unreasonable way. Furthermore, since war demands this obedience to orders from the soldier, it is essential to train him to treat the instigators of orders with respect. Should the instigators, the officers, be unworthy of respect the soldier's existence becomes intolerable. In looking to find the sources of the morale of the 2nd Scottish Rifles the place to start is at the top.

The importance of a Commanding Officer cannot be over-emphasized. It is perhaps fair to say that as far as the morale of an Army is concerned the Commanding Officers of battalions and Regiments are the vital people. At the higher levels of command one man's decision may be decisive in winning a battle, and perhaps a whole war. At the unit level one man's personality and efficiency are decisive in creating the spirit of his command, and it is almost frightening to see how the character of a Commanding Officer can be reflected in his battalion. It used to be said that a good horseman could tell in a few minutes from riding a young horse the character of the man who had broken it in. Certainly it is possible for the experienced eye to judge quite soon from working with a battalion the quality of its commander. At no level in the military hierarchy does anyone have such direct power over the lives of those below him. Not only does his approach to all the myriad activities which make up the life of a battalion permeate down to the humblest private, but all his subordinate officers, commissioned and non-commissioned, take their line from him in the running of their particular sub-units.

When he takes his battalion into action its conduct gives a full reflection of his ability. Not only will his skill in the tactical handling of his troops be reflected in their success or failure, but all that he has achieved before the battle will become evident. Every opportunity missed in the training of his officers will bring its inevitable harvest of mistakes and muddle. Any inefficiency which he has allowed to go unchecked will be paid for with the lives of careless men. If this is not enough, he has a further burden to bear in time of war, which is the appalling strain of ordering other men to undertake dangerous or even hopeless tasks. It is also the lot of a General to pass orders down the chain of command which may lead certain men to their deaths, and for a sensitive man this may be a great burden and source of worry. But distance lessens the impact a little. For the Commanding Officer the men in his battalion are terribly close. When he orders them into a dangerous situation he is probably there himself, which helps a little, but even so he is bound to feel a dreadful weight of responsibility.

So that it may not be felt that I have exaggerated the extent of the strains imposed on Commanding Officers, I would like to quote two passages in connection with their duties in the First World War. The first comes from the German side, and is taken from *My War Memories 1914–1918* by General Ludendorff:

The duties of regimental commanders were varied and exceptionally arduous. They were everywhere directly responsible for their troops, and had to answer to their superiors for the appearance and MORAL[E], the success or failure, the weal or woe, of every single man under their command. The outward appearance and inward bearing of the troops, and especially of the Corps of Officers, were indicative of the personality, the will, the capacity, of the commander. He had to inspire his officers and men with his own spirit; he was their example and their stay, their counsellor and friend in periods of inactivity as in battle.[2]

To show what this meant in terms of pure hard grind I can find no better short example than this passage from *General Jack's Diary*:

Nor is the office work light. In the Line and out of it, the volume of correspondence is astounding, between operations, training, administration and routine. Seldom are pen, paper and map laid down till bed-time. I have known battalion commanders pale with fatigue before a battle owing to the preparations for it.[3]

Only a man who was fit and strong could stand the pace. Field-Marshal Lord Wavell put robustness as the first quality of a General; it was certainly the main one required of a Commanding Officer in the First World War.

Perhaps the luckiest thing that could have happened to the 2nd Scottish Rifles was to have George Carter-Campbell on hand to assume command at Neuve Chapelle after the first hour was passed. His character was that required in a man who had to hold together a body of his fellows who had been badly shot up at the very start of a battle. The two outstanding qualities in him were his calmness, and his power to inspire trust. Calmness in times of great stress and danger is the finest expression of a man's inward robustness and courage. Carter-Campbell's calmness was probably the main contributory cause of this ability he had to gain the trust of the men. Over many years they had learnt to respect his fairness and strict determination, and when the real test came of all that they had so long been training for it must have been an enormous relief to see him calmly coming up to the front to take control.

It may seem odd that having stressed so much the importance of a Commanding Officer I should first have mentioned Carter-Campbell rather than Colonel Bliss. However, I cannot help regarding him as more the Commanding Officer than Bliss. Not only did he command at Neuve Chapelle for a much longer period, but during the months in Malta when he was in temporary command he had done so much to give the battalion a special sense of purpose and efficiency that it bore his stamp more clearly than that of Bliss.

Although I believe Carter-Campbell to have been the better and more inspiring officer, Bliss should not be underestimated. He had the fault of over-centralizing, and annoyed some of his extremely able Company Commanders by his insistence on taking things into his own hands which would have been better left to them. He was also very conventionally minded, and in this respect was blamed by many of his officers for the death of the Adjutant, Captain Maunsell, shortly before Neuve Chapelle. This arose because in the old peacetime way he always insisted on having his Adjutant with him when he went on any tour of inspection. Going round the barracks in Malta this was sensible; going up to the trenches in France it was unnecessary, and meant risking two valuable lives for no real purpose. Maunsell was killed in daylight by a sniper on his way up to a front-line position at Bliss's side. The whole episode was considered stupid and wasteful by most of the officers, and Bliss became more unpopular than ever. In spite of this he continued to run a good battalion, and the reasons are worth examining.

First, he was a man of integrity. He might have been, as one of his officers has written to me about him, 'Crimean in many ways—steeped in outmoded tradition and not prone to delegation of duties', but nobody doubted that he was genuine and sincere, and within his limitations a sound, practical officer. Such qualities are obviously best balanced by intelligence and imagination, but where it comes to a straight choice between solid honesty and integrity on the one hand, or quickness and intelligence on the other, then there is no doubt at all which a battalion commander needs most. To quote Wavell again: 'In the end character is more important than brains.'[4] Whether this will always be the case may be open to question, but it certainly was in 1915.

The second reason why Bliss could still have a good battalion in spite of being viewed critically by some of his officers was that he was known to be very loyal to the Regiment. Much could be excused on this score, and his subordinates therefore kept their complaints to themselves, and continued to give him their loyalty in spite of doubts about his competence.

The final reason was that he was strict. A martinet usually has a good effect on those he commands, and a man like Bliss could be respected for his high standards and insistence that they should be maintained. He might not have been very clever, but in a solid traditional way he got results. This should perhaps be his epitaph.

The influence of the Commanding Officer was the greatest overall factor in shaping the battalion's character, but close to it came the influence of his Company Commanders. Perhaps the most important sphere in which these men could have an effect was in training, and setting an example to their young officers. A Company Commander was in close contact with his second-in-command and his subalterns throughout most of any ordinary day. In peacetime they saw a great deal of each other, both in the Company lines and in the Mess. As all four Company Commanders in the 2nd Scottish Rifles were bachelors they had every opportunity in Malta to guide their juniors along the right lines. In time of war all the officers of a company lived together and messed together in one dugout in the trenches, and soon got to know most things about each other. Out of the trenches they often lived in much the same way by company groups in billets. Hayes, Ferrers, Lloyd and Ellis did a great deal to shape the characters of their young officers, both in working hours and off duty. Being a very sound and capable group this was an invaluable asset to the battalion. Had they been a poor lot they could have done irreparable harm.

The young officer coming out of Sandhurst in 1914 tended to be very impressionable: even more so perhaps than today. Arriving in his Regiment as a commissioned officer he was desperately anxious to do all the things that those around him did. He was unlikely to be very critical, as all his training and upbringing had been geared to making him obedient and ready to accept authority. C. E. Montague in his *Disenchantment* shows that he found an almost pathetic lack of intelligence and initiative in most young officers. He makes a very strong attack on almost every aspect of the old type of Regular officer. Having said that 'the fashion in sentiment in our Regular Army was to think hard work "bad form"; a subaltern was felt to be a bit of a scrub if he worried too much about discovering how to support an attack when he might be more spiritedly employed in playing polo', Montague goes on:

Consider the course of the life of the British Regular officer as you had known him in youth—not the pick, the saving few, the unconquerably sound and keen, but the average, staple article made by a sleek, complacent, snobbish, safe, wealth-governed England after her own image. Think of his school; of the mystic, aureole of quasi-moral beauty attached by authority there to absorption in the easy thing—in play; the almost passionate adoration of all those energies and dexterities which, in this world of evolution towards the primacy of the acute, full brain, are of the least possible use as aids to survival in men and to victory in armies. . . .

With an equal firmness your early power of supple and bright-coloured speech may be taken away and a rag-bag of feeble stock phrases, misfits for all your thoughts, and worn dull and dirty by everyone else, be forced upon you instead of the treasure you had. You may leave school unable to tell what stars are about at night or to ask your way to a journey's end in any country but your own. Between your helpless mind and most of your fellow-countrymen thick screens of division are drawn, so that when you are fifteen you do not know how to speak to them with a natural courtesy; you have a vague idea that they will steal your watch if you leave it about. Above all, you have learnt that it is still 'bad form' to work; that the youth with brains and no money may well be despised by the youth with money and no brains; that the absorbed student or artist is ignoble or grotesque; that to be able to afford yourself 'a good time' is a natural title to respect and regard; and that to give yourself any 'good time' that you can is an action of spirit. So it went on at prep. school, public school, Sandhurst, Camberley.[5]

As an attack on Regular officers it is vigorous and carries conviction. However, I would like to make three points. The first is that it is exaggerated, even though it no doubt contains a basis of truth. Secondly, I believe that Montague judged all officers by some of the relics of the Regular Army whom he met in his early days in training establishments in the United Kingdom. On the whole what he met in such places were the discards—the ones whom active service battalions would not keep. Thirdly, I think he slipped into the old human failing of judging the general by the particular. Soldiers are often subject to this treatment, as Colonel G. F. R. Henderson showed in connection with the Boer War:

Fame takes little or no notice of the shortcomings of the lawyer, of the parson, or the man of business; but the subaltern who rides into an ambush is criticized and derided at every breakfast-table, and his recklessness or misfortune furnishes smug common sense with a new and unanswered argument against the inefficiency of the whole body of his brother officers.[6]

Montague made a great mistake in condemning officers in general in a way that was only justified in respect of a minority. My own belief is that the good type of officer was much more in evidence than the 'sleek, complacent, snobbish' kind—certainly in the 2nd Scottish Rifles, where the 'unconquerably sound and keen' were there in numbers which made them much more 'the average, staple article' than merely 'the saving few'. On the other hand there is truth in what he has to say about schools and 'their almost passionate adoration of those energies and dexterities' which were of so little use; also about the taking away of the 'early power of supple and bright-coloured speech'. Knowing many men who were Regular officers before 1914 I feel that criticism of them for being too concerned with matters physical at the expense of matters intellectual, and also for being limited in their power of speech, is quite fair. But to criticize them for being 'sleek, complacent, snobbish' is not. Nor indeed do most of Montague's comments fit them well, at least as I have known them in their advancing years.

The young officer joining the 2nd Scottish Rifles in Malta was likely to be very receptive to the influence of his first Company Commander. If he started his service under a vigorous and intelligent officer, or a character like Ferrers, it could bring out all the best in him. Of Ferrers' particular power for good in this direction it is impossible to speak too highly. His immense enthusiasm, his emotional love of the Regiment, his quick wit, his courage, and perhaps most of all his eccentric approach to so many problems—all these facets of his character made his influence irresistible to his juniors. They were swept along into a world where all the virtues they had learnt about as children were actually being practised. Honour and high principles really lived in Ferrers, and were not just qualities to which he paid lip-service. At times he may have been a little ridiculous, but what a tonic this strange man provided!

Since the Commanding Officer and Company Commanders

had such an influence on the lives and the outlook of the other officers in the battalion, the effect of their influence must be examined. A fairly standard attitude to life developed among officers, even though there was nothing like complete conformity. The way I will explain my idea of the nature of this attitude will be by describing the ideal officer as he would have appeared to a young man of the time. Before doing that, however, certain factors which tended to reinforce this development of a common outlook among officers should be examined.

Factor number one was living in the Mess together. Only four officers in Malta were married. The rest lived in the Mess, and their ages varied from about twenty to forty-five. This meant that a certain tendency developed for the older officers to take charge of the conversation, and have things organized in the way that they wanted. The young officer was not particularly sat-on, but he inevitably slipped into a chair and listened to an argument rather than stood in front of the fire and started one. One could claim that young officers suffered from this sort of influence by being constantly indoctrinated against their will by their seniors and having no chance to air their own views. I am assured, however, by those who lived in the Mess before 1914 that this was not the case. Although a young man was not expected to hold the floor too freely he was perfectly at liberty to state his views, and was in no way crushed if his views were sensible. My own feeling is that having officers of all ages living together contributed towards a happy atmosphere. When all the older officers are married a Mess becomes, for much of the time, entirely the province of the young. It is easily forgotten that the young are just as capable of creating from among themselves a mental tyranny to crush individuality as any body of their elders. One usually finds that the most mature, balanced and individual people are those who have constantly mixed with other people of all ages. And on this subject of individuality, it is worth noting that in the Victorian and Edwardian eras, for all the deliberate efforts of older people to mould their young people into acceptable shapes, many 'characters' and eccentrics survived.

Also reinforcing a common outlook among the officers of the 2nd Scottish Rifles was their background. They came from near the top of the social tree in the most powerful nation in the world. From this fact most of them drew both satisfaction and strength. Some of course drew only satisfaction; really more self-satisfaction, or smugness. It could be thoroughly distasteful. In reviewing *Edwardian England 1901–1914** Cyril Connolly described the sort of people who battened on Britain's greatness:

I am old enough to be able to remember that greatness, the golden sovereigns, the sense of honour, the huge red blocks on the map, the delicious postage stamps with their handsome surcharges. But I also remember the incredible silliness and gigantic conceit of so many unimportant and self-satisfied people who were carried by the system: Anglo-Indian ladies, rentiers moving from one European resort to another, to the English clubs and tea-rooms, the vast network of poor relations whom Italian hoteliers or seaside landladies had to welcome. For one 'Edwardian' with a large income and a fine house there seemed a hundred self-important scroungers.

To the Anglo-Indian ladies and the rentiers must certainly be added a percentage of incompetent Army officers. There was undoubtedly a type to be found in most Regiments whose stock phrase was: 'It doesn't matter so long as the fellow is a gentleman.' But I believe there were never many. From my study of the Scottish Rifles in Malta I would say that there were hardly any officers of this sort; certainly no more than two, possibly three, out of twenty-eight.

This is not to say that the majority of officers did not think it important to be a 'gentleman', but that they regarded it as mattering a great deal more that 'the fellow' had other qualities as well as that of social acceptability. The whole structure of society was such that it was important to come from a good background, and the last thing I want to pretend is that his social position was not important to an officer, nor that he would be accepted in the 2nd Scottish Rifles if not a

* Sunday Times, *8 October 1964.*

'gentleman'. The thing is that position meant responsibility. This was where the strength came from. Most officers set themselves certain standards of behaviour below which their consciousness of their own status would not let them slip. Mostly this concerned honesty and courage. To lie or to run away were simply not conceivable, just as the idea would never enter the head of a gentleman to be dishonest over money or anything connected with it—no question, for example, of being 'sharp' over taxes. The cynic can point out that it was not worth being dishonest in small ways when you had so much already, but it went deeper than that. There was a fundamental conception of the word gentleman carrying with it much of its traditional meaning as well as referring purely to social standing. For every individual who used it only in the latter sense—the 'unimportant and self-satisfied' type of person just mentioned—there were six who understood it to connote qualities of chivalrous and honourable conduct.

Another factor which helped to form a common attitude to life among the officers of the Scottish Rifles was their inevitable involvement in the national admiration for physical courage and physical stamina. We still have this in Britain today, but to nothing like the extent of fifty years ago. There appear to have been two main causes for this obsession with physical 'guts' and strength of body. Partly it came from the Public Schools, and partly from memories of Regency days.

It has often been suggested that games first came into prominence at Public Schools in an effort to tire out the boys so that their thoughts would not stray on to matters of sex. Highly organized team games gradually developed during the nineteenth century, and became increasingly a part of the official life of schools. Certainly by the beginning of this century skill at games was a prerequisite for a successful school career. The possession of a good brain was in general estimation far less important than skill on the football or cricket fields. This aspect is of course well known, and of recent years many writers have drawn attention to it. The lingering influence of the Regency tradition on the British upper classes is much less appreciated. All the righteousness and high moral principles of Victorian upbringing could not wipe out an urge to go back to the days of prize-fighting, moonlight steeple-chases, and gambling on feats of endurance. In the Army this lived on very strongly.

Young officers took a great pride in being really hard and tough. One officer in the 2nd Scottish Rifles in 1910 made a bet that he could ride a mile, run a mile, swim a mile and row a mile all in the space of one hour. He achieved this feat with seven minutes to spare, and won his bet. To do something like this was looked on with great admiration, which to my mind it certainly deserved. To be a good horseman and to 'go well' out hunting was a sure way of gaining esteem. To be also an amateur jockey and ride in point-to-points and hunter 'chases was a tremendous feather in an officer's cap, which again was fair. Although there was definitely a tendency to overrate the importance of these sorts of activities at the expense of real ability, they had much to commend them. The man who rides a horse over a steeplechase course needs real courage to do it, and in doing so he learns to react quickly in moments of danger. It can well be said that to give an officer a confidential report, such as was quite common before 1914, of 'A good man to hounds', was rather silly in the age of the machine-gun and barbed-wire fence. But it was not wholly silly. Officers needed dash and quick reactions as much as brains and knowledge. What was wrong was to overemphasize dash while totally ignoring intelligence, or if not ignoring it putting it into second place.

Care for their men also made officers approach matters in the same sort of way. No officer could expect to have the respect of his fellows unless he took care of his soldiers. This was a fundamental principle. Some found it easy, and were genuinely and deeply interested in all aspects of their soldiers' lives. Such officers would know the name of every man in their own company and something about him, and probably the names of a very large percentage of the other men in the battalion. They would take infinite pains to sort out every problem brought to them by an N.C.O. or a Private, and would not dream of admitting that there could ever be better men than those they commanded. Some others might find it less easy to take a genuine interest, but these would never confess to such a weakness. The convention was absolute that an officer cared for his men. This was reinforced by such rules as the one on removing equipment after a route march. No officer in the Scottish Rifles was allowed to take off any of his own equipment on return from a long march until he had inspected his men's feet and had seen them have a meal. One's mind often finds it difficult to accept the fact that people many years ago did simple, efficient, methodical things in much the same way as they do today. Perhaps this is because history tends to dramatize situations. The imagination pictures the pre-1914 officer in almost any pose other than that of carefully examining a soldier's feet after a march.

An officer's outlook on life was much influenced by loyalty to the Regiment. Once a man was commissioned into a particular Regiment it was assumed that he placed its interest before everything else in his life. Demanding everything, the Regiment usually got it. In The Cameronians (Scottish Rifles) there was the rivalry between the two battalions which has already been discussed. Because of this an officer had a sort of dual loyalty; battalion first and Regiment second. But that is rather splitting hairs, and the main thing is to stress how much the Regimental spirit meant in all officers' lives. Although to modern eyes there may be something a little odd, even unbalanced, in the idea of a man being expected to put his Regiment before his own marriage and family life, it did not appear strange to young men before 1914. Deep down inside most of them there was a feeling that the true purpose of life was to serve some noble cause in an all-male community. This came from their upbringing both at home and at school, but whatever its roots, this insistence that the Regiment should be the prime interest in an officer's life certainly ensured his loyalty. Nobody was likely to treat lightly an organization which asked so much of him. Once he had accepted his conditions of joining an officer could not fail to become deeply involved in his Regiment, and to regard its good name and success as vital matters.

Finally, I want to mention a sense of duty. The devotion to duty of the best type of regular officer was perhaps his greatest quality. Whenever one is tempted to criticize the apparent coldness, the reserve, the inhibition of men like General Jack one must remind oneself that from these attributes sprang their formidable sense of duty. Having learnt to dominate their passions and feelings they could control their natural desire to take the easy way out of difficult situations. In his Foreword to the *Diary* Sidney Rogerson writes of Jack as he knew him in the trenches:

It is true to say that during those months I never really knew him, however much I grew to love and admire him. For one thing, his sense of duty was far too strict for most of us young men to understand. For another, he had an almost exasperating punctiliousness in what often appeared to us to be unimportant details of military etiquette as well as discipline.[7]

It is interesting to speculate whether the sense of duty could have existed without the punctiliousness. I have a feeling that it could not. Unless he is punctilious a man's natural reactions are always going to make him do things slightly less well than he should. The really conscientious person creates for himself a host of rules and observances by which he regulates his life. In times of stress he holds on to these and draws a strength from them which would rarely come to someone more easy-going.

Most Commanding Officers in the First World War would, I am sure, have said that the best officer was the one who was reliable. The man who was always there at the right time, always calm, always dependable was the sort of officer everyone wanted. The connection between reliability and sense of duty is obvious. It's a rather dull quality to talk about, but such things as courage, intelligence, drive, initiative, and good humour come to nothing in a man without reliability. A sense of duty could possibly be described as reliability with a spark—the same thing expressed more positively.

When an officer came to command a battalion himself his sense of duty became more important than ever. Not only was it an essential attribute if he was to do conscientiously all the varied things which clamoured for his attention, but also if he was to accept the full responsibility of his position. This meant protecting the interests of his subordinates, and when necessary taking the blame for their failings. No Commanding Officer with a high sense of duty would shirk accepting complete responsibility for what went on in his battalion. Jack, as a Commanding Officer, was driven by his sense of duty to go out at nights to watch patrols moving off:

My patrol leaders understand that I trust them to do their best, but nothing stupidly rash. When they are going in front with their men on important missions I take post in the advance trench to cancel the duty if conditions are unsuitable, and to be responsible if Higher Command are dissatisfied with the endeavour.[8]

How much easier it would have been for him to stay in his dug-out. How many Commanding Officers, even the best, would go to such lengths to do what they thought was their duty? This little passage covers in my opinion the fullest meaning of the phrase 'a sense of duty'.

With these factors which helped to mould a common outlook among officers in mind, I will try to describe the ideal officer as he would have appeared to one of his contemporaries in 1914. All human beings indulge in picturing themselves as they would like to appear to others. It is a harmless recreation at the worst; it may often be a good one. I am sure that no better clue to a man's attitude to life can be found than his private image of what he would like to be. Normally one gets an idea of this from even a close friend only from the occasional revealing remark. I am quite sure that one would never have succeeded in getting an officer of the 2nd Scottish Rifles to describe his inner feelings on the matter. However, I believe that if one could have done so the average young officer serving with the battalion in Malta in 1914 would have produced a word portrait along these lines:

The ideal officer is a tall man, about six foot, and lean. He has one of those thin, aristocratic faces with a faintly Roman nose which epitomize the well-bred Englishman. His eyes are blue, and very penetrating in their stare. Always immaculately turned out in uniform or civilian clothes he has a large wardrobe of expensive but unostentatious clothes, all of which come from the best tailors in London. His legs are very thin, enabling him to wear the straightest and narrowest boots imaginable. These, like his shoes, are made by the best makers, and are kept supple and highly polished under all conditions.

He is at ease in all company, and able to take part in conversation on most subjects, though tending to be reserved and quiet. He has the most courteous manners, and is unfailingly polite to women. In the company of men he is capable of quick and witty comment, and can give a good 'rocket' when necessary.

In manner he is dignified, and always carries himself erectly. Calmness in times of stress and danger is one of his main attributes. He is also very brave physically. Of moral courage he also has plenty, and will stand up for his subordinates whatever his seniors may say about them. To his seniors he is sometimes rather aloof, and refuses to be impressed by high rank. He will go to any length to avoid giving even the faintest impression of currying favour.

At field sports he excels, being an excellent shot and a skilful fisherman. Horsemanship is another sphere in which his skill is well known. He is a good jockey with great determination in riding a finish, and is always up with the first flight in the hunting field. Horsemastership, or the art of judging and caring for horses, is as important to him as the actual art of riding. His own animals are always beautifully turned out.

He plays all ball games well, having a good eye and a natural sense of balance which combine to make skill at games come easily to him. He never takes them too seriously, however, and is a very good loser.

He has had a certain amount of experience of active service in minor campaigns, where his courage has already been noted. As a peacetime officer he is known as a strict disciplinarian, and a stickler for good drill and turn-out. He is also a great believer in physical fitness, and is known to be exceptionally hard and wiry himself. His soldiers are devoted to him, and he is most conscientious over all duties connected with their welfare. 'Bumf', or paper work, he has no time for, and he cares little for the theory of his profession. Whenever possible he gets away from his Regiment on leave or some form of expedition or travel.

The Regiment, on the other hand, as an institution, is the first love of his life. He is not married, and such other loves as he has of the more conventional sort are fleeting affairs which never quite draw him away from his active life.

He is a reasonably religious man, and goes regularly to Church. On the other hand he makes little reference to this in his speech. His normal way of life is austere, and he eats and drinks fairly moderately because of his preoccupation with keeping fit. At the same time he knows all about wines, and is a sound judge of port.

His background is naturally impeccable. He comes of 'a good family' and was educated at a well-known Public School. Although by no means rich he has a private income sufficiently large to allow him to do all the social and sporting things expected of him.

He is in fact an excellent example of what an officer and a gentleman should be like.

Accepting that the picture I have drawn is reasonably accurate, there are a number of comments to make on it. The first thing that will strike most readers is the lack of ambition and deep professional interest. There is good ground for criticizing the general run of officers of those days on this score. At the same time the criticism needs to be qualified. There was a solid group of very serious professional soldiers in the Army, which, although small, was well up to the standard of any other Army in the world. To claim, as many do, that the stalemate on the Western Front was due to stupid and unprofessional British Generals being in charge of operations is to miss the truth. Field-Marshal Lord Haig is well described by John Terraine as 'the educated soldier'. Field-Marshal Sir William Robertson,* who had such influence on British strategy, was a man who had risen to the top of his profession from humble beginnings on merit, brains, and industry alone. The best answer to complaints about the stupidity of British Generals is given by pointing out the

* *Field-Marshal Sir William Robertson, Bart., G.C.B., G.C.M.G., G.C.V.O., D.S.O. was born in 1860, the son of a Lincolnshire villager. He joined the 16th Lancers as a trooper in 1877, and was promoted Troop Sergeant-Major in 1885. In 1888 he was gazetted 2/Lieutenant in the 3rd Dragoon Guards. He became a Major-General in 1910 as Commandant of the Staff College, Camberley. He was appointed Chief of the Imperial General Staff in December 1915, and in April 1919 was given command of the British Army of Occupation on the Rhine. In the same year he was created a baronet, and he was promoted to Field-Marshal in 1920. He was appointed Colonel of his old Regiment, the 3rd Dragoon Guards in 1925, and of the Royal Horse Guards (the Blues) in 1928.*

inability of the ultra-professional German High Command and General Staff to produce any better ideas.

Returning to the amateur approach of the ordinary British Regimental officer I am prepared to make a suggestion that his lack of intense professionalism was in some ways an asset. There is no doubt that the importance attached by the British officer to his Regiment and his men would have been greatly lessened if the prevailing attitude of mind among infantry officers had been more studiously professional. It is inevitable that men who become completely absorbed in the technicalities of their work should become ambitious. Ambitious men are necessary, but not too many of them. A whole Army full of eager officers all trying to reach the top of the promotion ladder would have resulted in far too many concerning themselves with their own advancement rather than such lowly matters as caring for their soldiers. If this seems to be overstating the case I can only submit that my personal experience of life bears out the truth of it. A few men, in any walk of life, can be both ambitious and thoughtful of others but most who catch the bug of ambition soon think of little else than their own advancement.

Also, in a paradoxical way the amateur approach of the pre-1914 officer became a very strong professionalism, though in rather a devious manner. By bringing his sporting and social life into his Regimental life the officer in fact bound himself more strongly to the Army than he probably realized. Admittedly he did not think of himself as belonging to 'the Army', but to a Regiment, and his loyalty was often limited very much to his own small Regimental world. But for all that the Regiment was part of the Army, and the nation got devoted service from many men who integrated themselves completely into a small part of its defence service. A parallel can be drawn here between the pre-1914 Regular officer and the executive in a great modern firm. The big corporation which ties up its executives' lives so much in the firm's well-being that they almost cease to have any identity outside their business is doing something similar to a British Regiment in pre-1914 days.

Another aspect of the unconscious professionalism of the

old Regular officer comes out in comparing him with his modern counterpart. Today's officer may be better qualified in many respects, and have a much broader view of his profession, but he is sometimes rather a '9-to-5' type of man. He may know more about strategy, but early marriage and small children can draw him away from care of his men in a way that officers of the 2nd Scottish Rifles in the days before the First World War would have thought disgraceful.

Finally on this subject of professionalism, there was a lot to be said for having officers in the Army who were uninterested in the higher science of war if only because they were not likely to involve the country in unnecessary wars. Thinking of themselves as gentlemen, administrators, keepers-of-the peace, sportsmen—anything almost rather than experts on war—Army officers in Britain were much better guardians of peace than their counterparts in other countries. The surge of enthusiasm for martial glory in 1914, was as much civilian in origin as inspired by the Army. There must have been many regular officers who shared the feelings of General Jack. His diary for 8 August 1914 reads:

But hating bloodshed as I do, and having had a hard if not dangerous fifteen months in the South African War (1901–1902) together with many racing, hunting, and polo accidents, I personally loathe the outlook. A queer soldier! . . .[9]

Perhaps it was a queer outlook for a soldier, but it was preferable to the professional militarism of the German officer of those days.

The obsession of the British Army with matters of dress was not an entirely military attitude, but sprang to a great extent from the social background of officers, which in its turn reflected the views of Royalty and the aristocracy. An example of the attention paid by Royalty to these matters is shown by this story about King Edward VII:

Like many monarchs, the king was apt to become unduly absorbed in ornamental detail, especially full-dress and mess uniform. His grandson, the Duke of Windsor, relates that King Edward caught him wearing the uniform of one regiment of Foot Guards, with the spurs belonging to another, and for long afterwards used to say over and over again how lucky it was they had met that morning.[10]*

King George V was also a stickler for details of dress being absolutely right. In John Betjeman's poem 'Death of King George V', which is so evocative of the old order and the approach to life of those who grew up before 1914, are the lines:

> The big blue eyes are shut which saw wrong clothing,
> And favourite fields and coverts from a horse; . . .[11]

In those days to appear wrongly or unsuitably dressed was social death.

In spite of the fact that people today in all walks of life devote an immense amount of time, thought, and interest to their own clothes and appearance, it is fashionable to mock the way in which earlier generations spent so much time dressing-up in fancy uniforms. To some extent this is justified. A good example of the lengths to which concern with matters of dress could take a soldier's mind away from the true interests of his profession is given in Margery Perham's *Lugard, The Years of Adventure, 1858–1898*. Explaining Lugard's struggle with the War Office over the appointment of officers for the West African Frontier Force, Miss Perham describes one of the Colonels who had already started to organize the Force before Lugard arrived on the scene:

He was a wealthy man and much interested in the sartorial side of the force, down to the design of the buttons, and he drew up a list of things needed by the officers which, Lugard remarked, were enough for a three years' campaign with elephants for transport.[12]

* *It is only right to add that Edward VII is shown, in the same chapter from which this is quoted, as being immensely knowledgeable on military matters of much greater import, and as having a great and beneficial influence on the reorganization of the Army during his reign.*

Although the date this happened was 1897 no doubt a number of officers still serving in the First World War would have looked on buttons as one of the more vital aspects of the military profession!

One should not, however, go too far in condemning concern with outward appearance. Take General Jack when, on 1 July 1916, he was Second-in-Command of the 2nd Scottish Rifles at the Battle of the Somme, and was put in charge of 'B' and 'D' Companies. He describes how he got ready for the battle:

About 4.30 a.m. on July 1st, following an almost sleepless night of work and tension, with the deafening cannonade, too, still ringing in our ears, I rose, shaved—there was not enough water for washing —slipped on tunic, boots, accoutrements and silver spurs in order to be properly dressed for, likely enough, the last time. Holden, who had cleaned my uniform and belts as well as possible, gave me a final brush before a breakfast of tea, bread and butter only, the more solid of our mess rations having been lost during shelling on the way up the previous night.[13]

During the day that followed Jack showed himself a fine leader and a highly intelligent soldier. I am sure that when he went out to his half-expected death with his spurs on, and his uniform as smart as he could make it, he was just that much better at his job because of these things than he might have been. He describes how during the morning his party were subjected to 'an infernal pounding from the enemy's howitzers. I could see nothing of what was going on in front. . . . Time and again we were covered with soil and débris thrown up by the shells. The strain on the waiting men was very great, so I took to joking about the dirt scattered over my well-cut uniform, while dusting it off with a handkerchief.' This extraordinary composure also enabled Jack to keep his head throughout the rest of the battle to such an extent that, by skilful handling of his men, he was largely the cause of losses in the 2nd Scottish Rifles being infinitely smaller than in other battalions of the brigade. I would not go so far to say that the smart clothes made Jack a fine officer, but I would suggest that his elegance at the height of battle was a symbol of his courage, and of his ability to be master of the turmoil around him.*

From describing the appearance of the ideal officer, I turned the attention of my imaginary subaltern to his skill at field sports, and his effortless ability to play games. John Arlott has written:

If Edwardian sport is to have one exemplar—which is not truly possible—it must be the Corinthians.† They seemed to personify, in their dashing, dilettante brilliance, the gay gallantry which a world war pillaged. Even in the twenties they were a nostalgically faithful echo of that earlier time. Simply to see them saunter on to a football field, scorning shin-guards, in fresh white cricket shirts, hands deep in the pockets of their uniquely shaped, dark-blue shorts was to feel a difference—deep, however out-dated—between their patrician negligence and the professional football of the industrial towns. Even their style of play was peculiarly their own, a blend of the artistic and the robust; in attack, keeping the ball closely along the ground with fast dribbling and short passing: defending with racing tackles and lusty shoulder-charging.[15]

This Corinthian approach to football reflected exactly the attitude to games of regular officers of the day; the combination of a casual manner and hard tackling epitomize the best of that generation's way of life.

The overall portrait of the ideal officer reflects a remarkable simplicity of outlook. This I believe to be important. Winston

---

* *In* Wellington: A Reassessment, *Sir Charles Petrie writes of dress in an earlier campaign in a different vein. 'Actually no general ever cared less about these matters than did Wellington, and he never worried officers or men about details of uniform on active service. Perhaps his indifference was due to his Irish back-ground.' 'Provided we brought our men into the field well appointed,' says Grattan of the 88th, 'with their sixty rounds of ammunition each, he never looked to see whether trousers were black, blue, or grey, and as to ourselves, we might be rigged out in any colour of the rainbow if we fancied it. The consequence was that scarcely any two officers were dressed alike. Some wore grey braided coats, others brown, some again liked blue: many (from choice, or perhaps necessity) stuck to the "old red rag".'[1]*

† *Stanley Clarke was a Corinthian.*

Churchill wrote: 'How these Victorians busied themselves and contended about minor things!'[16] When I read about Edwardian days I get the same feeling; when I talk to men who grew up before 1914 I am often astonished to find how much matters of only the slightest importance to me mean to them, and how easy they appear to find problems which to me present appalling difficulties. It is not so much that officers of 1914 and earlier were naïve—indeed they often knew more of the seamy side of life than their modern counterparts—but that they were uncomplicated. They saw things more in terms of black and white than most of us do today. Also their environment, at least until the First World War started, was so secure that they had time to be deeply concerned with matters of etiquette, dress, manners, and social precedence. The bigger affairs of life presented so few problems. As Alan Clark has written of the men of Kitchener's New Armies: 'Behind them stretched the ordered childhoods of Victorian Britain; decency, regularity, a Christian upbringing, a concept of chivalry; overriding faith in the inevitable triumph of right over wrong; such notions were imbued in them.'[17] In this passage, although it was not actually written about regular officers, I find explained very neatly the roots from which sprang the simple philosophy of life of the officers of the 2nd Scottish Rifles.

To sum up these officers, at whom we have looked so closely, I would say that they were men well suited to the life of the Army in which they served. The good ones, who formed the majority, drew assurance and strength from their social position without becoming unduly arrogant and snobbish. Their uncomplicated approach to life, with its consequent lack of intellectual inquisitiveness, make them no doubt a little dull and reactionary. At the same time it enabled them to carry out their simple duties efficiently and enthusiastically, and also gave them a strong faith in the virtue of their own way of life. Doubt was not one of their worries. From their admiration of physical strength and courage came obvious military advantages: they were almost all brave, fit, and capable of enduring hardship and pain cheerfully. Finally, out of their upbringing in an age and country where traditional institutions of all sorts flourished they slipped naturally into acceptance of the Regiment as the centre of their life, and from this came the priceless virtue of *esprit de corps*, on which their morale was to such a great extent founded.

Other Ranks

*But above them all towers the homely but indomitable figure of
the British soldier, the finest all-round fighting man the world
has seen; who has won so many battles that he never doubts of
victory, who has suffered so many defeats and disasters on the
way to victory that he is never greatly depressed by defeat; whose
humorous endurance of time and chance lasts always to the end.*

Field-Marshal Earl Wavell, THE SOLDIER AS CITIZEN[1]

HAVING TRIED TO show how some of the other ranks in the
2nd Scottish Rifles reacted to the conditions they had to face
at Neuve Chapelle and how their morale was such that they
were able to withstand all the horror of the battlefield and
remain a properly organized and disciplined body of men
although reduced to a fraction of their original numbers, I
must look much deeper into the structure of the other rank
world. My approach to matters of background is naturally
tied up, as it was with the officers, with questions of social
class. The classes mainly dealt with in this chapter, the working class and the real lower class, were very much apart.
Sociologists know that at the lower end of the social scale
class distinctions are just as fierce as at the top, largely because
relatively small differences in income can mean big differences
in living conditions. This certainly was the case in the period
up to the First World War. The working class, with steady
jobs and a certain security, were able to feed reasonably well,
and were often big and well set-up. They were able to play
a part in community life, to have ambitions, and to think of
bettering their lot. The real lower class on the other hand

could barely exist, and physically were generally stunted and unhealthy. Life was simply a question of remaining alive from day to day. Planning and foresight could rarely be applied by them to their lives. These tremendous differences colour much of the content of this chapter.

Trying to balance the proportions of men in the 2nd Scottish Rifles who came from the different classes I would estimate it to be:*

Lower-middle class	—	5 per cent
Working class	—	25 per cent
Real lower class	—	70 per cent

The 'gentleman ranker' was of course a fairly common type of the day, but like 'the trooper of the forces who has run his own six horses' in Kipling's poem,[3] he was usually found in the cavalry. I can certainly find no trace of any 'gentleman ranker' in the 2nd Scottish Rifles, though one of the officers, Fergusson, who later became a famous figure in the Sudan, had come to the battalion after doing three years in the ranks in the 8th Hussars instead of entering through Sandhurst.

Examples of men from the different classes fall into place quite easily. Graham, who at Neuve Chapelle was Quartermaster, was an example of the small element who joined the ranks from the lower middle-classes. Chalmers came from the upper end of the working class, as did such Warrant Officers as C.S.M. Culley and C.S.M. McBeath. C.S.M. Conway, who was a commissioned officer by the time of Neuve Chapelle, came from the lower-middle class. Men like Privates McHugh and Murray were, on the other hand, from the real lower class, and so were the majority of their fellows.

One notices from these examples a pattern forming, which was that the Warrant Officers and N.C.O.s tended to come from higher in the social scale than the Privates. This is not

* *Rowntree*, Poverty. *In a footnote Rowntree says that 90 per cent of the recruits in 1900 belonged to the working classes, 7 per cent were shopmen or clerks, 3 per cent boys under 17, and only 1 per cent belonged to the servant-keeping class ('gentleman ranker'). Since his definition of working class covers both what I call working class and real lower class I think my division is reasonably accurate.*

by any means a fixed pattern, but it forms a useful guide for further investigation. A triumphant example of the flaw in the pattern was Tommy Finn, who it will be remembered was Quartermaster in Malta at the beginning of 1914. He came from the slums of Glasgow, of Glasgow-Irish stock which is almost the classic example of the real lower class, and rose in the end to be a Lieutenant-Colonel. But on the whole the men who had been born into the working class tended to rise to higher rank than those who had had the misfortune to be born in real poverty.

Starting with those who came to the 2nd Scottish Rifles from the lower-middle or working classes, one must appreciate that in most cases they came in direct opposition to their families. Lord Wavell wrote of the Army in pre-1914 days: 'There was in the minds of the ordinary God-fearing citizen no such thing as a good soldier; to have a member who had gone for a soldier was for many families a crowning disgrace.'[4] There are numerous examples of this attitude among respectable middle- and working-class families. Brigadier Stanley Clarke has written to me of one case as follows:

In October 1918 I was Commandant of the VIII Corps Battle School. My R.S.M. was a Drill-Sergeant from the Grenadier Guards (a splendid man of the Chalmers type), and I remember him telling me that his father was a small farmer in Gloucestershire. When he told his parents he wished to join the Army he was abused for wanting to join 'that scum' and told that if he did they never wished to have anything more to do with him. I asked him what he had answered. He said he was joining, and as far as their ultimatum went it was a game two could play. He added: 'I never did have anything more to do with them.'

Where a man joined with the blessing of his family it was usually where a strong connection already existed with the services. Thus the son of an old soldier, who had left the Army and settled in a good job, might get active encouragement from his father. But such cases were rare. Most men who did well in the Army and came out to a good job were more anxious to see their sons learn a skilled trade than follow in their own footsteps.

Perhaps following from this opposition to the Army from the working classes it is an interesting fact that many of the soldiers who joined the 2nd Scottish Rifles from this category were English, particularly Londoners. I think that this can be explained by the need to make a clean break with their outraged families, which led them to enlist in Regiments from distant parts. Since Scottish Regiments were well known for their fighting qualities vacancies in them were always in demand, and also the romantic appeal of things Scottish was strong to a young man brought up no doubt to look on Scotland as a distant and exciting land. A good example of the Cockney soldier was R.S.M. Wood, who it will be remembered succeeded Graham in Malta, and in his turn was commissioned as a Quartermaster after handing over to Chalmers. One of the great advantages which Londoners had over Scotsmen was the ability to talk both wittily and coherently. However great their personal qualities many Scots suffered from being dour and silent. In peacetime soldiering, where the ability to instruct and take drill were so important, they were often outshone by N.C.O.s from the South who were naturally better equipped for this sort of thing. Wood had an endless flow of quick talk and repartee which enabled him to carry a group of men with him where a more silent man would have failed to make such an impression. Since he was an intelligent man as well as a 'character' he had a very successful career. Also from London, it will be remembered, was Sergeant Bryant who had this gift of quick, humorous talk—almost back-chat—as well.

To succeed in the Army was most important to a man who came from the lower-middle or working classes. Not only was it necessary to justify himself if he had joined up in opposition to his family, but he was naturally caught up in the tremendous drive for improvement which spread through those classes in the early days of the century. Nowhere in society were the Victorian virtues of respectability, thrift and success more admired than at that level. A man braving the scorn and opprobrium of his family and friends to join the Army would feel compelled to spare no effort to gain promotion. Having gained it, he would insist on being given the respect due to his

1. The 2nd Scottish Rifles on parade in Malta in 1913. There are twenty-one officers on parade and seven hundred and thirty-eight other ranks. Each company has eighty-one other ranks on parade. The Pipes and Drums and Military Band number eighty-two men combined. This photograph was taken shortly before the reorganization of battalions into four companies.

2. OFFICERS OF THE 2nd SCOTTISH RIFLES 1913
All names reading from left to right. (Just what happened to all of
them eventually can be seen at Appendix 'B'.)

Back row: Lieutenant R. N. O'CONNOR, Lieutenant W. B. GRAY
BUĊHANAN, Lieutenant L. WANLESS O'GOWAN, 2/Lieutenant
The Hon J. DE BLAQUIERE, Lieutenant A. C. L. STANLEY
CLARKE, 2/Lieutenant D. C. FOSTER, 2/Lieutenant T. E. D.
DUNN.
Middle row (standing): Lieutenant R. V. CLERK, Lieutenant J. P.
KENNEDY, Lieutenant W. J. KERR, 2/Lieutenant J. F. EVETTS,
2/Lieutenant H. A. C. SIM, Lieutenant H. R. CRAILSHEIM,
Lieutenant and Adjutant W. L. MAUNSELL, Lieutenant R. D.
HUNTER.
Front row (sitting): Captain W. H. MacALLAN, Captain E. B.
FERRERS, Major E. de L. HAYES, Colonel C. H. P. CARTER,
C.M.G. (BLISS'S predecessor), Major G. A. ELLIS, Captain
A. C. NORTHEY, Captain and Quartermaster T. FINN.

Officers on the strength of the battalion at the time but not included
in the photograph were:
Major G. T. C. CARTER-CAMPBELL, Major H. D. W. LLOYD,
2/Lieutenant C. R. H. STIRLING, 2/Lieutenant C. R. I.
HOPKINS, 2/Lieutenant T. L. LODER-SYMONDS.

3. THE SERGEANTS' MESS
The Commanding Officer, Colonel Carter, sits in the middle with
the Regimental Sergeant-Major, R.S.M. Wood, on his left and the
Adjutant on his right.

4. The Signallers of the 2nd Scottish Rifles.
The officer in the centre is Lieutenant R. N. O'Connor, later
General Sir Richard O'Connor, G.C.B., D.S.O., M.C.

5. Shells of a German barrage bursting close behind the British trenches during Neuve Chapelle to prevent reinforcements coming up. These shelter trenches are probably the ones built just behind the front line for the second wave of the attacking battalions to occupy. *(Imperial War Museum)*

6. The German machine-gun position from which such terrible execution was done to the 2nd Middlesex and the 2nd Scottish Rifles. It was only destroyed in the second bombardment on the morning of 10 March 1915. This was the gun which killed so many of 'A' Company in particular. *(Imperial War Museum)*

7. This rather blurred photograph was taken in front of the 2nd
Middlesex position after the battle. It brings out the horror and
ugliness of the battlefield. *(Imperial War Museum)*

8. A hideous picture of the front-line trench from which the 2nd
Scottish Rifles attacked on the morning of 10 March 1915. Taken
shortly afterwards, it shows over twenty bodies in a small area.
(Imperial War Museum)

9. This and the next three photographs were taken at a place called Doulieu towards the end of April 1915. This one shows the battalion on parade, now very strongly reinforced after Neuve Chapelle. This collection of photographs was taken by Captain R. C. Money, M.C., Adjutant of the battalion. *(Imperial War Museum)*

10. Musketry in an orchard near Doulieu. A fine spring morning—29 April 1915. *(Imperial War Museum)*

11. The Quartermaster, Lieutenant J. Graham (extreme right), with some of his men at Doulieu on 29 April 1915. Rations are being divided up for issue to companies. *(Imperial War Museum)*

12. Brigadier-General R. J. Pinney talking to the Mayor of Doulieu. General Pinney commanded the 23rd Brigade of which the 2nd Scottish Rifles were part. *(Imperial War Museum)*

13. The 2nd Scottish Rifles Cemetery in the orchard of 'La Cordonnerie' Farm, Rue du Bois, on 5 May 1915. *(Imperial War Museum)*

rank and position. Regular Warrant Officers and Sergeants of those days knew their own worth.

The standard of education among those who sprang from the working classes was often remarkably high. The Pipe Corporal of the 2nd Scottish Rifles, Corporal J. C. Horn, wrote a poem about Malta in 1912 of which the following are the first two verses:[5]

> I sing the praise of a beauteous isle,
> An ocean jewel, rich and rare;
> Creation carved it with a smile,
> Of beauty, gave it liberal share
>
> 'Tis Malta, beautiful, unique.
> That poesy's Muse bids me appraise;
> The ancient home of Turk and Greek,
> Who loved and fought in bygone days.

It is not great poetry, but it shows that there were men in the ranks of the Army who were both sensitive and highly literate. In fact the 30 per cent coming from the lower-middle or working classes were in general well brought-up, intelligent men of reasonable education who would have held their own in any walk of life.

From this 30 per cent we must now turn to the 70 per cent who came from the real lower class. I intend to say a lot about the background from which they came, as it is impossible to appreciate their true qualities unless one understands the dreadful conditions in which most of them were reared.

The bulk of the men in this category in the 2nd Scottish Rifles came from Glasgow and the industrial towns of Lanarkshire: a few from London, Newcastle and Birmingham. Less in proportion came from farther afield than in the groups just looked at.

Even today the South side of Glasgow and the industrial towns of Lanarkshire form for the most part a grey, smoky, and unattractive complex of ugly factories and mean houses. Fifty years ago it was as depressing an area as the human mind can envisage. The life lived by the poor in these parts was cold, hungry, and generally miserable.

But although such appalling poverty and discomfort existed, people in the 1890s and 1900s were at least awakening to the fact, and starting to do something about it. The first requirement was to record the facts, and important studies were those made by Charles Booth, a shipowner and social reformer, and Seebohm Rowntree. Booth's contribution was the monumental seventeen-volume *Life and Labour of the People in London*. Rowntree based his investigations on the city of York, and called his book *Poverty, A Study of Town Life*. Unfortunately nothing of the same nature was written about Glasgow, though a certain amount can be found in reports such as those of the City's Medical Officer of Health.[6] However, the conditions in Glasgow can be assumed to have been very similar to those in York and London. Both Booth and Rowntree make the point that there was considerable similarity in their findings, and that it is reasonable to suppose that the same conditions existed in other industrial centres.

Booth wrote about Rowntree as follows:

Mr Rowntree's study of poverty in York has widened the area of observation, and involved the suggestion that a more or less uniform standard of poverty exists in all urban centres.[7]

Rowntree himself took this a stage further, and pointed out that:

. . . when the result of careful investigation shows that the proportion of poverty in London is practically equalled in what may be regarded as a typical provincial town, we are faced by the startling probability that from 25 to 30 per cent of the town populations of the United Kingdom are living in poverty.[8]

Conditions in Glasgow were not only as bad as in London or York, but if anything worse. In Glasgow itself the real lower classes lived mainly in tenement blocks. In the surrounding towns they were more likely to live in rows of small terraced houses. The worst features were overcrowding, and lack of sanitary facilities. Rowntree produces a table of overcrowding based on the 1891 census of Great Britain.[9] This shows Glasgow as far the worst town in Britain, with 59 per cent of the population living more than two persons to a room. This scale, he points out, was generally accepted as constituting overcrowding—a modern reader should realize that it means more than two persons per room in the house, not just bedrooms. In a footnote Rowntree also opens one's eyes to the seriousness of overcrowding in Scotland.

In Glasgow, Edinburgh, and some other towns, the sanitary authorities have ascertained the cubical contents of a number of tenements chiefly in block dwellings, and have placed tickets on the doors of these tenements indicating the number of persons who may sleep in them. Should a larger number be found sleeping in the tenement than is indicated on the ticket, the householder is liable to prosecution.

In Glasgow during 1900 no less than 51,544 visits were paid to these 'ticketed' houses for the purpose of detecting overcrowding, with the results, viz:

Total number of cases of overcrowding detected	5,051
warned by inspectors	3,620
summoned before magistrates	1,395[10]

The lack of decent sanitation is even more incredible to modern understanding than the overcrowding. Often forty or more people would be expected to use the same lavatory in a tenement block. The result of this was that the lavatories were used more as slop-emptying points than for their proper purpose. Chamber-pots and other receptacles were used in the rooms; sometimes children simply performed on newspapers on the floor, or went out on to the stairs or into the street to urinate.

Some of Rowntree's 'case histories' of slum dwellings and their sanitary facilities are appalling. He points out that one of the worst evils was the 'midden privy', which was really no more than a latrine sitting straight over a concrete pit. This was a type of lavatory also used in Glasgow, and he quotes the Chief Sanitary Inspector of Glasgow on the subject:

None but those who have spent days in the slums can adequately realize the difference it makes when an ashpit can no longer with truth be called a midden. To be in one of these midden-courts when the satellite of cleansing is busy at his operations can only compared with the experience of poor Falstaff in Mrs Ford's buck basket, 'that *there* is the rankest compound of villainous smell that ever offended nostril'. The midden even in its undisturbed state, if the weather is mild, 'smells to heaven' every hour of the day, and no house-wife with any remnant of an olfactory nerve will open her window if it be 15 feet from it.[11]

The main reason why such dreadful conditions existed was, of course, poverty. Rowntree coined the phrase 'poverty line', and divided people living below the poverty line into two categories. Families living in primary poverty were those 'whose total earnings are insufficient to obtain the minimum necessaries for the maintenance of merely physical efficiency'.[12] Those suffering from secondary poverty would have had enough if some part of the family income had not been absorbed in extra expenditure of either a useful or wasteful nature. The most common useful expenditure would be travel of the man of the house to and from work; the most common wasteful expenditure, drink.

A tiny margin existed between relative comfort and one or other of the degrees of poverty. Among the real lower classes the average weekly wage was about 25s. in Britain as a whole. In Glasgow wages were probably slightly lower on average, but so were prices. A man earning this sum was most likely living in a state of secondary poverty. If he was lucky enough to have a small family of three or less children, to live near his work, and to be very temperate, he and his family could no doubt live a reasonably healthy life on this amount, and eat well enough to work efficiently. But of course in most cases either too many children, travel, drink or some other cause would upset the balance.

Rising above the average to 30s. a week would enable a man to support his family quite comfortably. Another 10s. a week and he would be into the working class, and have a very different way of life open to him. Often, of course, there were families where big sums came into the house but the way of life changed little. Charles Booth quotes one: 'As showing the large sums which are often coming in, in apparently poor streets, a district visitor mentioned a family living in a cottage whose combined income for father, mother, son and daughter was about 75*s.* a week; yet their home was always a den.'[13] Such a family need not have lived in a 'den'; the awful thing is that many who received less than the national average of 25*s.* a week could do nothing else. A family living on £1 per week or less was in the state of primary poverty, and doomed to wretchedness.

To give an example of what it meant to live on less than £1 a week I cannot do better than quote a case of Rowntree's.[14]

He produced family budgets in great detail for two dozen families of widely differing circumstances. Budget No. 1 is for a labourer's family with a total income of 17*s.* 6*d.* per week. The household consisted of a father, mother and five children, and also, during the last nine of the twenty-one months surveyed, the mother's mother as well. The father was unable to earn a good wage on account of physical disability left after a long illness, and the mother, although a capable woman and a good manager, looked underfed and overworked. The eldest boy was deformed and threatened with tuberculosis, and could not go to school because of his health. The other children mostly bore signs 'of the privations they have so long endured'.

The menu of meals provided in this household during the week ending 31 August 1900 was pathetic. On Friday the meals were as follows:

Breakfast	Bacon, dripping, bread, tea
Dinner	Bread, butter, tea
Tea	Cheese, bread, butter, tea

The family never had any supper. On Sunday they had beef, Yorkshire pudding, potatoes and cabbage for dinner, but this cannot have been a lavish meal. The amount of beef bought was 3½ lb., and it had to do Monday's dinner as well. Among eight people, for two days, 3½ lb. of beef, even without bone, does not allow very large helpings.

The difficulties of life were often made intolerable by having too many children. The connection between the size of the families in poor areas and the surrounding poverty exercised Charles Booth's interest:

. . . and as we descend the scale and find marriage earlier and children more numerous, it may well be questioned whether these features are more the causes or the consequences of the poverty that accompanies them. To my mind, while no doubt to some extent a cause, they appear more definitely as consequences.[15]

Whichever way it was, there were always too many mouths to be fed—and this in spite of an appalling rate of deaths among children.

Averil Stewart, in *Alicella*, quotes a letter from Mrs Stewart of Murdostoun, in Lanarkshire, about families in the industrial part of the county in 1900: 'The families appal one; one poor woman who is expecting and looks more dead than alive, had twins last May, and buried them in six months. They generally say: "We've six alive and buried ten." If Mrs —— wants to start a family, I think a few months' residence in Lanarkshire would easily bring that about!'[16] Throwing an even grimmer light on infant mortality is this comment, taken from Marghanita Laski's chapter on Domestic Life in *Edwardian England 1901–1914*, on the rate of deaths among children born in Poor Law institutions. It was a case of '. . . something like a third of all children born and staying there (in Scotland, a half) dying within their first year'.[17]

For those children that survived, a healthy youth, with a proper chance to grow mentally and physically into intelligent and well-developed adults, was extremely rare. To quote Miss Laski again:

. . . the health of the Edwardian poor was appalling. At the very beginning of the period some public unease had arisen over the low standard of recruits for the army. Of those who offered themselves in 1900, the health and physical development of one-half was below the comparatively lax standard required by the authorities who had, in any case, already taken the practical ameliorative step of lowering the required standard; the required height, which in 1883 had been 5ft 3in. was brought down in 1900 to 5ft.[18]

Rowntree devoted nearly four pages to the physical condition of Army recruits. One of the points he makes is that even the low standard of health found in men being examined for enlistment did not really reflect the state of health among the poor generally. The reason for this was that, as he quotes for the Annual Report of the Inspector-General of Recruiting for 1900: 'All officers concerned in recruiting have instructions not to send a recruit up for medical examination unless there is a reasonable probability of his passing.' Even though one allows that recruiting officers probably permitted a number of unlikely looking men to go forward on the off-chance of passing, there must have been many they interviewed who obviously had no chance at all, and could not even be sent for examination. Of those actually examined, the largest percentage were failed for being 'Under-developed (i.e. chest, weight or height)'.[19]

The other manifestations of poor health, besides stunted growth, were bad teeth; rickets, often known as 'the Glasgow disease' which frequently led later to bandy legs; a tendency to develop tuberculosis; constant colds, which were thrown off with difficulty; and premature ageing. This latter disability was very marked in women. Women of thirty in the real lower classes often looked about fifty by modern standards. Being in bad health their pregnancies took a tremendous amount out of them, and lack of rest and good food after having babies never allowed them to recover again.

Bad health was often due to lack of hygiene. Sanitary conditions, as we have already seen, were often shocking, and at the same time there was often a complete lack of understanding of ordinary cleanliness. Charles Booth has a quotation from a relieving officer to illustrate this:

Fever and ill-health, to a certain extent, may be attributed to the amount of personal and domestic uncleanliness. There is not enough soap and water going, and dirty bedding is a special feature. The quite unnecessary dirt and filth sometimes found are appalling. In hot weather there are plagues of flies, like nothing seen ordinarily. In one house, the table was fairly black with them, and the woman of the house was helpless; she did not know how to get rid of them. It had never occurred to her to wash the table.[20]

But if washing and scrubbing of articles of furniture and houses was sometimes neglected, the cleanliness of the

human body was almost universally ignored. Not unreason-
ably were the lower classes often referred to as 'the great
unwashed'. Many adults might not wash their bodies below
the waist more than three or four times a year. Brushing of
teeth was totally unknown at the lowest level of society, and
even young children were often bathed only once a week. The
smell of a crowd of people in a slum area was powerful and
nauseating. The man of the house might wash his face and the
top half of his body on return from work in the evening, but
rarely would he dream of taking a bath. Baths, of course, were
never the fitted article known to all social classes in modern
times, but were tubs set down in the kitchen and filled by
kettles. Quite a number of proper baths were available in
big towns on a payment basis—usually provided by Town
Councils—but to spend money on hiring one of these would
be looked upon as a waste of money below the working class.

The sort of work that a man of the real lower class might
do was likely to be of the labouring variety, and also usually
of a casual nature. Working hours were long, and the jobs
open to the real lower class were boring and ill-paid. They
were usually unable to do the sort of regular manual work
which earned reasonably good wages through being physically
too weak. They were thus found in jobs such as working in the
docks, labouring on a building site, or any other form of
manual work done on a casual basis. The accent was always
on 'casual'. Miners earning £2 a week at the coal face did hard
and dirty work, but they were members of the working class,
by my definition, and went home to good meals and clean
houses. It was the lower grade jobs which came the way of the
man from the slums.

When not working, men of the real lower class had little to
do. In the house all work was done by the women, who were
constantly employed, and usually at a point verging on
complete exhaustion. Booth quotes a London vicar: 'The
men have a good time compared to the women, who lead
fearfully hard and almost slavish lives.'[21]

To fill his free time the man of the house would normally
sleep, loaf at the street corner, or go to the nearest bar. The
idea of doing anything constructive with his free time was

likely to be beyond him—he simply was not educated or organized enough to think of it. A visit to a football match, or to a fairground boxing booth, was as far as his conception of sport went. In the Glasgow area football matches were often the scene of fights and riots on a large scale. The annual Celtic versus Rangers match had to be stopped in 1909 because the rioting got out of hand,* and even in a quiet year it was always the scene of a number of vicious incidents, as indeed it still is. There was always a good crowd at a boxing booth, and always a good supply of men and boys to provide the entertainment. That the man who fought regularly in the booths was inevitably destined to become a 'punchie', a sort of wreck with all his intelligence and co-ordination knocked out of him, worried scarcely anybody. It was a hard, rough world, and when men watched a fight they wanted to see a hard, rough battle. Tough young men prepared to fight up to a dozen bouts a day were easy to find, and would take their punishment willingly in return for a few shillings and the chance of a good meal that this brought.

In Scotland the social drinking which is a feature of the English pub was quite unknown in the early days of the century. Men went to bars in the poor areas with the idea of getting drunk, or at least on the way towards it. Earlier on in the book I said that one should remember how miserable life was, and that drinking was often just a means of escaping from the misery. Even so, one must also remember that when a man or woman escaped from misery themselves in drink for a short time they usually increased the misery of those around them. The truth is that they just could not afford it; the real evil was not found in the fights, the vomiting and urinating in the streets, the wife-beating, and the general brutalizing effect of a surfeit of cheap spirits, but in the hunger of children which so often followed a 'binge' by the father of a young family. Drink was the main reason why families fell into the state of secondary poverty. To find a man spending over half his tiny income on drink was not unusual; to find

* *The ticket booths were burnt down in this year, which was thought to be stretching things a bit.*

him giving all his money to his wife was almost unheard of. Many men in the poor areas saw little wrong in keeping as much money as they could for their own spending and giving as little as possible to their wives.

Turning away from all the unhappy aspects of the life of the real lower class, one must look for the better side of things. There were a number of points about life in the slums which were most inspiring—it is surprising to find how many virtues existed among people who had so little chance to develop properly, and who were so inadequate in many ways. The first of these was kindness. Amidst all the roughness of a poor area in Glasgow there could be found a generosity and helpfulness which was the result of true kindness of heart. Booth quotes comments from a nurse and a Nonconformist social worker: 'How the poor live when they are helpless remains a mystery, save for their great kindness to each other, even to those who are strangers. This is the great explanation. It is nearly always the neighbours.'[22] And then: 'It is only the poor that really give. Personal help and timely relief are the key notes of the charity of the poor. They know exactly the wants of one another and give when needed.'[23] This generosity to each other cannot wholly be explained on the grounds that it was wise for the very poor to help others so that they could expect it themselves when they fell on bad times: it was also due to a great extent to a very real compassion and goodness which is often found in people who have themselves suffered a lot and can therefore appreciate fully the plight of others.

When looking at the life of these families in their miserable conditions it is easy to think that they all lived in squalor and wretchedness. Unfortunately most of them did—they had little chance of doing much else—but there were a few who contrived to rise above the circumstances around them, and these deserve special mention. The achievement of running a clean home in the slums and rearing a healthy family was something very remarkable. When it was done it was usually due to the energy and determination of the woman of the house. A woman who did achieve the near miracle of running a good, clean home in a tenement building had to have qualities of character far beyond those that most of us require in life.

When one looks at the general character of the real lower classes before 1914, in the context of the conditions in which they existed, one should try to see the good qualities rather than the bad. A few could rise above everything, as I have just shown, and a few of course became really vicious and evil. But the great majority turned out surprisingly well. They were inclined to be apathetic, and they showed little sign of intiative or imagination in trying to better their lot. On the other hand, they were able to preserve many of the decencies of life, and were cheerful in adversity and ready to make the best of their few chances of happiness. Anyone who criticizes their weakness should think carefully about how they themselves would have reacted in the same environment.

The moment has now come to look at the products of this environment, on coming into the world of the Army. In discussing those who joined up from the lower-middle and working classes I showed that the men themselves were enthusiastic about the Army, and joined it in most cases in the face of strong opposition from their families. In the case of the real lower class the men were usually reluctant to join and did so as a last resort to avoid starvation. As Booth was told by one of his many informants: 'Boys living at home pay for their food, and if out of work cannot pay. Then they often enlist, which they seldom do willingly.'[24] The attitude of their families was unlikely to be strong either way; in most cases they were quite glad to see the boy off somewhere else where he could be fed by another hand, but rarely would they take much interest in his career. Occasionally strong feelings existed amongst the real lower classes against the Army, but not for the same reasons that those a little higher in the social scale despised it so much. Among the small minority of the very poor who had strong political interests the soldier in the ranks was looked on as renegade, a lackey of the bosses and an enemy of his own class. The sight of any sort of uniform was anathema to the really 'red' Clydesider, and a soldier was only slightly less abhorrent than a policeman. A soldier on leave in uniform in the poor areas areas of Glasgow might at times be jeered at by people at the street-corner, though strong anti-military feelings really belonged to the days after the First World War as far as Scotland was concerned. Before the War there was a more ready acceptance of the existing order than in later years.

It is interesting to note that Kennedy had a Private Mason in his platoon, whom he describes as a 'great gaunt Clydesider', who had rejoined as a reservist after several years out of the Army working in the mines. There he had become involved with some men of violent Communist opinions and at times in the trenches he would tell Kennedy of what he and his friends intended to do to the capitalists and bosses after the War. It was blood-curdling stuff, in spite of which Mason was a most loyal and willing soldier, and went out of his way to almost mother Kennedy, and to give him cups of tea and extra rations at frequent intervals. Apparently officers of his own Regiment were exempt from the fury of his class-hatred.

Whatever the reactions of his family when a man joined from the real lower class, if he was successful in the Army it was inevitable that he grew apart from his origins. Almost invariably the soldier who started to rise in rank tended to lose touch with his people at home and to drift away from them. If he rose to be a Sergeant he became in effect, by virtue of his income, security and pension prospects, a member of the working class (or even the lower-middle class) and so usually made a complete break with his background.

I have written of the life of a soldier in the ranks in Malta, and mentioned how much a man reared in a slum could appreciate the order, cleanliness, and regular life. On the other hand, for a man coming from a prosperous working-class home where order and cleanliness were natural, and where good food, comfort and gentleness were also to be found, the life of a barrack-room wore a very different aspect. For a while my approach to the other rank world based on background and upbringing must be left in order to look at conditions of life in the Army from a general point of view as they affected all soldiers regardless of where they came from. Next I will briefly refer back to the two different groups to show how particular factors influenced soldiers in different ways according to their original social class. Finally, I will attempt to show the characteristics which were common to all other ranks, and to assess the way in which their tremendous morale and *esprit de corps* developed.

One of the most important points to remember about the Army was that it was a long-service Army. At Neuve Chapelle there was not a man in the ranks of the 2nd Scottish Rifles with less than five years' service. Some of course had only returned to the battalion in 1914 after a spell on the reserve, but all these men had completed at least seven years before becoming reservists. Not only did soldiers serve for a long time, but they usually remained for most of their service in the same company, or at least the same battalion. The average man in an infantry battalion abroad had spent six months at the Depot doing his basic training, and then had spent up to six months with the Home Service battalion of the Regiment before being drafted overseas. This pattern had been somewhat disrupted in The Cameronians (Scottish Rifles) because the 1st Cameronians and the 2nd Scottish Rifles had changed roles in 1910 and 1911; the former coming home from South Africa to take over Home Service duties and the latter going abroad to Malta. Even so, when the attack was launched at Neuve Chapelle many men in each company had been in it for up to seven years or more. The result of this was that there were ties between many soldiers which were stronger than one can easily imagine. And remember that these men had not only worked together, but had lived every minute of the day together. Remember C.S.M. Leggatt: 'It didn't matter what continent you were in, it was always the same. Everything was organized inside the battalion. . . .' Two men who had become mates or 'muckers' in the Army were closer to each other than most brothers, and often developed a joint identity so that no sensible N.C.O. would dream of telling one to do a job without detailing the other at the same time.

Another reason why men grew so close to one another was that very few of them were married. Only a handful had wives with them at their station, and the lot of the wife who married 'off the strength' was enough to deter any decent man from marrying unless he could have his wife with him. The situation is explained in this passage by Cyril Falls from *Edwardian England 1901–1914*:

One dreadful scourge afflicting the rank-and-file had been the lack of any provision for marriage except for a select few. If a soldier obtained his commanding officer's permission to marry, his wife was henceforth 'on the strength', was moved with the unit, obtained fair quarters abroad or, if she had to be left behind, a small allowance. But the commanding officer was not his own master in the matter. He had only a handful of tickets to wedded bliss. The fate of the wife married off the strength was grisly. Even if she and her children could be kept alive while her husband remained on one station, what was to happen when the unit moved. Theoretically there was one answer only: they must starve. In practice this did not occur, but the sufferings of soldiers' families in this plight were often atrocious.[25]

A modern reader should remember two points. First, that this objection to marriage applied to officers as well as the men, and that about the same small proportion were married in each category. Second, the age for marrying throughout Britain as a whole was older that it is today. A man joining at eighteen years old and waiting for fifteen years before being given permission to marry was only thirty-three when he finally entered wedlock. Thirty-three was considered a very normal age to get married at the turn of the century. As a matter of interest, 20 per cent of men in Scotland in 1899 married between the ages of 30 and 40, 68 per cent between 20 and 30, and only $2\frac{1}{2}$ per cent before they were 20.[26]

This bachelor existence by most of the men was a major contributory cause of the strong comradeship among soldiers. Men turned their natural affection towards each other. This does not mean that they became homosexual. Homosexuality was extremely rare in the Army, particularly among other ranks. It is well known that sexual deviations are much less common at the lower levels of society than among better educated people. Furthermore, public opinion in those days was very strongly opposed to any kind of irregularities in the sexual field, and a man with the reputation for being homo-

[150]

sexual would be completely ostracized—as well as being likely to get a 'hiding' whenever a couple of drunks were looking for someone to beat up. In speaking of 'natural affections' I am referring to the sort of love and kindness one finds in a happy family between parents and their children, and between one child and another. Having no family to turn to, many soldiers lavished all their affections on their friends. Anyone who has had experience of Army life will remember many examples of very deep friendships between men in the ranks, and also an amazing power of self-sacrifice on occasions from the most unlikely people. When a man has a family he naturally thinks more of them than of other friends, and tends to withdraw from all but the strongest of his links with other men. Army life brought about the sort of relationship that existed between Kipling's *Soldiers Three*: 'Once upon a time, very far from England, there lived three men who loved each other so greatly that neither man nor woman could come between them.'[27]

Having described at some length the sort of life led by men of the 2nd Scottish Rifles in Malta, and having described how they were trained, there are some aspects of this life on which I would like to elaborate. One of the strongest criticisms that can be made about the general attitude towards soldiers in the ranks was the lack of effort made to encourage them to think for themselves. As Cyril Falls puts it:

. . . good as were the bulk of the regular rank-and-file, little was done to stimulate their intelligence or initiative. 'We make the private soldier in many cases a fool', wrote an officer, 'because we start with the assumption that he is a fool.' A familiar but to the imaginative a pathetic sight was that of three or four soldiers being marched across a square by a non-commissioned officer, presumably incapable of doing some little job otherwise.[28]

It should not be thought that no effort was made to teach men their jobs, or to educate them. The trouble was that instruction was hammered into them with little attempt to arouse their interest. They learnt like parrots; not only military training but also the subjects covered by Army education. The battalion had an Education Sergeant who endeavoured to make up the gaps in the knowledge of the rank and file, but his contribution was looked on as a little unnecessary by the officers and as a bore by most of the men. As a result he did little more than instil some elementary Regimental history into the bulk of his pupils, and perhaps some basic arithmetic. This was a great pity: with the time available, and the opportunities presented by having so many men about with almost virgin minds, great things could have been done by lively instruction to bring soldiers up to a reasonably high standard of education.

Military skills were driven home by constant repetition. For the ordinary private the two subjects which occupied most of his training time were weapon training and drill. The standard achieved in the former was remarkable. 'One accessory of training,' writes Cyril Falls, 'the small-arms cartridge, cheap in a small army, had never been stinted, and off the range soldiers had spent much time simply working their bolts. Reservists and young soldiers alike could shoot steadily and accurately at a relatively slow rate for long periods, or in an emergency fire what they called their "mad minute". A good man fired eighteen rounds in the period; supreme experts, often non-commissioned officers, claimed so many that one hesitates to set down the figures for fear of perpetuating a legend. The blast of fire produced was paralysing. . . . It was without a parallel in the contemporary continental armies.'[29]

The 2nd Scottish Rifles were not quite as keen on drill as some battalions, but they devoted a lot of time to it. In paying such attention to drill the Army was of course really looking backwards to the days when armies went to war in close formations and carried out complicated manœuvres as drill movements on the battlefield. Drill had good points, but the obsession with it was part of a way of warfare which had departed long before 1914. In criticizing the training of the private soldier for being backward looking and unimaginative one is probably putting a finger on the main weakness of the old Regular Army. It was so good in many ways, but it sometimes lacked understanding of the problems of its own day.

Recruits who joined the Scottish Rifles started their service at the Regimental Depot at Hamilton. I will deal first with the man who came from a lower-middle or working-class background, who usually arrived because he was desperately keen to be a soldier, and often in defiance of his family. In most cases his early days in the Army were a shock. To start with he would find that the great bulk of his fellow recruits came from the real lower classes, and were much rougher than any people he had ever met before, particularly if he came from a quiet village in the country. Not only might they be rough, but frequently verminous and smelly, as well as foul-mouthed and noisy. Coming on top of the shock of having to live with these people would be the shock of finding that he was treated exactly like them, or if he made any pretensions to gentility, slightly worse. He would be forced to have his hair cut very short, would be made to bath, possibly even being scrubbed by two N.C.O.s as though he had come from a slum with 'filthy flesh' (the Army term of the day for bodily dirt) himself, and would be shouted at and driven from pillar to post all day from 6 a.m. to 'lights-out' at 10 p.m. Recruits were definitely 'broken in' before 1914; their introduction to the Army was meant to be rough.

Some young men of good upbringing found this life too much for them, and these could buy themselves out of the Army for a few pounds if they could persuade their families to provide the money. Then a sorrowful figure would return home to his parents, head hung low, to admit his mistakes and settle down in a respectable job. But most of course stuck it out, and the good ones usually determined to rise right to the top of the promotion ladder as quickly as possible. The challenge of the harsh start to their Army careers usually stayed with them, steeling them to accept strict discipline and a hard life, and to excel at their professional duties. It was amongst these men of solid background serving in the ranks that one probably found the strongest military ambition in the Army. Some of course just drifted through their service, but the majority were set on promotion—much more so than the average officer. Arrived at the top, they were in no doubt as to their own importance. A typical Warrant Officer is described as follows:

The Regimental Sergeant Major remains vividly in my recollection —a leather-faced, hard-bitten old soldier of a type now extinct. Even other sergeant majors stood to attention in his presence and spoke only when spoken to. . . . In his eyes, the Army consisted of a vast number of officers and men and a small elite of Warrant Officers, Class One, who rose on merit alone. In this select band he alone was unique in that he could recite the King's Regulations by heart.[30]

One catches in this description a glimpse of the rigidity of mind of the sort of men who rose to be Warrant Officers. It would be fair to say that a Sergeant-Major became, whatever his start in life, a member of the lower-middle class on reaching his rank. I have mentioned the intense respect for the virtues of thrift and ambition which this class had in pre-1914 days, and how much they prided themselves on being respectable. Of all the classes, it is in the lower-middle (followed closely by the upper-middle) that one sees the strongest signs of the so-called Victorian approach to life. It produced in men at times a very hard and unsympathetic streak, but it had great value in the military field. The absolute trustworthiness and reliability of the good regular Warrant Officer or N.C.O. more than offset any lack of originality he may have had. He was a man entirely suited to his job—in much the same way as were his officers.

Army life for the boy from the real lower classes was different again in the impression it made. His first few days were likely to be unhappy as well, but mainly because of the few things that his more carefully brought-up counterpart clung to for comfort—the regular hours, hard work, enforced cleanliness, and constant activity were strange, as was being constantly ordered about by someone to whom he could not answer back. Furthermore, many a boy from a slum had done so little for himself in civilian life that even cleaning a pair of boots or making a bed up in the neatly folded way demanded by the Army were skills which needed time for him to absorb. But it was not long before most recruits settled down to the routine of Army life, and began to develop in every way.

Mentally, the soldier was given a great stimulus by finding

himself a wanted member of an organization rather than being a creature on his own without anyone to care much what happened to him. The effect of being given his uniform was a great help in creating this sense of belonging and being of importance, as is shown by this quotation from Booth:

Of the type embruted by perpetual dependence on casual employment, it is hopeless to make men, while they remain in this condition; but give a man a uniform and a badge, any token that he is something more than a casual, and there will be a complete change in his moral character.[31]

The way that boys from the slums grew physically was also

COMPARATIVE DIETS

Article	Amount issued to one soldier in a week	Amount purchased for family of 8
Bread	8¾ lb.	32 lb. (flour and
(or biscuit)	7 lb.	meal)
Meat, frozen	8¾ lb.	
(or Meat, preserved)	5¼ lb.	4 lb. meat, 2 lb. fish
(or M. & V. ration)*	7 lb.	(Note: The family also bought 3 eggs during the week)
Tea	5¼ oz.	6 oz.
Sugar	1 lb. 10 oz.	4 lb.
Cheese	1 lb. 5 oz.	¼ lb.
Bacon	1 lb. 12 oz.	2 lb.
Jam (or dried fruit)	1 lb. 12 oz.	1 lb. (currants)
Butter	¼ lb.	1 lb.
Vegetables (except when M. & V. issued)	3½ lb.	7 lb. potatoes, 1 cabbage
Pea soup	7 oz.	1 quart (a gift)
(or Oxo)	7 cubes	
Rum	1 gill	—
Tobacco	2 oz.	1 oz.
Milk	2 tins	5½ pints fresh, 1 tin condensed

* *Tinned meat and vegetable ration.*

remarkable. In a few months they put on pounds in weight, and changed into entirely different looking men. From being pale and thin they grew broad and ruddy-faced. They did not put on many inches in height, but they filled out enormously across the shoulders so that the term 'stocky' is the one often heard to describe their build. Fresh air, exercise, and food worked this change—particularly the last. To see how much food they got in the Army it is worth making a simple comparison (see p. 155) between the amount of food provided in a week to a single soldier in the trenches during the winter 1914–1915 and the amount bought for the entire family living on 17s. 6d. a week whose diet has already been discussed on page 141.[32]

In time of peace the rations were not quite as plentiful, but even so the soldier had a very good balanced diet on which he thrived. Grumbles about the cooking were often heard, of course, but to the man who had grown up on the edge of starvation even the worst cooked Army meal was a feast.

Another physical advantage of Army life, as well as making men bigger and stronger, was that it gave them facility with their hands and physical co-ordination. Although the countryman of pre-1914 days was often a remarkably well-developed man with great skill at many manual tasks, the town-dweller was amazingly clumsy and inept, as well as carrying himself badly and moving awkwardly. Much of this came from never having small jobs to do about the house as a child because 'mum' did everything, and small boys were always pushed out of the house to play. At school there was no physical training, and when the boy finally got a job it was usually one requiring little skill. If it required physical effort nobody bothered to teach a youth how to use his body correctly to do it; he learnt either by watching others, or, more likely, by straining or hurting himself first. On this score, the rate of injury to manual workers throughout the country due to clumsiness, carelessness or stupidity was appalling. The Army, to give credit where it is due, was already taking great pains over physical training. Not only did men do P.T. regularly and often as part of training, but they played games a great deal as well. Furthermore, they were taught most carefully how to stand and carry themselves when learning to drill, and how to hold and work their weapons when learning to shoot. As a result of all this training the soldier stood out in a crowd of people from the same upbringing not only on account of his healthy appearance but also because of his bearing and co-ordination of movement.

One of the great things the Army could do for a bright boy from the slums was give him education and an opening into an altogether different way of life. Although heredity and environment combined to rob most slum children of the ability to rise in the world, there were some who had the potential to do great things. Usually this potential was frustrated, and burnt itself out in bitterness, and sometimes in crime. But often a bright boy came into the Army and discovered his ability to absorb knowledge and lead his fellows. Within a few years he would start to rise in rank, and might well come eventually, like Tommy Finn, to be a senior Quartermaster. Few other walks of life could offer the same openings.

Of the average soldier in the ranks it would be fair to say that he was by nature very much a child. Physically a man, he remained mentally a boy. Most recruits from the real lower classes came into the Army with a mental age of about ten. Their training and instruction as soldiers would raise this to about twelve or thirteen, but few of them ever developed a truly adult approach to life.

One sees these childish characteristics in many forms—and I would be chary of decrying them. Looking at it from an entirely practical point of view, there was a lot to be said for having a slightly simple mind when in the trenches. First, because the childish mind is resilient and recovers very quickly from shocks and frights; secondly, because it is normally optimistic rather than fearful. The immature soldier was more likely to be bolstered up by optimism and excitement than overcome by childish fears.

First among the three main characteristics that I would describe as 'childish' was a capacity for hero-worship. Naïvety played a big part in this; better educated people are less prone to adulation than the simple. Many soldiers perhaps gave rather too much credit to admired officers in the way a boy can give too much credit to any well-respected adult. The opposite to this is true as well—those who were 'agin' authority were often as violent in their antipathy to those they did not like as a thwarted child can be.

The second immature characteristic was the ability to be carelessly cruel. This took various forms; often completely at variance with the general kindness and good-humour which has always characterized the British soldier. Teasing of an unpopular figure could be carried to lengths where it was in fact gross cruelty. One aspect of life which has undoubtedly improved tremendously among the young in recent years is the decrease in bullying. But before 1914 it was one of the nastier things that went on at schools, in particular, and in most other places where a communal life was led. Soldiers often found it hard to grow out of the habit of tormenting the misfit. Another odd example of a streak of cruelty was the indiscriminate killing of small animals. A man would be ridiculously sentimental about a dog of his own or a horse he looked after, but would kill a mongrel dog, a cat, or a small creature like a mouse or a frog with no scruples at all. It was not so much the killing as the amusement it caused which is hard to understand. On the other hand things were perhaps better in the big cities in 1900 in respect of cruelty to animals than they had been earlier: 'Moral improvement', an old Londonder told Booth, 'among the people is immense, owing mainly to education; shown amongst other ways in kindness to animals. The day was when no cat could appear in the streets of Bethnal Green without being hunted and mal-treated; now such conduct is rare.'[33]

The third characteristic is irresponsibility. It took the soldier who had been brought up in a real lower class home years to develop a sense of responsibility. Often it happened that the influence of early years in a disorganized and feckless home could never be completely thrown off. A very common type among soldiers was the man like Private Murray who would go for months on end without putting a foot wrong, and then suddenly go off the rails, usually by throwing a drunk at an inopportune moment. Such men often gained promotion, rising to Corporal or even Sergeant before a major 'black' put them back at the bottom of the ladder again.

In addition to these three 'childish' characteristics, as I have called them, there are two others to mention. One is humour. In defining morale I said that cheerfulness is one of the surest signs of good morale. The average soldier in the 2nd Scottish Rifles was an amazingly cheerful character. There were dour and gloomy ones—often among the more intelligent—but the 'wee Jock' from the Glasgow back-streets was usually an irrepressibly cheerful figure. Like other men from the big cities he had his own form of quick wit, and although to an outsider his jokes would be quite unintelligible, within a group from the same background the repartee often reached quite a high standard. In the presence of strangers it tended to dry up: the most garrulous Scot has always been liable to become tongue-tied in the company of a group of Englishmen.

The final thing I want to mention is the 'old soldier' attitude. This at its worst was a glorification of laziness and 'lead-swinging', springing from a deeply ingrained suspicion of enthusiasm, and a consequent determination never to show keenness in case of becoming involved in extra work. I believe that in this form it was less evident in Scottish regiments than others from the South. There certainly were a few 'old soldiers' in the 2nd Scottish Rifles who got into 'cushy' jobs where they were seldom disturbed, and who were rarely seen by anyone except on pay parades, but they were rare. Certainly none of the N.C.O.s had even the slightest chance of becoming work-shy with an R.S.M. like Chalmers watching over them. Readers of Montague's *Disenchantment* will remember his description of the Sergeant-Major who took him out on his first route march and went straight to the nearest pub to pass the day being stood drinks by the wealthier recruits. Montague draws unfortunate conclusions from this, forgetting first of all that an old rogue such as he describes was only likely to be found, in the same way as the incompetent officer, in a home training establishment. In a battalion such as the 2nd Scottish Rifles on active service no Warrant Officer would have had a chance of getting up to such tricks, nor indeed would the idea of doing so have entered his head.

The 'old soldier' at his best, however, was another case altogether. Charles Carrington, in *Soldier from the Wars Returning*, has described his own idea of 'Old Bill', the hero of the famous Bruce Bairnsfather cartoons. He sees him like this:

Completely cynical about national or political issues, he is never-theless a dedicated man, immersed in his military tradition, exemplified by the use of Hindustani words picked up from the Indian Army. On duty he is irreproachable, punctual in his duties; his buttons are always polished, his rifle clean, a state of affairs which he attains with the minimum of effort. Having thus adjusted himself to the routine his whole endeavour is directed towards the ease and comfort of 'number one'. Though recognized as a good soldier, he avoids promotion since responsibility calls for extra duty. He never shirks and he never volunteers. Since he has the trade of soldiering at his fingertips, he knows exactly how to make himself comfortable under the worst conditions, and never misses any good thing that is going. . . . He is not a very honest man, retaining old-fashioned notions about a soldier's right to plunder. . . . But we must do justice to Old Bill by saying that in the line he never fails. He can and will fight, and the young officer will be wise to use his experience. When the sergeant is killed it is Old Bill who takes command and carries the platoon through, without waiting for promotion.[34]

It is a delightful picture of an invaluable type of man.

Some basic characteristics existed among all men in the ranks regardless of their individual social origins. The first was loyalty, which I see as a three-way virtue, starting with the Regiment. It was an intensely felt emotion, whose inten-sity has been brought home very much to me in the letters and talk of men who served in the ranks before 1914 and during the First World War. In an age not devoted to institu-tions, it may be hard to comprehend the extent of even the humblest private's love of his Regiment. Next came the loyalty of the soldier to his officers. The final direction in which the soldier turned his loyalty was to the other men in the ranks around him. This was partly in order to survive both the rigours of peacetime training and the dangers of active service; it was also partly comradeship. One feels the strength of it even today at reunions and meetings of old soldiers, and it is much stronger among 1914–1918 veterans than those of the 1939–1945 days. Fierce loyalty of any sort is perhaps, sad to say, a slightly simple virtue, and as men grow cleverer they lose the capacity for it.

From loyalty, a spiritual strength, I would turn to physical strength. The other ranks of the 2nd Scottish Rifles shared their officers' admiration for toughness and readiness to withstand hardship. They exulted in their fitness, and particularly their ability to march. The battalion was very proud of its achievement in 1911 of marching from Harwich to Colchester, just over twenty miles, in full equipment and at 'forced march' pace, four miles in the hour, without a man falling out. A term of admiration was to describe another soldier as a 'hard' man. This implied a two-way ability to give or take punishment of any kind. The 'hard' man could give or take blows without mercy or complaint, depending on which way they came.

As with officers, this obsession with physical toughness had its obvious corollary in a contempt for intelligence. Many of the men were ignorant and illiterate, and even those who were neither would affect to some extent their fellows' antipathy towards learning and intelligence. To be obviously clever was not a good thing; the answer for the bright man was to conceal his mental ability as much as possible.

Allied to this stupidity, whether real or feigned, was a readiness to accept orders and discipline without demur. Soldiers were expected to do what their superior officers told them, and not to ask questions. Those who did question the orders they received earned the title of 'barrack-room lawyer'. As such, they were strongly objected to by both their superiors and their equals. His superiors realized that the 'barrack-room lawyer' was unlikely to understand the full implications of the regulations he quoted; his fellows knew only too well that it was better to keep quiet than make a fuss about some small injustice. As the saying went: 'The Army will always win.' It usually did.

If these last three general characteristics are turned into adjectives, the description of other ranks arrived at is 'loyal, hardy, and obedient'. Many could show more than these three qualities; of few could less be said.

I come now to the final stage of this chapter, which is an attempt to assess how all the different factors I have brought into it influenced the men of the 2nd Scottish Rifles at Neuve Chapelle.

The bulk of the men in the battalion were those I have described as originating from the real lower class. One could almost say that for them the whole of their lives had been a conditioning for the trenches. As children they had learnt to live happily with so many of the things that made life at the front unbearable for those reared in gentler surroundings. Cold, ragged clothes, dirt, lice and fleas, bad food, hard beds, overcrowding, rats, ugly surroundings; these were nothing new to someone whose boyhood had been passed in a Glasgow slum. Even the violence and bloodshed of war was not entirely strange, although on a bigger scale. Nobody could grow up in Glasgow before 1914 without seeing an occasional fight, and meeting men from time to time who were hideously disfigured by a razor-slash or a broken bottle.

From this hard and rough environment, where he had learnt to endure discomfort and privation, the soldier came, often reluctantly as I have shown, to the very different world of the Regular Army. A great change now came over his life. First, he found that he was important. Officers and N.C.O.s were interested in him; people cared whether he wore his uniform correctly, whether he progressed in his training, and whether he was a credit to the Regiment. His comrades also cared about him. It was important that he should not let them down by failing to do his fair share of communal tasks, or by bringing the wrath of the Sergeant on to the whole squad by making mistakes at drill. He found himself a member of a small community, with certain obligations to the other members of it, and certain privileges which are part of communal life—companionship, cheerfulness, and a sense of belonging. Secondly, he started to live in an ordered way. Time ruled his life—his daily routine, the training programme, even the moment he went to sleep were all ruled by the clock. Adjusting to this orderly existence was not easy, but it made

[162]

him learn how to run his life and organize himself. Combined with plentiful food, fresh air and physical exercise, the highly controlled life of the soldier had an immensely beneficial effect on the young man from the real lower classes, and developed his natural hardiness and resilience into the best qualities of a soldier.

For the man from the lower-middle or working classes the Army provided not so much a developing process as an outlet. Many of the qualities demanded in war had grown in this type of person with his upbringing. He was obedient, industrious and dutiful almost by nature; what he wanted was adventure, travel, and the chance to hold authority. Also he often looked for colour and romance. From the steady, ordered existence of a respectable home the Army offered an exciting escape. He joined up determined to show his mettle, and to prove himself a leader. Usually he found what he was looking for. The magnificent Warrant Officers and Sergeants of a battalion like the 2nd Scottish Rifles were in every sense dedicated men, who achieved more of their early ambitions than most men do in their lives.

Finally, all the other ranks in the battalion were caught up, whatever their origins, in the powerful grasp of the Regiment. By the time they had lived for two or three years in the atmosphere of Regimental tradition, had made the strongest friendships of their lives within the Regiment, and had been constantly reminded of their duty to it, the Regiment could claim them as its own. They might at times curse it, or even want to leave it, but they were in fact so much part of it that they could never break from its clutches. I do not suppose Regimental spirit will ever mean so much again as it did to those regular soldiers of 1914. In the changing world we live in only fifty years later such loyalty is not altogether easy to believe in. But if anyone wants to know what was the quintessence of the morale of the pre-1914 Army—what was the rock of its foundation—then the answer is the Regiment. Everything else was important, but if the actions of the soldiers of the Scottish Rifles at Neuve Chapelle are to be explained in a few words one can only say that they did it for the Regiment.

The Officer–Other Rank
Relationship

No officer ever asked me to do something that he was not prepared to do himself. Lieut. Kerr, 'A' Coy, was killed working with a party building a sandbag wall. He could have remained in a safe place.

9549 Sergeant J. Noble, 2 Platoon, 'A' Company,
2nd Scottish Rifles at Neuve Chapelle

IN ORDER TO explain the background of members of the Scottish Rifles there has been more discussion of class in the last two chapters than I would have liked. The subject should be put into its right place. Too great a preoccupation with it is bound to lead to a misunderstanding of how the British Army of 1914 worked. Class was important, but only as part of a big picture which displayed many different aspects of human life. In this picture I doubt if class should even be in the foreground—its place is probably as an interesting feature of the middle distance, an essential and integral part of the composition but overshadowed by more significant features in front of it. To show the danger of overemphasizing class differences I am again going to quote John Connell. His thesis in the following passage is the evil influence of class hatred. Having said that the theme of seventeenth century revolution was religious intolerance, he goes on:

The theme of revolution in the 20th century is class hatred. We are going to all sorts of shifts, by legislation and other means, to demonstrate our hatred of racial hatred. But class hatred flourishes as never before. It is not merely unrebuked or unconfined; it is actively promoted. It is preached from the pulpit, it takes its seat in the House of Lords, academics expound it in lecture halls, it is sapping the foundations of our educational system, and you cannot read a newspaper or watch a television programme but its slimy, sick tide pours over you. As religious hatred did, it horribly perverts the concept of the brotherhood of man; and it poisons the roots of the affection, the kindness, the trust, and the respect which can knit men together in trouble and in joy, and indeed give the word 'society' the only meaning it possesses.

To try to write history with this hateful bias is inevitably to twist it. It happens that the military history of recent times can, with brazen ease, be interpreted in terms of class hatred. But it is twisted history all the same.[1]

The essential thing to understand about British life in the early part of the twentieth century is that the class system was readily accepted. In general it is in the minds of later generations that the bitterness has grown. Although we can observe today inequalities and injustices which surprise and even shock us, it would be entirely wrong to assume that those who lived under the social system of fifty or sixty years ago were particularly concerned about this unfairness or that they resented it strongly. Most people knew their place on the social ladder, and were content with it. Indeed the majority probably gave it little thought. Those who did, writers, politicians and social investigators, were not particularly heeded. It was not until after the First World War that widespread bitterness along class lines developed in British life. I have no interest in the rights and wrongs of the matter, but only wish to record that for the greater part of the population of Britain in 1914 the class system was a fact of life which was little discussed and little resented. Modern writers who assume that it was a cause of bitterness because to them, fifty years later, the inequalities are to be deplored, are making a false assumption. Further, they are mistaken in thinking that the limits set by the class system could not be broken, and that no opportunities for advancement lay open to the clever man of humble origin. To quote John Connell again:

The society in which anybody now over 40 spent his most formative years was not egalitarian, though it was by no means as rigid, as hierarchic, or as stupid as its modern critics think. The Services, like the other professions, the law, the Church, medicine, diplomacy and the administrative civil service, were manifestations of this non-egalitarian pattern; but in the Services, as in the others, the outstanding youngster without means or connections was not necessarily deprived of his chance to rise. For example, the class-hatred merchants slither past the career of Field-Marshal Sir William Robertson because it knocks a big hole in their tight little thesis.[2]

One of the important points to realize about life before 1914 was that throughout much of the country traditional patterns of life were still carried on which have now almost completely disappeared. I am referring here to life in the country villages and small towns rather than the big industrial centres. In rural and small urban communities people of all classes met each other more than they do today. Divisions might be sharper and more obvious between different classes, but at the same time there was a great deal of mutual interest to draw people together. In many places the old families still played their traditional roles in local life; not only did this apply to squires and lairds, but to doctors, lawyers, farmers, merchants, shopkeepers, craftsmen, and labourers. Between them all flowed far more powerful currents of interest than do today; they all knew about each other's doings. This intimate knowledge softened the feeling of inequality.

A good picture of the way rural society operated in Scotland in Edwardian days can be obtained from this description of life at Murdostoun Castle in Lanarkshire. It is interesting because the writer* sees the injustices so clearly, and has no illusions about the life of the servants. Because she has no illusions the last sentence is especially valid.

To a generation with a different outlook it seems extraordinary that Robert, kind landlord as he was, never built a bathroom in a single

---

* *The writer is the daughter-in-law of Sir Robert and Lady Stewart (Robert and Alice in this passage) and lives in the Castle at the time of writing. Sir Robert's second son served with The Cameronians (Scottish Rifles) throughout the First World War (6th and 9th Battalions) and won the M.C. and Bar.*

farm or cottage, and that Alice, wearing herself to exhaustion with innumerable good works, thought it unnecessary to give her kitchenmaids a regular day off. But so it was. Hours were long, work beginning at seven on the estate, while housemaids rose before six. Footmen panted up from the basement laden with coals, girls carried heavy trays along dark corridors for the servants' hall meals; knives were cleaned and sharpened by hand in a kind of circular frame; silver ornaments, all requiring polish, littered the tables in the drawing-room. No sweeper ever defiled the many rugs and carpets—all were ministered to on hands and knees with dustpan and brush. Hot water was taken three times daily to the bedrooms, slops were emptied and dozens of fires made up. Brass taps were burnished, ranges black-leaded, and muslin curtains sent continually to the house-laundry, where weighty irons and mangles worked by hand wrought them to snowy whiteness. All provisions were fetched from the village or station, sheep and pigs were killed, cut up, and hung in the outside larder. The groom was constantly on the road with messages and notes. When the house was full for a party it was rare for the servants to be in bed before midnight. Yet wages were unbelievably low, even the head-gardener receiving no more than thirty shillings a week. The house staff was paid only once in three months, since Alice thought that this encouraged thrift. Taken by and large the lavishness so often said to be the hall-mark of the Edwardian epoch was confined to a fortunate few. Yet, for all that, the personal interest and friendship between master and man was rewarded at Murdostoun, as it was in most other places, by willing and faithful service lasting, in very many instances, for close on fifty years.[3]

The pattern described so skilfully here was followed all over Great Britain. It applied, on a smaller scale, to other levels of society right down to near the bottom of the ladder. A similar way of life could be found in the homes of the professional classes, of tenant farmers, of small businessmen, and of shopkeepers. Just as the life of the estate was mingled with the life of the Castle at Murdostoun, so the working of a farm was mixed up with the running of the farmhouse, where many of the hands lived and were fed, and the keeping of a shop was closely integrated into the owner's private existence in the back premises. Outside the industrial areas, most workers were involved in occupations which brought them into close contact with other people of different social levels. Domestic servants, farm-labourers, and shop-workers constituted between them the major part of the working population of Britain; '. . . her farms employed more labourers than either her mines or her textile factories; and more men and women were engaged in paid‚ domestic service than in all the metallurgical industries—from pin-making to shipbuilding—put together.'[4] It was the element of personal contact which made overworked and underpaid domestic servants and agricultural labourers accept their lot so readily. Because they knew the people they were working for intimately they accepted the long hours and the low wages which they might have resented in the service of strangers.

If this is so, why did the workers in the industrial centres not show resentment at their conditions of employment, even harder and worse rewarded as they were, and not eased by much contact with their employers? The answer is partly apathy, partly ignorance, partly preoccupation with simply keeping alive, and partly that the time was not ripe. Before the First World War the bitterness of the real lower classes about their own harsh existence was only starting, and those who pointed it out were little heeded. It takes time for human beings to become fully conscious of social movements, and the men and women who preached dissatisfaction in 1900 were not to see their ideas fully accepted for another twenty years.

One should think of the majority of the population of Edwardian Britain living in harmony in spite of vast differences in the standard of living between the rich and the poor. One should remember the thinkers and writers who were drawing attention to the differences, but one would be wrong to imagine that their words were taken note of by more than a handful of people. In the country and small towns one should think of employers and employed living much closer than today, and seeing more of each other, thereby avoiding much of the bitterness of inequality of wealth and living standards. In the centres of industry one should imagine sections of the population living in deep poverty, but on the whole unwilling to do much about their misfortune. In a sentence, one should see Britain as a nation of distinct classes, with widely differing ways of life, but in general contriving to live together with little friction.

The first thing to record about the officer–other rank relationship in the 2nd Scottish Rifles is that it was a success story. The officers and men lived and worked together in remarkable harmony. To achieve an understanding between leaders and led of quite such a successful nature is something which more often eludes than crowns the efforts of human beings. I would not claim that the battalion was unique in respect of this harmony of relationship because I am sure it was shared by most good front-line battalions in the First World War. But it is still a rare enough success story to be worth careful study. One must look at this remarkable affinity between officers and men in both peace and war, seeing how it was rooted in the peacetime life of the battalion, and then how it flowered in the harsh, stark existence of the trenches.

All ranks were linked together by the fact of belonging to the 2nd Scottish Rifles. For officers and men alike the battalion was at the centre of their existence. Anything could be forgiven if it was felt that the person concerned was loyal to the Regiment. A strict, unbending officer could be excused his harshness on the grounds that he was concerned with the good name of the battalion. An ignorant and incompetent subaltern—not that there were many—would be devotedly guided and assisted by the Sergeant-Major of his company and his platoon Sergeant as long as they thought his heart was in the right place and he was really keen on the Regiment. This worked the other way as well. Some of the stricter officers tolerated the drunkenness and misbehaviour of a few of the old reprobates among their men for year after year because they knew that they were unfailingly loyal. And many a reprobate knew that his punishment for being involved in a drunken brawl with soldiers of another Regiment could be halved if he put in a word or two about the other side having dared to insult the Scottish Rifles. One might say that the cornerstone of the relationship between officers and other ranks was their common devotion to the Regiment.

The care which officers were expected to take of the soldiers under their command I have gone into fully already. This care was more a matter of concern for the men's efficiency than in making them contented, or sympathizing with their troubles, but it provided a link of mutual interest between them.

The interplay between the relative simplicity of mind of officers and the childishness of outlook of many other ranks should be noted. The two qualities, or defects, depending on which way one looks at them, went well together. Because they were brought up to believe implicitly in certain values and ways of doing things the officers assumed their position of authority over their men as a King might take his throne: confident and assured, they never doubted that they would be obediently and loyally served. The men, being generally rather like children, fell into place in this scheme of affairs without question. There were very few individuals in the ranks to whom this pattern was not readily acceptable.

Each generation has its hero. The warrior, the saint, the film-star, the business tycoon, the pop-singer, or some other type of person fills for a time a place in the imagination of the immature. When dreaming to themselves people of every age have transformed themselves into the shape of the current idol. In Edwardian days this idol was the rich young English gentleman. He had a magic which enthralled not only his own countrymen but people of many other countries as well. The picture which day-dreamers conjured up in their minds was similar to that of the ideal officer described in Chapter 5. The youth standing at the street-corner fifty years ago envisaged himself in his happiest reveries as an elegant young squire standing at the door of his country mansion. When he came in contact with the gentry he often gave them credit for many qualities which may well not have been there. If in due course the youth left the street-corner and joined the Army he liked to find that his officers came from the type he so much admired. He was ready to follow 'a real gentleman' to the ends of the earth. In contact with members of an admired and envied world—almost a story-book world*—he

* *The story books that were read in those days all reinforced a respect for the English gentleman, as did the magazines and journals which the lower-middle and*

felt a fascination which never quite died away even after he became older and wiser. It may be that I have made too much of this idea, but I do not think so. It is the explanation of the affection, bordering on adulation, which the majority of soldiers were prepared to lavish on officers who particularly appealed to them. It went far beyond the normal respect and goodwill which one might expect from a subordinate towards a competent and kindly superior. Officers who combined efficiency and fairness with the obvious qualities of a gentle-man received from their men a devoted loyalty which one might almost say no human being deserves from another.

A very important point is the friendship which existed between commissioned officers and Warrant Officers and Sergeants. In Malta before 1914 there was not a great deal of direct contact between officers and the rank and file. This does not mean that officers did not know the privates, nor that they did not speak to them. What it does mean is that in the ordinary course of the daily round orders were passed to the rank and file through the Warrant Officers and Sergeants. This body of men acted as the channel of com-munication between the officers and the privates. If a Company Commander wanted the company paraded he told his C.S.M. to do it; if a Platoon Commander was ordered to carry out a task he told his Platoon Sergeant to get the men ready and move them to the place where the job was to be done. For this reason, a very close and important form of contact developed between the officers and the senior N.C.O.s.

Keeping this special contact on the right lines was one of the unwritten responsibilities of the R.S.M. By his own example and careful words of guidance he insured that young officers learnt how to treat the senior N.C.O.s with a correct balance of politeness and respect for their length of service while not losing their own proper authority. At the same time he showed the N.C.O.s how to be obedient without being

working classes were starting to read so avidly. The Boy's Own Paper was not only full of good stories and exciting adventures (see also Chapter 10), but it sang the praises freely of the officer class. (It is worth remembering also that even Tarzan was originally a British peer when out of the jungle, an aspect which has been less stressed in recent years.)

obsequious, and how they should correct a young officer's faults without undermining his confidence. An R.S.M. like Chalmers became for many young officers almost more important a figure than the Commanding Officer. They knew that they could turn to him for advice and help in any circumstances. And the effect that he had on the young officers of the 2nd Scottish Rifles is particularly vivid to me because of a relatively small point. In his study, Captain Kennedy, whose name has appeared so often in these pages, has one photograph on his desk. It is a simple, oval photograph of R.S.M. Chalmers. Fifty years after Kennedy left the battalion, never to go back again, he looks at a photograph every day of the R.S.M. If one can appreciate from this very simple little illustration the extent of the respect and affection that must have existed between these two men one can start to understand the bonds that linked the officers of the pre-1914 Regular Army to the men who served under their command.

One of the most perceptive descriptions I have seen of the *rapport* that can exist between an officer and a senior N.C.O. does not come from the British Army, but from the French. This passage is from *Portrait of an Officer* by P.-H. Simon.

Brahim Sadoun, who was my senior non-commissioned officer, never left my side; he was beside me in the turret of my tank, a second pair of eyes to locate the enemy, a second pair of hands to aim the gun or the machine-gun; he was beside me when we had to fight as infantry and advance under fire, and I really don't know how often we were instrumental in saving each other's life; and he was with me in my jeep, bumping over the African tracks or driving along the roads of France. . . . And I do not believe that this complete fellowship between two men, this sure knowledge of a loyal presence, can occur outside the military life, or in any case outside a life of danger. We were brothers, and yet not equals: it was not by age, but by rank and professional experience that I dominated Brahim; his submission was only the more complete, and without a shadow of bitterness, rancour or denial, as my power was without contempt or pride. Between Captain de Larsan and and Sergeant Sadoun there had developed quite naturally a perfect, simple and age-old link, which was both intimate and traditional:

a devotion of man to man, a friendship within a hierarchy, in fact an honourable feudal relationship.[5]

Change the nationality of the names, and substitute a bay of a trench for the turret of a tank, and the passage would fit exactly a British officer and Sergeant in the line in the First World War.

When the 2nd Scottish Rifles went into action in the trenches the close relationship which had in peacetime been limited to officers and senior N.C.O.s extended its bounds. Not only did officers and Sergeants know each other well, but a good Platoon Commander established real friendships with the junior ranks from whom he had been a little distant before. Of the reward he found in this Kennedy has written:

The trenches, for all their drab unpleasantness, soon showed up what a man was worth, and enabled an officer to know and appreciate his men as never before. It is, moreover, hardly too much to say that, by being thrown into such constant and intimate contact with his men in trench warfare—far closer contact, in fact, than with most of his brother officers—the average regimental officer came to establish with them such a bond of mutual understanding and liking that, when they were killed or seriously wounded, he felt their loss, as a rule, far more deeply than the loss of any but his closest friends in the commissioned ranks.

On this last score, I find his words at a later stage about the death of Private McHugh most moving. He had last seen McHugh as he himself lay wounded beside the hedge shortly after the start of the battle of Neuve Chapelle. He writes of McHugh's death:

I heard afterwards that he had been killed later in the day, helping to carry our own wounded out of danger while exposed to heavy fire. He should, of course, have left that to the stretcher-bearers; but it was typical of McHugh to sacrifice himself to help others. Absolutely fearless, a first-rate worker, and always ready to volunteer for any unpleasant job that was on hand, he was one of the best men out. Of all those who met their death that day there were few, if any, whose loss I felt more deeply.

If Kennedy felt in this way about his men, it is interesting to consider what they thought about him. A very revealing passage in his manuscript describes how he kept in touch with his platoon after he had been evacuated from the front and had eventually reached the Royal Herbert Hospital at Woolwich. Having described how his family came regularly to visit him, he goes on:

What pleased me as much as anything, however, were the occasional visits from men of my old platoon. Their numbers had been sadly reduced at Neuve Chapelle, but several of the survivors kept up a regular correspondence with me from the Front; and when, later, they returned to England in ones and twos on leave, they never failed to devote an afternoon of their short time at Home to make their way out to the hospital at Woolwich, if they could possibly manage it. Little wonder that one forgot all the horrors and discomforts of the trenches and longed to return to the Regiment at the Front in order to be with these men once more.

There may not seem to be anything very unusual in this passage, but I believe that there are two remarkable points about it. One is that 'several of the survivors kept up a regular correspondence' with Kennedy. Just think what it meant in terms of effort to privates of those days to write a letter. To write one letter a week to their families was probably quite a strain amidst the weariness, discomfort and awkwardness of their existence at the front or just behind it; for them to make the effort to write as well to a young officer, who had only been a year or so with the battalion before he was wounded, I find astonishing. Even more astonishing I find the fact that they devoted 'an afternoon of their short time at Home to make their way out to the hospital at Woolwich' to see him. Other ranks did not get much leave from France, and rarely more than a week at a stretch. For privates to struggle out to Woolwich to see their Platoon Commander— and it is still a struggle to get to the Herbert Hospital—speaks for a depth of comradeship which was a unique feature of the First World War. Good relations between officers and men have been known in other wars, but rarely with quite this degree of warmth seen in 1914–1918.

The main cause of this wonderful relationship between good officers and their men in the trenches was that all the trappings of life were removed, and the real worth of an individual was revealed. All the aspects of normal life which divide men from each other became of secondary importance. Between men in the front line there was: 'neither East nor West, Border, nor Breed, nor Birth'; where a man came from and where he might go after the War was of little account; wealth, background, and education only mattered in as far as they had fitted a man to play his part in the structure of the battalion; whether he was a saint or a sinner nobody cared, but only that a man could do his job.

In this environment the leader assumed heroic proportions. I should qualify this by saying the good leader; the bad one became an object of contempt and quickly vanished from the front line. But officers in the 2nd Scottish Rifles who proved themselves in action to be brave and conscientious, as indeed nearly all of them did, earned a trust and respect from their men that transcended anything they had known in peacetime.

If the leader, whether officer or N.C.O., found a reward in this happy atmosphere, the ordinary private found an even greater one. The chance was open to any soldier to prove his real worth. It was as though the slate had been rubbed clean, almost as though men had been born again. Every private, however unimportant he may have felt himself before, quickly discovered in the line his true value. As he stood on sentry duty at night, cold and tired though he was, he knew that on him depended the safety of his section and platoon. More than this, he knew that this importance was recognized. He knew that before long the shadowy figure of one of the company officers would be beside him for a moment or two as he went on his round of the sentries. A whispered conversation would take place for perhaps half a minute, then with perhaps a muttered: 'Good man—keep at it', the officer would move on. Not much, perhaps, but the trust and harmony between those two figures caught together for a moment in the night made up for much of the apparent misery and squalor of their lot.

One of the gravest mistakes in human relationships is to

underestimate the need of human beings to have a sense of the value of their work. We all know, however pompous it may be to say so, that the only real happiness in life is to be found in doing a useful job well. The man who does the simplest and lowliest work needs the satisfaction of knowing that it is important even more, perhaps, than the man at the top of an organization. After all he probably gets little other reward. One must remember this fact when considering the reaction of the private soldier to the appalling conditions he endured in the First World War.

Though he cursed and swore his way through those miserable winter months before Neuve Chapelle, and though he dreamt of getting a nice 'blighty' wound which would get him away from the front, the private of the 2nd Scottish Rifles was, I am sure, far happier than one would imagine. He knew that he was doing an essential job in a good battalion, and that his worth was fully recognized. Under good officers whom he trusted, who shared his life, and who gave him the recognition he wanted, he could be relied upon to do his best under any conditions. This was proved at Neuve Chapelle. So strong was the mutual trust between officers and men that it seemed to carry on after nearly all the officers were out of the battle killed or wounded. The experienced officers knew that this would happen, as Ferrers' story of Neuve Chapelle shows. To the young officer who doubted that the men would follow Ferrers replied with complete conviction: 'Don't you worry about the lads, they'll come all right.' And in a moment or two they did. When soldiers and their leaders have developed trust in each other to this extent only annihilation can stop them.

Having said so much about the successful side of the officer–other rank relationship something must be said of the occasions when it was not entirely happy. Rare though these were there were times when an officer found difficulty in establishing a good *rapport* with his men. The most usual cause was a tendency on his part to laugh at the men unkindly, or to be sarcastic about them. Sergeant Noble, whose overall opinion of the officers of the 2nd Scottish Rifles is recorded at the head of this chapter, has told of a small incident

shortly after the battalion arrived in France in 1914. At this
stage it was thought that spies behind the British lines might
be sending information to the Germans by carrier pigeon.
The order therefore came down from G.H.Q. for troops at the
front to watch out for pigeons crossing their lines in the
direction of the enemy trenches. Noble's story is this:

Newly arrived officers sometimes seemed to treat N.C.O.s as
inferior. One morning I was posting a sentry, day duty in the trench,
and I said 'Keep a sharp look out for pigeons.' The officer went
'Ha, ha', the sentry likewise. I felt humiliated. I reported to my
C.S.M. (Culley) who reported to the Major, and through the
batman I learnt that the officer received a good ticking off.

The indignation of a first-rate N.C.O. at being laughed at
in this way was intense. It was more than a matter of personal
pique; it was a feeling that the officer had abused his position
by mocking someone who could not answer back. He had
destroyed for a moment the all-important channel of mutual
trust and respect between himself and his subordinates. And
this was obviously what the Company Commander, Major
Hayes, felt when he heard the story by one of the methods
through which an officer could keep closely in touch with
what was going on among his men. A quiet word from a
sensible soldier servant, or batman, to his officer often put
right similar small grievances. It was part of the family
atmosphere of the old Regular Army.

In reading the story of the battle of Neuve Chapelle one
cannot fail to be struck by the extent of casualties among
the officers. Was it right to lose so many trained leaders in
such a way? General Jack had to answer this question almost
a year after the battle, as this extract from his diary for
19 February 1916 shows:

At dinner a few nights ago a New Army officer made scathing
remarks about the waste of officers' lives in my battalion at Neuve
Chapelle. The best defence to the charge that I could think of at
the moment was to suggest that it is an officer's duty to 'go down
with the ship' if necessary. This he countered by saying that the
taxpayers expected better value for their money.

I consider that in this and similar assaults our casualties in officers of irreplaceable value were far too high. Too many of them were sent charging across open, bullet-swept ground when experience and training were largely at a discount and little more was required than bulldog courage. At the same time one must weigh the effect on the morale of the men if their officers do not share their dangers. The mistake was in having so many valuable officers present with battalions at all. . . .[6]

It is far from simple to answer this question. The obvious practical solution would have been for a number of officers to have been kept out of the battle from the start, but more was involved than pure logic. Much of the quality of the 2nd Scottish Rifles was due to having a good supply of officers of a high calibre, who were in close and harmonious contact with their men. For many of these officers to have been left out of the battle would have been unthinkable. Between an officer kept out of the line at Neuve Chapelle and the men he had lived with until the eve of the battle there would have grown afterwards a distrust which would have been the complete antithesis of everything that had gone before. The soldiers could not have failed to feel a faint contempt for their officer when they met him again after the battle:

> There would be doubt, hesitation and pain,
> Forced praise on our part—the glimmer of twilight,
> Never glad confident morning again![7]

My belief is that the morale of the 2nd Scottish Rifles was so closely bound up with the excellent relationship in the battalion between the officers and the other ranks that anything done to upset that relationship would have upset morale disastrously as well. As long as the officers were there on the strength of the battalion they had to do everything their men did.

The correct answer is indicated in General Jack's suggestion that there should have been fewer officers with the battalion in the first place, that is that its official establishment of officers should have been less. It obviously helped in many ways to have a lot of officers with the battalion, and it was easier for a Company Commander to run a good company with five officers than with only two. But these advantages were marginal. Two good officers per company, especially when one considers the high quality of the Warrant Officers and Sergeants, were enough to have produced very nearly as good results as were in fact produced. Had more careful and sparing use been made of trained Regular officers in the early days of the War, particularly in this way of limiting the numbers posted to each battalion, some of the difficulties, and huge casualties, of later years might have been obviated.

To sum up the officer–other rank relationship in the 2nd Scottish Rifles, I would say that it was conspicuously successful. It was rooted in the peacetime traditions of Regimental life, where all ranks regarded loyalty to the Regiment as the supreme virtue. From the slightly distant relationship of peace officers and men found themselves in the trenches in close and intimate contact. The innate trust and respect between them blossomed in these conditions, where the true nature of each man became quickly apparent, into a deep and warm friendship—to repeat P.-H. Simon's words '. . . a perfect, simple, and age-old link, which was both intimate and traditional: a devotion of man to man, a friendship within a hierarchy. . . .' From this simple friendship both groups drew great strength and satisfaction, and its existence must be taken to be a big factor in the battalion's high morale.

Discipline

The sterner the discipline the better the soldier, the better the army.[1]

It was a platitude of the fighting period that discipline would win the war, as it is now a platitude that discipline has won it.[2]

Stephen Graham, A PRIVATE IN THE GUARDS

MILITARY DISCIPLINE HAS two purposes. The first is to ensure that the soldier does not give way in times of great danger to his natural instinct for self-preservation, but carries out his orders even though they may lead to his own death. The object of discipline in this case is to leave no doubt in the mind of any officer or man about where his duty lies. The soldier in battle is subject to many temptations to give way to his fear. As a private of the American Civil War put it: 'The truth is, when bullets are whacking against tree trunks and solid shot are cracking skulls like egg shells, the consuming passion in the heart of the average man is to get out of the way. Between the physical fear of going forward, and the moral fear of turning back, there is a predicament of exceptional awkwardness, from which a hidden hole in the ground would be a wonderfully welcome outlet.'[3] In these vivid words is caught the essence of the problem. When discipline is seen at its best it provides a buttress to support the soldier in his struggle against his own fears. The end should be that: 'The avenue to the rear is absolutely closed up in the mind. Such equanimity is produced by discipline. Stern discipline can manufacture collective heroism.'[4]

If the primary purpose of military discipline is to produce

staunchness in battle, the secondary one is to keep order within an army itself, so that it may be easily moved and controlled, and so that it should not abuse its power. In this latter respect, it must be remembered that even the army of a highly civilized nation can slip easily into disorder, particularly on active service. Men living together without feminine influences, armed and trained to fight, can behave in a way that would be unthinkable in ordinary life. The only antidote to potential disorder is strong discipline.

The British Army of 1914 was very conscious of discipline. It was regarded as the foundation of training, and indeed of the whole of Army life. I doubt if much consideration was given to the reasons for regarding discipline as such an important matter: it was readily accepted as the keystone of military efficiency by General and private soldier alike, and nobody had any doubt that the first test of a unit's quality was the state of its discipline. What discipline meant to the average British soldier was obedience. The current phrase was: 'Orders is orders'; every man was instructed from his earliest days in the Army that any order given by a superior officer, whether commissioned or not, had to be obeyed instantly. He was also told that questions could be asked after obeying the order, and not before. 'You do what you are told, and ask questions afterwards'; that was the doctrine, and there was no challenging it.

It is interesting to note that more or less the same doctrine applied to the German Army. The equivalent phrase was used: 'Befehl ist Befehl'. It may well be that the answer to why the First World War went on for so long lies here. As Stephen Graham wrote: 'never in history have such disciplined armies fought one another'.[5] Had one of the armies been less well-disciplined it would have given way; the very excellence of both in this respect meant that the reaching of a decision between them was bound to be a bloody, long drawn-out business. No contest is more savage than that between well-matched opponents.*

* *General Jack's views on this are in the general notes at the end of the* Diary *(p. 307):* 'When determined and equally matched opponents meet there is no short cut to victory; the struggle must be long; the way hard. . . .'

Before looking into the nature of discipline, and the ways in which it affected members of the 2nd Scottish Rifles, I want to take up briefly Stephen Graham's comment above which he wrote in 1919. My belief is that it was not only true then but will always remain so. It is my contention that a stage was reached in 1914–1918 in the development of man, certainly European man, when he was at his zenith in this particular respect. This is not to claim that he was at his zenith in other respects, but simply in the field of military discipline.

Going back to the first organized army in history of the type we know today, the Roman Army, Gibbon shows how its remarkable discipline was achieved:

. . . it was impossible for cowardice or disobedience to escape the severest punishment. The centurions were authorized to chastise with blows, the generals had a right to punish with death; and it was an inflexible maxim of Roman discipline, that a good soldier should dread his officers far more than the enemy. From such laudable arts did the valour of the Imperial troops receive a degree of firmness and docility, unattainable by the impetuous and irregular passions of barbarians.

Later, he elaborates on the authority of a general:

In his camp the general exercised an absolute power of life and death; his jurisdiction was not confined by any forms of trial or rules of proceeding, and the execution of the sentence was immediate and without appeal. [6]

From this autocratic control, with power of life and death, it is a huge jump to the relatively small powers of coercion vested in a General today. In the British and other democratic armies there are still heavy penalties for serious crimes of disorder within the body military itself. Mutiny, looting, or wilful defiance of authority could still be punished severely, even in certain circumstances with a sentence of death. But failing to control his fears in battle is not likely to earn a soldier a very severe punishment. Whatever he may be told about the appalling consequences of running away in the face of the enemy, the truth is that the modern soldier is unlikely to get more than a year or two in prison for the most blatant cowardice. What this means is that civilized countries now depend on the soldier himself to provide the discipline required to resist his own instinct of self-preservation. Naturally he is helped by leadership, by training, and by use of such factors as public opinion and loyalty to his comrades in his efforts to do his duty, but it is still basically a matter of self-discipline. The primary purpose of discipline is now fulfilled by the soldier from his own resources. Although the antithesis of self-discipline, which I will call imposed discipline, still exists, it is enforced almost entirely for the preservation of good order, and has little influence on a man's courage in battle. Many revolutions have taken place in the twentieth century, particularly with regard to social attitudes and matters of conduct, and this is one of them. This particular revolution, which has gone almost unnoticed, is one of those which accelerated rapidly in the first years of this century. In 1914–1918 the influences of self-discipline and imposed discipline were very delicately balanced. A point had been reached about half-way between the absolute control from above imposed by the Romans, enforced with savage and frequent punishment, and the complete reliance of modern armies, such as the British, on a soldier's own willingness to do his duty.

When one starts to consider self-discipline it is apparent that the term is nearly synonomous with 'high morale'. The primary source of self-discipline in the 2nd Scottish Rifles was public opinion within the battalion. One of the strongest reasons for men behaving well and trying to do their best is to earn the respect of their fellows. Put in a negative way, it is to avoid the contempt of others, particularly such people as they themselves admire. For most men an essential part of courageous behaviour is their desire to gain the admiration of their comrades, and also of their leaders. Nothing can cause a man more unhappiness than to incur the scorn of someone he admires. By the same token a word of praise from a well-respected figure can steel a man's self-discipline as nothing else can.

In the 2nd Scottish Rifles the finest personalities drew the best out of those around them. Men with this power developed to a high degree were Carter-Campbell and Ferrers among the officers, and Chalmers, Culley, and Docherty among the other ranks. A great part of this power was due to their own high standards of personal discipline. From their example others drew strength. This applied not only to that aspect of discipline which led to courage in battle, but also that which applied to good order in peacetime conditions.

Also a source of self-discipline among members of the 2nd Scottish Rifles was *esprit de corps*, which is another way of saying group loyalty. It is a better term in this context, however, because it implies concern for the reputation and success of the group in addition to its well-being and security. Men controlled their fears, and their conduct, not merely to avoid letting down their comrades, but also for the good name and efficiency of the battalion. Charles Carrington has written: 'Discipline without *esprit de corps* is a damnable thing for which no humane person is likely to offer a defence; discipline based on *esprit de corps* is the dynamic of human progress towards any goal.'[7]

An organization with a strong *esprit de corps* powerfully influences the conduct of its members. Discipline becomes natural; to do anything selfish, anything to detract from the good name of the organization, becomes unthinkable. So it was with the 2nd Scottish Rifles, though they would not, one hopes, have put it quite so smugly.

Having a bearing on the self-discipline of the officers more than the men, was the dual influence of two divergent traditions. One was that of the early nineteenth century, and the other of Victorian times. The former, what one might call the tradition of the Regency 'buck', laid great emphasis on physical courage, contempt for pain, and the importance of cutting a fine figure under any conditions. The archetype of that age was John Mytton (1796–1834), whose life was recorded in a book which many young Regular officers of 1914 would have read. Mytton was grossly lacking in self-discipline in many respects, being a notorious gambler, drunkard, and loose-liver. On the other hand he had certain qualities of endurance which were remarkable. His biographer records that: 'He never wore any but the thinnest and finest silk stockings, with very thin boots or shoes, so that in winter he rarely had dry feet . . . and in frost and snow he waded through all water that came in his way.'[8] As a horseman '. . . he performed immense distances on the roads on his hacks. He would ride, several times in the week, to cover nearly fifty miles distant from Halston, and return thither to his dinner. Neither could any man I ever met in the field walk through the day with him *at his pace*.'[9]

As well as endurance of this sort,

Mr. Mytton appeared, at least wished to be supposed to be, indifferent to pain. A very few days after he had had so bad a fall with his own hounds as to occasion the dislocation of three ribs, and was otherwise much bruised . . . he took the lead off of all the field, upon the horse he called 'The Devil', and was never headed by any man, till he killed his fox, at the end of a capital hour's run. He was very near fainting from the severity of this trial; but I remember his telling me, *he would not have been seen to faint for ten thousand pounds*.[10]

The colossal vigour and hardihood of men like Mytton was a potent factor in Britain's rise to greatness in the nineteenth century. Stories of their feats of endurance and fearlessness lived on to the end of the century, and the young man growing up before 1914 was strongly influenced by them.

To balance this early 19th-century tradition there was the earnestness, moral purpose, and high-mindedness of the later years of Queen Victoria's reign. When one found the two traditions influencing one man a most remarkable form of self-discipline appeared. The best example, in whom the two influences can be strongly seen, was General Jack. His sense of duty, his meticulousness, and his reserve were part of his Victorian upbringing, while his elegance, his independence of mind and his physical courage sprang from an older tradition. The pattern seen in him was obvious in many others. It provided a fertile ground on which self-mastery could flourish.

From the discipline which officers and men created for themselves I now turn to that which was imposed from above. Broadly speaking, in 1914, men in authority in all walks of life were expected to enforce discipline strictly. This applied to schoolmasters, employers of labour, foremen, parents, policemen, and every type of person one can think of with the least vestige of authority, as much as to officers and N.C.O.s of the Army. And there were few doubts about how to enforce discipline. The schoolmaster told a boy to learn something, and if the boy did not know the answer the next day the master beat him; the foreman ordered a man to do a job, and if it was not done the man was sacked; in the Army, an N.C.O. gave an order, and the private who failed to obey was doubled off to the guard-room, and put in close arrest.

Although this enforcement of discipline in the Army was often unnecessarily brutal, there were a number of things to be said in favour of a rigid imposed discipline which are easily forgotten. Many of the men found in the strictness of their daily routine a security which more than compensated for a lack of obvious liberty. In a paradoxical way the soldier of pre-1914 days was perhaps freer than other people living apparently less controlled lives. The demands made on him were simple, and absolutely clear. As long as he did his own job well and observed the rules nobody worried much about what he was thinking, or whether he liked doing what he had to do or not. As long as he went through the motions correctly he could think his own thoughts; his daily round was ruled by Military Law, but his soul was his own.

A reason why soldiers often preferred to be ruled with a heavy hand rather than in a more liberal fashion is that a strictly imposed discipline is not condescending. Strict obedience is a challenge which sets a man on his mettle. To allow a soldier to disobey orders is really to insult him. A good man, in any walk of life, knows what he can do, and what he should do. If he fails, he expects the just reward of failure—punishment, disgrace, ruin or whatever it may be. If for some reason he avoids his just reward, he knows perfectly well that it is due to luck, or to pity on the part of someone else. Neither luck nor pity are things he wants, because they simply add to his own sense of failure. The old saying that an ounce of spite is worth a pound of pity has a lot of truth in it, and harsh, even spiteful discipline, has usually been more acceptable to soldiers than tolerance—though not likely to be admitted.

[186]

Perhaps the root of the matter is that tolerance of poor performance implies that a person's efforts are unimportant. A man in authority who lets his subordinates get away with poor performance implies in doing so that they, and their actions, are of no consequence.

At the head of a military formation where discipline is strict there must be a strict Commanding Officer—a martinet. Both Bliss and Carter-Campbell could be described as martinets, and both were effective Commanding Officers in their own ways. Why should Bliss, in particular, have had such success, when in many respects a rather stupid man? Usually in the First World War a strict, old-fashioned Commanding Officer achieved much better results than a more liberal man of greater intelligence who tended to be too understanding of his subordinates' weaknesses. Although there is a temptation to say that this is a sad reflection on human nature, it needs to be looked at more carefully.

Everyone in a military formation knows how things ought to be done. Even the stupidest soldier learns very quickly the difference between what is correct and efficient and what is incorrect and slip-shod. This applies of course to other organizations as well as military ones. For most men life is a constant struggle between doing what they know they ought to do, and the temptation to get out of making the effort to do it. When they find a superior who insists on them doing things properly, and takes action if they do not, they are happy. Also, they are not faced with the problem of making decisions for themselves. Harshness and strict insistence on matters of discipline are for this reason preferred to tolerance. Tolerance is not only disliked by the soldier for its implication that his efforts do not matter much, but also because it is to some extent an abnegation of duty by his superior. In allowing a man to do less than his best without taking action the officer or N.C.O. throws on to the man a decision which is properly his own. Beyond this, he gives the man that let-out from doing his best which he is already struggling against. The man feels cheated and insecure. For all these reasons that a 'Crimean' character like Colonel Bliss could have a good battalion in spite of his limitations. Any criticism of the unsympathetic approach of men of his type to their subordinates must be qualified by recognition of their success.

A problematical subject is that of the means by which discipline was enforced. Although precept and example played their part, maintenance of discipline in the pre-1914 Army was mainly a matter of punishment. And there is little doubt that it was at times used excessively. Cyril Falls has written: 'Punishment was still altogether too severe, at its severest verging on the brutal in units containing a large element intractable in character.'[11]

Death was the severest punishment that could be inflicted. The death sentence was used in the First World War for cowardice in action, desertion, and mutiny. The actual numbers executed were just over three hundred. I am not going to go into the rights and wrongs of the use of the death penalty as no member of the 2nd Scottish Rifles was executed during the period this study is concerned with, and to the best of my knowledge throughout the War. Although most people knew at second-hand about an execution by the firing squad it was extremely rare for anyone to have personal knowledge of one. What I want to look at are the more commonly met forms of punishment.

On active service a court martial, and a Commanding Officer administering summary justice, were empowered to sentence a soldier to undergo what was called 'field punishment'. The rules for this, as contained in the Sixth Edition of the *Manual of Military Law* printed in February 1914 are, by modern standards, rather horrifying. Rule 2 reads as follows:

Where an offender is sentenced to field punishment No. 1, he may, during the continuance of his sentence, unless the court martial or the commanding officer otherwise directs, be punished as follows:

(*a*) He may be kept in irons, i.e. in fetters or handcuffs, or both fetters and handcuffs; and may be secured so as to prevent his escape.

(*b*) When in irons he may be attached for a period or periods not exceeding two hours in any one day to a fixed object, but he must not be so attached during more than three out of any four consecutive days, nor during more than twenty-one days in all.

(*c*) Straps or ropes may be used for the purpose of these rules in lieu of irons.

(*d*) He may be subjected to the like labour, employment, and restraint, and dealt with in like manner as if he were under a sentence of imprisonment with hard labour.[12]

Many Commanding Officers of the day took advantage of the latitude allowed them by the Rule to dispense with attaching the man to a fixed object. They felt that it was degrading and bad for morale. There were those on the other hand who thought it important to make an example of offenders, and always insisted that the tying-up part of the punishment, known to soldiers as 'Crucifixion', be carried out. Kennedy does not remember many cases of field punishment being awarded in the 2nd Scottish Rifles, but thinks that when it was the men were usually tied up for two hours a day to a fixed object.

However offensive such punishments may seem to a modern reader, and however surprising it may be that such barbaric language was used in an official handbook only fifty years ago, one must try to see things in perspective.

One must consider the whole attitude of people to matters of crime and punishment in the last hundred years. Writing in 1924 George Bernard Shaw recorded:

. . . that when I was already a grown man I saw Richard Wagner conduct two concerts, and that when Richard Wagner was a young man he saw and avoided a crowd of people hastening to see a soldier broken on the wheel by the more cruel of the two ways of carrying out that hideous method of execution. Also that the penalty of hanging, drawing, and quartering, unmentionable in its details, was abolished so recently that there are men living who have been sentenced to it. We are still flogging criminals, and clamouring for more flogging.[13]

The British Army had at least stopped using the lash as a method of punishment well before 1914. And in curtailing the use of cruel methods of execution Britain was well ahead of most other countries in the nineteenth century. Seen in this light the hang-over from crueller days contained in the rules for field punishment are less disquieting.

There is also the fact that soldiers of pre-1914 days were

extraordinarily tough. And although normally well-disciplined and well-behaved, they could be amazingly rough and savage when drunk. In fact practically all their crime, such as there was, sprang from moments of drunkenness. For example, my father remembers two drunken men murdering an N.C.O. in 1910 by beating him to death with hockey-sticks in his bed. It was men such as this who tended to find themselves on field punishment, and one cannot believe that tying them up for two hours to a gun-wheel did them very much harm.

A final point about harsh punishment is that there was no other method by which those in authority could bring home to a possible offender the full extent of their resolve that he should not commit the offence. However barbaric the firing squad may have been it brought home to those who had knowledge of its existence a realization of the lengths to which their superiors would go to ensure that their orders were obeyed. One will never know how many men were frightened into or out of various courses of action by the threat of execution, but it was certainly a threat that was not trifled with.

Sentences of death for purely military offences, and of field punishment, could not be awarded in peacetime. When the battalion was in Malta, the most serious punishments that the Commanding Officer could award were detention in the guard-room and fines for drunkenness. Lesser punishments, which could be awarded by a Company Commander, were confinement to barracks, extra guards and picquets, extra fatigues or duties, and admonition, the legal word for an official 'telling off'.

When a man appeared in front of an officer charged with a breach of discipline he was normally punished, and very rarely was the charge against him not upheld. It would be fair to say that officers were more concerned with reinforcing the authority of the N.C.O. who had charged a soldier than with examining the evidence in the case in minute detail. If there was any doubt the word of the N.C.O. was taken before that of the private soldier. Any occasional minor injustice that arose from this approach to the administration of justice was considered of far less importance than the need to maintain overall standards of discipline in the battalion. The extent of such injustice was not great. There may well have been cases when the evidence against a soldier was not as complete as it ought to have been to ensure a conviction, but on the whole officers used their powers of summary jurisdiction with a strict fairness, and showed little desire to abuse them. One must remember too that very few soldiers appeared on charges regularly. The Commanding Officer probably dealt with no more than a dozen cases a week, or 1 per cent of the battalion, and these would tend to be the same men time after time. Usually their crime was something to do with drink, and very rarely would any of them offer any form of defence. Officers and men in those days used the saying, in respect of earning the displeasure of their seniors, 'never complain, never explain'. The Scottish soldier stuck to this, and in nine cases out of ten accepted his punishment without a word.

John Brophy says much the same with slightly different emphasis to mine:

Ninety-nine men out of a hundred never ran any great risk of the more drastic punishments but this was only because the spirit in which King's Regulations were administered was more flexible and humane than the spirit and letter of the regulations themselves. The possibility of severe punishment hung perpetually over the private soldier and indeed some Regular N.C.O.s boasted that if they really wished to they could make sure that any man under them would be sent to a military prison. As soon as the private soldier realized the power of the organization to which, body and soul, he now belonged, he realized also that, while he might learn certain ways of outwitting it, outwardly he had no choice but to submit. Any form of direct defiance was worse than useless.[14]

If the impression has been given that summary justice in the Army was meted out with more concern for the maintenance of general good order than the rights of the individual, the exact opposite applied in more serious cases dealt with by courts martial. Unfortunately the court martial has often been used in novels, plays, and films as a vehicle for carrying stories of the persecution of innocent soldiers by stupid, reactionary, and vindictive officers. Thus the very term itself has become almost suspect in the minds of many people who have never seen one at work. In ninety-nine cases out of a hundred a court martial in the British Army has always been utterly different. It has normally produced exactly the same reaction in the minds of the officers forming the Court as that of the members of a jury. Being thoroughly conscious of their own inexperience, and anxious at all costs to avoid bringing in an unfair verdict, the members of a court martial tend to lean heavily towards the interest of the accused. Whatever anyone may have heard to give them ideas to the contrary, I am prepared to state categorically that soldiers who were tried by court martial in the pre-1914 Army were given thorough and scrupulously fair trials, and indeed usually had the scales of justice tipped in their favour. Commenting in general on death sentences awarded by courts martial General Jack wrote of: 'a sickeningly terrible end for these poor fellows'. But he went on to record:

I know that presidents and members of courts martial impose this penalty with extreme reluctance, and only on irrrefutable evidence which is minutely examined by the Judge Advocate-General at Army Headquarters before the sentence is carried out by a firing party.[15]

So far the official methods of enforcing discipline in the Army have been mentioned. There were other methods used, which were not always so reputable. On occasions, irregular punishments were thoroughly justified. Sergeant Noble has described one of them in vivid words. During the meal halt on the march to Neuve Chapelle on the night 9/10 March 1915 this episode took place:

I saw three drunks and Regimental Police arrive. Colonel Bliss ordered the three drunks into a nearby shell hole, water waist high. Soon he let them out, an issue of stew and everybody was happy.

But there was also a tendency for N.C.O.s to deal with many matters themselves. Although quite illegal, the practice was one to which many officers turned a blind eye. In a well-conducted Regiment it did little harm: the trouble was that it was open to grave abuse, particularly in a battalion where the officers did not supervise their subordinates carefully. An N.C.O. could develop too easily into a bully if given power beyond that legally allowed to him.

Bullying was much more prevalent before the First World War in all walks of life than it is today. In a works or factory, and at school, the odd man out was liable to be persistently and cruelly bullied. The same thing applied in the Army; perhaps it was seen at its worst in the treatment of new recruits. With a harsh N.C.O. in charge of his squad a recruit's life was grim. Particularly offensive, to modern eyes, was the way he was likely to be sworn at, insulted, and berated incessantly with a view to crushing his tendency to answer back. On the other hand, most men lived through the breaking-in process with little harm done to them. Also, bullying by a superior was never as hard to endure as bullying by equals. The men who deserve real sympathy are those who were bullied by their comrades. One can only be grateful that this sort of human nastiness is rarer today than it was fifty years ago.

Imposed discipline in the pre-War Army was mainly enforced by punishment; another way in which it was enforced was through drill. Although the 2nd Scottish Rifles did not pride themselves particularly on drill, as did many regiments, it was none the less an important part of military training. Out of the line for even a few days, everyone was put on to drilling. General Jack wrote of his spell in charge of a party of Scottish Riflemen at No. 8 Infantry Base Depot a few months after Neuve Chapelle:

This Depot holds reserves for the 8th Division and I command 93 men of the 2nd Battalion of my regiment. . . .

Parades are held daily from 8.15 a.m. till 12.30 p.m. and from 2 o'c. till 3.30 in the afternoons. On the top of the hill there is a good level training ground with practice trenches, assault courses, and a rifle range. In addition to tactical exercises, route marches, lectures and other training we carry out daily a little close-order drill, in which I firmly believe as a solid foundation for making soldiers. Detachments of the Guards are continually at drill, performed, as are all their duties, with the thoroughness that places them, perhaps, the first soldiers in the world.[16]

[193]

Mention of the Guards brings to mind a passage from *Good-bye to All That*. Robert Graves records that as an instructor at Harfleur in 1916 he had to answer some Canadians who:

. . . asked what sense there was in sloping and ordering arms, and fixing and unfixing bayonets. They said they had come across to fight, and not to guard Buckingham Palace. I told them that in every division of the four in which I had served—the First, Second, Seventh, and Eighth—there were three different kinds of troops. Those that had guts but were no good at drill; those that were good at drill but had no guts; and those that had guts and were good at drill. These last, for some reason or other, fought by far the best when it came to a show—I didn't know why, and I didn't care. I told them that when they were better at fighting than the Guards they could perhaps afford to neglect their arms-drill.[17]

Writing of the Burma campaign in the Second World War Field-Marshal Lord Slim has much the same to say:

At some stage in all wars armies have let their discipline sag, but they have never won victory until they made it taut again; nor will they. We found it a great mistake to belittle the importance of smartness in turn-out, alertness of carriage, cleanliness of person, saluting, or precision of movement, and to dismiss them is naïve, unintelligent parade-ground stuff. I do not believe that troops can have unshakeable battle discipline without showing those outward and formal signs, which mark the pride men take in themselves and their units and the mutual confidence and respect that exists between them and their officers. It was our experience in a tough school that the best fighting units, in the long run, were not necessarily those with the most advertised reputations, but those who, when they came out of battle at once resumed a more formal discipline and appearance.[18]

The true value of drill is not often recognized. Done badly, or under bullying instructors, it is an unhappy way of wasting time. But so are most human activities when poorly performed. However reluctant any soldier might be to admit it, drill done well under good instructors is an inspiration. The corporate action, the carrying out of complicated manœuvres as though one man, the crash of boots on the ground, the thrill of marching to a band, all these appeal to most men's natural instinct for theatre and display. However primitive, even childish, the critical may say such things are, they do have a strong effect on human beings. Military formations are wise to make use of them. For the soldier of pre-1914 drill also provided useful training in co-ordination and, perhaps more important still, something that he could really master however limited his intelligence. It was something that even the simplest could do well by trying hard, and I am sure many a man who was none too bright at other things gained confidence through being smart on the square. After many years in the Army drill got into a man's blood, and Kipling catches this in his lines about the old soldier coming back into the Army after a spell outside in civilian life:

> I 'eard the feet on the gravel—the feet of the men what drill,
> An' I sez to my fluttering 'eart-strings—I sez to 'em 'Peace, be
> still'.[19]

Another aspect of drill is that of learning to do things as drills. This is not quite the same as drilling on the barrack square. Before 1914 most military skills were taught in the drill fashion. This particularly applied to learning to shoot. The practice handling of weapons in barracks was referred to as 'pokey drill'. Much of the superb musketry of the B.E.F.* was due to constant 'pokey drill', and in particular to bolt manipulation and reloading practice with drill rounds. A man would spend much time each week lying on the ground loading his rifle with these dummy rounds, and then practising the quick movement required to flick one out of the breech by opening and pulling back the bolt before pushing another into it with a sharp forward movement. The skills taught as drills, and regularly practised in the same way, were what soldiers remembered in times of stress and danger in the

---

* *The story is often quoted that the Germans believed that the British Army had numerous machine-guns in the early days of the War because the soldiers fired at such a tremendous speed with their rifles. In fact each British battalion only had two machine-guns.*

trenches. They automatically carried out the correct action however frightened they were. All the long years of constant repetition of simple movements were eventually proved worth while, however dull they may have seemed in time of peace.

The final aspect of imposed discipline to look at is its effectiveness. It is easy enough to understand the importance of self-discipline, but how valuable was the imposed type? An interesting answer can be found in an article written recently by an officer who served in the First World War under the title 'Discipline or Enthusiasm'. He describes two occasions during the War when he was with battalions whose morale had become less good than it might have been: it is worth seeing how things were put right.

The first case was after the retreat from Mons in August 1914, and the battle of the Aisne in September. The author records that:

. . . not all had gone as they should, and the Colonel used the first opportunity, which came about a week later, to overhaul and discipline the battalion. There was one execution for cowardice, and many were the FP No 1 that were given out for straggling. 'You were with the Loamshires, you say? But you are paid to fight with this regiment. 28 days Field Punishment No. 1.' Draconian punishments, yes! But it was a vastly improved battalion that returned to the line, with the more ineffective N.C.O.s deprived of their commands and their places taken by what we subalterns judged were stouter-hearted fellows: and when, a few weeks later, we marched from Hazebrouck to Ypres we all felt we were something to be proud of with our fours tightly covered off and the swinging stride of thoroughly fit men.

The second was when he was with the 8th Division, the Division of which the 2nd Scottish Rifles were part, in 1917.

General Heneker took over command at the beginning of 1917. The division was out of the line at the time and he came like a storm through the billeting area, insisting on a smarter turn-out all round. He put the fear of God into adjutants, and sundry officers were sent down to the base. Smartness of arms drill, the gleam of buttons, immaculate waggons, all these things he insisted on, and all those things, in short, that today are derided as 'bull'.

Of course, he insisted on other things too, but these were the most important so far as the regimental officer was concerned. The effect was to transform the division in a few weeks into a reliable fighting unit. Of course I knew it was right, so that when in early March I was given the honour of leading the battalion in an assault at Bouchevesnes I was glad. I was sure it would no longer be difficult to get the men forward, and my expectations proved correct. For the first time since I had known it—that is, over 21 months—the battalion really 'went'.[20]

In the face of evidence such as this, from someone who saw its effectiveness, it is difficult to doubt that imposed discipline was a very important ingredient in the extraordinary fortitude of the British Army in 1914–1918. If the 2nd Scottish Rifles are taken as typical of that Army, what is the picture that appears of their discipline?

Starting at the top, there were officers whose whole background and upbringing might have been designed to engender military discipline into them. The traditions of their class, the training in their homes and at their schools, and the conventions of their Regimental life all subscribed to make the subjugation of their natural weaknesses one of their main concerns. To be brave, to master fear, to ensure that they never 'let the side down'; these were their most cherished desires. Though the odd one might fail the test of battle, most were ideally conditioned to pass it with credit.

Below the officers, the Warrant Officers and N.C.O.s were men who had reached their positions of trust through their ability to accept, and administer, discipline. It was an essential part of their personalities. In the best sense of the term they were thoroughly indoctrinated with the virtues of 'good order and military discipline'.

Providing the base were the private soldiers. Mostly used to rough living from an early age, they were hardy, loyal and obedient. They were ready to give of their utmost for their battalion and their friends. They were long-service soldiers at their best—well trained and steady.

Here then was the potential. The secret was to make the best use of it. This, I believe, was achieved by a careful balance of self-discipline and that imposed from outside.

The generally cordial relations between all levels of the battalion hierarchy were balanced by the understanding that nobody could expect poor performance of duty to go unpunished. Everyone was encouraged to do his 'bit' willingly, while being quietly reminded that there were plenty of ways of ensuring that he could be forced to do it unwillingly if necessary. Praise was given for good work, but punishment was just as freely doled out for bad. Above all, every officer and man was expected to put the interests of the battalion before his own—and to look for no mercy if he did not.

Earlier armies failed to realize the importance of appealing to their soldiers' own sense of service, and recently many, Western ones at least, may have drifted too far from a proper standard of imposed control, leaving too much to an individual's own resources. The British Army at the start of the First World War had got the mixture between the two disciplines just right, and much of its excellence sprang from this fact.

Religion and Morals

He faced me, reeling in his weariness,
Shouldering his load of planks, so hard to bear.
I say that He was Christ, who wrought to bless
All groping things with freedom bright as air,
And with His mercy washed and made them fair.
Then the flame sank, and all grew black as pitch,
While we began to struggle along the ditch;
And someone flung his burden in the muck,
Mumbling: 'O Christ Almighty, now I'm stuck!'

Siegfried Sassoon, THE REDEEMER[1]

JUST AS THE class divisions in Britain in 1914 were generally accepted without rancour, so one can say that people at that time were generally religious. They were by no means all devout, but the majority were ready to accept the Christian religion without much question. In the same way that servants did not question their master or mistress's social position and authority so the bulk of the population did not question the validity of the Church's teachings and its authority in moral fields. A few men and women openly rejected the Christian religion, but most of those who turned away from it were careful to keep their doubts to themselves. It was 'not done' to be an atheist and likely to incur social discredit—for a member of the middle classes at least.

In order to see how much religion affected the officers and men of the 2nd Scottish Rifles one must first look briefly at the place it held in national life.

The officer, coming from an upper-middle-class home, and

having been educated at a public school, had normally been subjected to prolonged religious indoctrination from his earliest days. The teaching staff at public schools frequently included many members of the clergy, and many famous headmasters were clergymen. In these bastions of the Church many hours a week were spent undergoing enforced religious instruction. I know from my own experience many years after 1914 that half-an-hour's compulsory religion each weekday and two hours on Sundays, a total of five hours a week, was the minimum one could get away with. In earlier days, when prayers and services in school chapels were much longer, about eight hours a week might be normal. The result was to make religion loom very large in a boy's life, and even if in later years he might give it up, his mind could never completely free itself from these influences. It was also normal for the boy who went to a public school to go to church with his family in the holidays at least once every Sunday, and often twice or three times, especially after his confirmation. Since habits enforced so rigorously in youth can never really be broken, it can be seen that church-going meant a great deal to members of the upper and upper-middle classes in the early days of the century.

Among the other classes of society, particularly in the cities, attendance at church was not nearly so common. Rowntree estimated that only 28 per cent of the population of York went regularly to church.[2] This was far more than today, but not nearly as high a percentage as those who enthuse over the great days of the Church would suggest. Of this 28 per cent Rowntree reckoned that two-thirds were working class, and that among them were more women than men. He found that they tended to come from the middle of the group, that is slightly above what I would define as the dividing line between the working class and the real lower class. Church attendance was rare among the skilled workers or artisans, and also among the poorest families. It seems that the better informed members of the working class were often contemptuous of religion and resisted it as unprogressive, while the very poor simply had no knowledge or experience of it. It was the middle-of-the-road working-class family which felt the need of religion.

Finally, in looking at religion on a national basis, it is worth remembering that regardless of individual belief, the Church was considered 'a good thing'. It was connected in people's minds with the Crown and the hierarchy of the country: what is known today as the Establishment. Since the Establishment was generally trusted and respected, so was the Church and its ministers. Clergymen were regarded as good men, and what they said was felt to be right and proper. A man might make no effort to follow the teachings of the Church, but on the whole he would agree that to do so was desirable.

The overall position of religion in Great Britain in 1914 was this. At the top of society were people who had been brought up on a strong educational diet of religious instruction, and who made the Church a big part of their lives. Below them about a third of the adult population were regular church-goers. Among those who took little part in religious life the vast majority were respectful of the Church and its teachings, and only a minority were actively opposed to it. The Church was very much tied up with the structure of society, and the clergy were an influential and admired profession.

Looking at the members of the 2nd Scottish Rifles, a certain pattern appears in their religious beliefs. Most of my material here is direct from men who fought in some part of The Cameronians (Scottish Rifles) in the First World War, and who have been kind enough to answer my questionnaire. Some of them were in the 2nd Scottish Rifles; those who were in other battalions reflect, I am sure, the same opinions as would have come from members of the 2nd.

In answer to the question whether they thought religious faith was a help in the trenches about 50 per cent of the officers I wrote to were definite that it was. Their replies were much along the lines of one who answered: 'Yes. I know in my own case a wonderful help.' One catches in these very simple words something of the security and confidence which I am sure came to men with a definite faith.

Against this, another group shared views similar to the following: 'My answer is No. In ——'s time as C.O. Sunday service before battle was always optional and very few attended, and those who did were mostly not very stout soldiers. The general feeling among officers and men was, I think, that they hadn't lived a particularly Christian life before and they weren't going to cry for help now at the last moment. Pride perhaps but who knows?'

My guess is that only 15 per cent of the officers of the 2nd Scottish Rifles at the time of Neuve Chapelle had this sort of attitude. It was one which was more likely to be found among temporary officers, of whom there were very few in the battalion early in 1915, than regulars. The regulars, most of whom came to the Army through Sandhurst, rather than the Universities with their more inquisitive and questioning climate of opinion, were not in most cases the sort of men to have doubts. They might not have taken their religion very seriously, but they were not likely to doubt that the teaching they had been subjected to in their youth, and still had drummed into them each Sunday on Church Parade, was fundamentally true. The complete dissenter was therefore a rare bird, though there must have been a few. It is of course impossible to know just who they were, as no doubt they kept their views to themselves. A regular officer who paraded his doubts on religion in 1914 would be thought unreliable by his superiors, and an appalling bore by his equals.

So far I have given the attitudes of some 65 per cent of the officers. The remaining 35 per cent were probably a little vague in their approach, and would have shared these reactions to my question: 'Possibly. But not noticeably. If it did it was private, as it should be. It's not much use walking about a trench filled with flies feeding on a disintegrating tin of marmalade shouting the odds about believing in Jesus! It would go down even less well than the marmalade.'

There is a final view of religion covered by General Jack in his diary. It is not one to which I can allot a percentage value, as I believe it was common to all the three groups mentioned above, even those who had no beliefs at all. On 17 October 1915, when with the 2nd Scottish Rifles in divisional reserve, he noted: 'Today I attended church parade—as an example to those whose Faith is still intact. Besides, the practice helps to screw up one's sense of duty.'[3] This was a sound approach, and typical of many of Jack's type.

In examining the attitude of the men I will start with those who were fully committed Christians. One was a young Corporal in 1915; he was later to earn the Military Medal (M.M.) as an N.C.O. in the First World War and the M.C. as an officer in the Second. His view is: 'I consider religious beliefs helped officers and men. I still can remember quite clearly the day before we went into the Battle of Festubert, June 1915. Our Padre giving a short sermon and the Holy Communion to the Battalion. I was very impressed and uplifted. We knew we were going into battle and this service did help.'

My estimate of the percentage of men in the ranks who were affected in this way is 10 per cent. On the other hand, those who were supported by Christian faith of this sort were largely men of the same calibre as the writer of these words, and so in terms of influence they were probably far more important than their numbers would indicate.

The help a man got from religion was affected, as were so many other things, by the sort of home he came from. This is very clearly brought out by the comments of an ex-Sergeant, another man who earned the M.M. as an N.C.O. in the Regiment: 'This entirely depended on the upbringing of the man. In many cases religion has no effect.' Those who were reared in the worst areas of the big cities could hardly be expected to find strength in beliefs which never came into their lives as children.

My estimate is that to 50 per cent of the other ranks in the 2nd Scottish Rifles religion was of no importance at all. I think that Robert Graves exaggerated the case when he wrote: 'Hardly one soldier in a hundred was inspired by religious feeling of even the crudest kind. It would have been difficult to remain religious in the trenches even if one had survived the irreligion of the training battalion at home.'[4] So many of the ex-Privates who have answered my questionnaire have been certain that religion was a help to them that I am reluctant to accept Graves' figure. There is no doubt that there were few real believers, but the number of complete unbelievers I would not put much above half the men in the ranks.

What happened was that many of the men got intermittent

help from religion. Many would laugh at religion one day and pray most sincerely the next, particularly if under heavy shell-fire. My estimate is that 40 per cent reacted in this way. Among them were those who had been given slight religious instruction as children, or had absorbed a little elementary Christianity since joining the Army. It is likely that they would be men of average or above natural intelligence, and the sort who were susceptible to the influence of a good padre or a religiously-minded officer. I also believe that a number of the Roman Catholics in the battalion reacted in this manner. The Glasgow-Irish Catholic has always had a wonderful facility for switching his religious conscience on and off as it suits him, or as conditions demand.

Out of all this, the best way to summarize the influence of religion on morale is to say that it had three possible effects. It could be an important influence, giving immense strength and inspiration; it could be of no importance at all; or it could be something rather vague and intermittent. I offer the following table to show the percentages included in each of these three categories:

	To officers (%)	*To soldiers* (%)
An important influence	50	10
No importance	15	50
Vague and intermittent	35	40

Turning from the members of battalions such as the 2nd Scottish Rifles, one must look at the men whose job it was to bring religion to them—the chaplains. One comes up immediately against the difficulty of getting an objective view. This is due to the respect for the clergy, already touched upon, among people who were young in 1914. It was based on respect for the Establishment as much as anything. One group of people firmly upheld the padres because they were part of a class and social system. Robert Graves has written of 'the respect that most Commanding Officers had for the cloth'.[5] This was natural enough, as many officers were sons of clergymen, or had close relations in the Church. 'Dog don't eat dog', and so few officers looked particularly critically at padres.

When anyone did so, he felt that he was being offensive, and knew that his efforts would be considered bad form. The result was that he tended to overstate the case, feeling no doubt that the only thing to do was to plunge in right up to the neck.

Trying to come to a very general, but fair, conclusion; I would say that the padres of the Protestant Churches proved to be rather inadequate, but that the Roman Catholic padres were of an averagely high level. Very little appears in the official history of The Cameronians (Scottish Rifles) about padres, and few of the people I have been in touch with have strong recollections of them. Kennedy, for example, remembers vividly a Christmas Communion Service in a barn about 25 December 1914, but apart from this has no recollection of seeing a padre at all during his time in France, certainly nowhere near the front.

It is only right to point out that there were a number of remarkable exceptions to the ordinary run of Protestant padres. One famous character was the Reverend Theodore Bailey Hardy who won the V.C., D.S.O. and M.C. in the space of eleven months for great gallantry in the forward areas. The King tried to persuade him to return to England as one of his personal Chaplains, but in spite of the fact that he was fifty-four years old and had more than done his share of dangerous duty Hardy refused. As had been expected, he was killed in action shortly afterwards.[6]

An officer of the Scottish Rifles, whose written comments to me about chaplains are largely unfavourable, has also said: 'To be fair, I believe there was one Protestant Padre in the division who was extremely good and beloved by the troops but I never met him.' There obviously must have been a number of Protestant chaplains who did go up into the line regularly and were not afraid to risk their lives, and there was certainly one very brave chaplain with the 2nd Scottish Rifles in 1918. This is the story of a man who was with the battalion at the time of the great German onslaught in the spring of that year which so nearly defeated the British and the French. Describing how he was firing at a group of advancing German soldiers, he tells of his surprise at suddenly seeing the padre standing beside him digging with a spade:

He should not be up here in the firing line, with Jerry only a hundred yards away, and bullets snapping viciously close. Our eyes meet, he smiles, and says as he turns a sod: 'Get on with your work, soldier, I'm making a bit of head cover for you to roll over to.'[7]

Needless to say only a few minutes later this brave chaplain was killed. But the main impression gained from reading about the First World War and from discussing it with those who fought in it is that the average Protestant padre kept very well back from the dangerous areas. Robert Graves suggests that they were actually instructed to keep away from the front;[8] whether any exact instructions on this score were given on an Army basis is hard to discover. The likelihood is that the head chaplains in different formations made 'local rules' for their own areas. It has been suggested to me that normally padres were told to go only to the Regimental Aid Post,[9] which would normally lie about half a mile from the front line, but no farther. It is probable that this was the usual practice. Although no doubt sensible enough a ruling from a logical point of view, it created a barrier between the fighting man and the chaplain which could rarely be broken down.*

Perhaps the strongest condemnation of chaplains in the First World War is that contained in Montague's *Disenchantment*. He devotes a whole chapter to 'The Sheep that were not Fed'. His argument can be summed up as follows. Men facing great danger and living in a world cut off from normal material influences felt a strong need of spiritual guidance. They were waiting for someone to bring it to them; if not consciously waiting, they were at least ready for a message. Because as a rule the chaplains did not go into the front line,

---

* *But from* The Army Chaplain *by the Revd. P. Middleton (A. & C. Black, 1942), in the chapter 'Duties of Chaplains' comes this note: 'At the beginning of the Great War in 1914 and the early part of 1915, chaplains were not allowed in the front line. But it was soon found that this had to be countermanded. It militated against the influence of the chaplain if he did not share the dangers of the men and confined his activities to times when they came out of the line. In addition the presence of the chaplain in the line was a source of inspiration and good cheer. The troops were able to talk to him in a way in which they were not able to talk even to their own officers, and some of the best work done by chaplains in the last war they were able to do in the front line.'*

the men who should have brought the message never came. Instead nice, jovial, hearty padres turned up at odd moments to have a few words of friendly banter, mainly secular, and then shot back to the rear areas. The following quotation from this chapter highlights the missed opportunity:

Thus would these inexpert people hang unconsciously about the uncrossed threshold of religion. With minds which had recovered in some degree the penetrative simplicity of a child's, they dis-interred this or that unidentified bone of the buried God from under the monumental piles of débris which the learned, the cunning, and the proud, priests and kings, churches and chapels, had heaped up over the ideas of perfect love, of faith that would leave all to follow that love, and of the faithful spirit's release from mean fears of extinction. In talk they could bring each other up to the point of feeling that little rifts had opened here and there in the screens which are hung round the life of man on the earth, and they had peeped through into some large outer world that was strange only because they were used to a small and dim one. They were prepared and expectant. If any official religion could ever refine the gold out of all that rich alluvial drift of 'obstinate questionings of sense and outward things', now was its time. No figure of speech, among all these I have mixed, can give the measure of the greatness of that opportunity.

Nobody used it: the tide in the affairs of churches flowed its best, but no church came to take it. Instead, as if chance had planned a kind of satiric practical epigram, came the brigade chaplain. As soon as his genial bulk hove in sight, and his cheery robustious chaff began blowing about, the shy and uncouth muse of our savage theology unfolded her wings and flew away. Once more the talk was all footer and rations and scragging the Kaiser, and how 'the Hun' would walk a bit lame after the last knock he had got. Very nice too, in its way. And yet there had been a kind of savour about the themes that had now shambled back in confusion, before the clerical onset, into their twilight lairs in the souls of individual laymen.[10]

This attack on chaplains has the ring of truth about it. It seems strange to think that men whose main purpose in life was to carry into the world the story of Christ and his death should have been willing to stay away from the front line. What a religious revival might have been started if padres had shared fully the dangers of life in the trenches.

In contrast to the general condemnation of Protestant chaplains one has the praise given to Roman Catholics. How much this was due to a slightly subjective approach is hard to say. Many Protestants who are dissatisfied with their own branch of Christianity are always ready to point out the strength of the Catholic Church. Furthermore, it is possible that many of those who attacked their own padres felt a strong urge to blame the failings on to men rather than their faith. Having said how inadequate the Anglicans were, they felt obliged to put in a few words of praise, and so gave this to the Catholics. Even allowing for this, one gets the impression that Catholic padres really were better. Robert Graves has written: 'For Roman Catholic chaplains were not only permitted to visit posts of danger, but definitely enjoined to be wherever fighting was, so that they could give extreme unction to the dying. And we had never heard of one who failed to do all that was expected of him.'[11] One of my informants has written of 'the padres, of whom by far the most successful and effective were the Roman Catholic priests, who succeeded in getting quite reasonably close to the enemy, and sometimes got into danger'. Another says: 'Some Protestant padres were not too good because they appeared to be afraid to die or even to expose themselves to danger if they could avoid it. The R.C. padre who stayed with us for a year on the other hand appeared fearless, attended to and encouraged men in the front line quite regardless of their religion.'

From religion I would like to turn to the closely allied subject of morals. If asked what morals meant, the average man in 1914 would have said refraining from extra-marital sex, swearing, and drink. There are values of much more importance in judging the relationship between morale and morals, but these three things loomed large in men's minds at the turn of the century.

Sex is obviously a most important influence in human life: to many who grew up before 1914 it was also an appalling problem. For this reason it is essential to look at this aspect of sex with some care, although it may not at first sight have a very great bearing on the subject of this book. The problem angle was much more a concern of the better educated section of the population, and therefore the attitude to sex of the average First World War officer will be examined at more length than that of the other rank.

The first thing to say is that he thought of sex as being 'wrong'. This was due to a long and thorough process of indoctrination, starting in the family and rigorously enforced at his different schools. A Victorian mother, and perhaps more important still, a Victorian nanny, made it clear to a small boy at an early age that certain parts of the human body were 'not nice'. Leaving the nursery for his preparatory school, he found that the excretory functions were the subject of endless jokes and stories which were definitely naughty. He might well be caught telling one, and find himself being soundly beaten by an angry headmaster for retailing 'filth', as it was always known. Then in time came the shock of discovering that these same wicked organs were involved in the process of human reproduction. This knowledge, gained more likely from other children than adults, opened the door to further corridors of guilt. Whereas a dirty story about the lavatory might earn a beating, the same thing about sexual intercourse might lead to expulsion from school, and certainly would involve the unfortunate boy in a lasting reputation for being thoroughly disgusting and unpleasant.

At his public school, the life of a boy was overshadowed to a strong degree by the idea of sex as something vicious. One of the evils he was constantly warned against was that of masturbation—usually referred to in indirect terms as 'impure trifling with God-created instincts', or 'beastliness'. Instead of being a normal outlet for sexuality it became a hidden vice, practised with an unhealthy delight and regretted shortly afterwards with exaggerated shame and humiliation. Worse still was the fate of the boy who drifted in this atmosphere into homosexuality. Discovery of anything of this nature led not only to instant dismissal from school, which was understandable, but also, most likely, to complete rejection at home and in society in general. Fortunately homosexual affairs were much rarer at public schools than is often made out.

What happened to a large number of men in the upper-middle classes who grew up under this repressive attitude to sex was that they removed it from their lives altogether.* Even when fully mature they blotted out thoughts of sex as though they were something evil. A high proportion never married, and many of them felt that it was almost virtuous not to do so. Although this attitude is hard for us to understand today, there were advantages in it. Indeed, it is fair to claim that in many ways his repression of his sexual instincts was a valuable asset to the Army officer in his military life.

One reason was that it made him contented with his lot as a bachelor. He felt that in living as a single man in a semi-monastic community he was fulfilling the highest purpose of life. The temptations of sex, of lust and 'filth', were removed. He could meet girls occasionally, admire them and possibly flirt with them a little, but he could avoid the messy, animal business of having intercourse with them. However much reason might tell him that this side of human relations was essential for reproduction of the race, however much he might sometimes want to do it, the teaching of his early days had imbued him with a subconscious fixation that it was wrong. So the life he led in the Army, untrammelled by more than fleeting contact with women, suited him well.

The second reason was that being single he was inclined to devote more of his time and energy to his profession and the life of his Regiment rather than dividing his interest between these concerns and his family. Although he did this for the most part willingly, care was taken to ensure that he understood that it was also expected of him. Kennedy records his arrival with the 2nd Scottish Rifles. His Company Commander, Ferrers, met him when his ship docked at Malta:

He held very decided views on what a subaltern should and should not do; and in the short space of time required to cross in a dhaisa from Marsamuscetto, where the ship lay at anchor, to the landing stage at Sliema, he made it quite clear to me that the one

---

* *Some of the aristocracy were more liberal-minded about sex, and very free with their affections. But only a tiny proportion of the very rich and very arrogant chose to ignore the rigid moral climate of the day.*

unforgivable sin was to get married. With this was coupled 'poodle-faking', by which was meant dancing attendance on the feminine element of society.

As marriage at an early date was about the last thing I was contemplating at the time, his strong denunciation of this particular offence made little difference to me. When, therefore, having arrived at the Mess and been introduced to such officers as were present, I was instructed (in defiance of King's Regulations!) to sign a document promising to pay a fine of £50 if I married before attaining the rank of captain, I appended my signature without demur. This done, it was impressed on me that there were only two married officers in the battalion.

Something of the same outlook was apparent in this attitude to the Catholic Church's insistence on a celibate clergy; the profession, the calling, came very much first, and the individual second.

The final reason why the officer was better able to do his job well as a bachelor was that he was not made reluctant to face danger because of family commitments. The dangers faced by soldiers in distant parts of the Empire were considerable even in peacetime. Small campaigns, riots, disease, and accidents took a steady, small toll. The fewer the families the more eager would the officers be to meet dangerous situations.

Living alongside those officers who held their sexual urges strongly in check—who 'sublimated' them, as it is sometimes called—were another group, those who indulged freely in sex, but always with prostitutes. Their reaction seems to have been this. They accepted that sexual intercourse was wrong, but they found that their urge to do it was so strong that it could not be resisted. They therefore went periodically to brothels and had intercourse in a completely unemotional way. Many of this type were the most confirmed bachelors of all, and the strongest objectors to their brother officers getting married. Someone who was a subaltern in the Scottish Rifles before 1914 has told me of hearing two members of this group talking in the Mess. One turned to the other and said: 'Have you heard that old So-and-So is getting married—the bloody man?' The other replied: 'Another good officer lost. Well, they won't catch us—we'll whore it out to the end.'

If it be thought my two types—the men who sublimated their urges and the ones who indulged them purely on a commercial basis—are drawn too strongly, I can only refer back to the 2nd Scottish Rifles. Out of twenty-eight officers in Malta in 1914 only two were married; the Commanding Officer and his four company commanders were all bachelors. None of them homosexual; what other explanation can there be?

Enough has been said about the sexual habits of officers. Among the men, apart from a few of the better educated ones who shared similar views to the officers, there was little problem. Most soldiers were ready to have sexual intercourse with almost any women whenever they could. In France this was not often possible. Even when there were brothels available few private soldiers could spare the money to use them. Sex given for nothing on the basis of affection was unlikely to come the way of the front-line soldier once the War had settled down into its static pattern. Within the area in which his life was lived women were rare. The few attractive ones by all accounts became expert in rebuffing the amorous advances of the hordes of soldiers who passed daily through the villages they lived in. The only soldiers in France who had a chance of making love to a French girl were those who duties kept them far behind the lines. Once again the despised 'base-wallah' had all the luck.

In the environment from which the average soldier of the 2nd Scottish Rifles sprang, that is the real lower class of the industrial cities, sex was a primitive business untroubled by pangs of conscience such as afflicted the middle classes. The men rarely had any scruples about it at all; they looked on every woman as fair game. The resistance always came from the feminine side. Girls wanted to be protected, and to have a chance to rear their children in a proper home with a mate who would bring home a regular wage. Thus they feared more than anything 'getting into trouble' and having to rear a baby outside the relative security of matrimony. Many of course failed, and in Glasgow the overall illegitimacy rate was 7 per cent in 1913. In the Blackfriars district of the City there were ninety-nine illegitimate births in 1913, representing 15·6 per cent of all births. Many of the poorer districts had a rate of around 14 per cent.[12] The mothers of these children were often the victims of rape, or of getting involved with men whose enforced attentions were very close to it. Others were simple-minded creatures who probably scarcely understood what they were doing.

Along with promiscuity and its danger of giving birth to a bastard went the even worse danger of catching venereal disease. Glasgow's Medical Officer of Health reported in 1913: 'That about 8 per cent of all classes of children from the poorer classes of Glasgow give a positive Wassermann reaction, and, if this reaction is to be taken as pathognomic of syphilis, that a considerable proportion of the children of the poorer classes are infected with this disease.'[13] The obsession of moralists of the day with the evils of sex looks more reasonable in the light of information such as this.*

Even though these figures of illegitimacy and venereal disease are shockingly high they still represent a relatively small proportion of the population. Most men and women in the poorer sections got married and raised families in a per-fectly normal way. Their way of life, however, accepted sex as the main object of marriage, leading to a large family as an automatic, and usually desired, result.

One reason why there was no place for prudery or worry about the rights and wrongs of sexual behaviour among the real lower class was overcrowding in their homes. Big families, in small houses with few rooms, grew up with no inhibitions. Parents normally shared rooms with their children, and often a whole family might use one bed. It was far from uncommon for a husband and wife to have intercourse while in the same bed as some of their children. Regrettably, incest was also prevalent in the Glasgow slums for the same reason. But even if they never went to that length, the products of tenement homes could not avoid having a very full knowledge of the facts of life and human anatomy by an early age. As a result it was all quite a normal part of life to them. A man raised in such an environment never really understood the fuss that the better educated members of society made about sexual

* *See also Appendix 'D'.*

morals. As far as the average private soldier of the 2nd Scottish Rifles was concerned I do not believe that sex had any bearing on morale at all, except that he might consider himself a bit hard done by if he had to go too long without having intercourse.

On the other moral failings, it is doubtful if, from the other rank's point of view, swearing made much difference to morale. On the whole the British soldier has always been pretty foul-mouthed, and it has not affected his performance very much. Indeed it could almost be claimed that a good bout of swearing releases tension, and is a definite aid to morale. However, it is worth mentioning in opposition to this theory that in 'B' Company of the 2nd Scottish Rifles Ferrers would allow no swearing at all—at least not use of obscene swear-words. He would even check a man for swearing in the trenches when under fire. This helped morale for two reasons. First, it played down the danger. The very fact that his Company Commander was able to tell him off for a relatively trivial matter while shells were falling all around forced the soldier to look on the shells as just a little less frightening. Second, it reminded him that he had in a small way lost his self-control by using language which he knew Ferrers would find offensive when in his presence. This point I think important. An officer who disliked swearing showed weakness by allowing soldiers to do it in his presence, and such weakness might lead to a lessening of his authority.

Swearing by officers themselves depended very much on personal character. Some fine fighting commanders were famous for their propensity for foul language, while others were never known to use it. As long as it was in keeping with normal habits it mattered little whether an officer swore in the trenches or not. When it did matter was when a man who usually refrained from swearing started to do so. From such small points might a keen observer spot the start of a man cracking up.

Much more indicative, however, of approaching breakdown was undue reliance on the bottle. Nearly everyone I have discussed this matter with, and all books as well, agree that once an officer became a regular heavy drinker in the trenches the end of his usefulness was approaching. This should not be mixed up with having an occasional 'blind' when out of the line. In fact a surfeit of alcohol after a hard spell in the trenches could relieve tension in a remarkable way, and do a tired man a lot of good. It was regular soaking which did the damage. In fact it was a very rare thing to meet: many people seem to know of odd cases but usually at second-hand.

In France unhealthy drinking was largely an officer problem. Soldiers could, and did, get drunk occasionally. But they could not afford to become soaks. As an officer of the Regiment has put it: 'Other ranks in the infantry received a paltry sum when they came out of the trenches—a fraction of the pathetic pay due to them, and they could not afford anything but a little beer or cheap vin blanc and cigarettes.'[14]

The moral qualities which had an important effect on morale were sense of duty, kindness, and unselfishness. Sexual licence, swearing and drunkenness were trivial matters in comparison. On the pre-1914 Regular Army's feelings about the value of a high sense of duty Charles Carrington has this to say:

Though it had always been customary in the Old Army to affect a certain cynicism about such matters as honour, glory, and patriotism, a habit of mind which sharply distinguished British from French soldiers, this derogation of the martial spirit did not apply to matters of plain duty. A soldier of any rank was expected to 'do his bit' and to take pride in doing it thoroughly. It was one thing to make jokes about 'swinging the lead' (shirking duty), or 'working your ticket' (getting your discharge papers), and quite another thing to avoid a dangerous task which someone else must do if you did not.[15]

The kindness of the British soldier was one of his greatest strengths in the First World War—as indeed it has been throughout history. It is something which has always puzzled me a little; why should becoming a soldier and fighting wars bring out this quality of gentleness and kindness in ordinary men to such a degree? My theory is that it is usually to some extent a form of reaction against the cruelty of war. Surrounded by horror, men either submerge themselves in it and become brutal and callous, or else turn against it and try to soften the impact of their surroundings by kindness and thoughtfulness to their comrades. Although not understood by the soldiers themselves, their compassion sprang largely from the tradition of the British Army of fighting wars without allowing looting and pillage. Cromwell, Marlborough and Wellington, each in his own century, laid down the principle that British soldiers should fight without the reward of loot. From this grew, over the years, the feeling that war was something to be suffered and endured, but never enjoyed for any prospect of pillage. Out of this tradition soldiers learnt to adapt themselves to war with patience rather than to exult in it. This approach automatically cut out for the British soldier the possible course of submerging himself in horror, and left him only that of softening his lot through compassion. The usual outlet was found in kindness to his comrades, and to civil populations.

Examples are endless of unselfishness in the First World War. The story has been told me of a stretcher-bearer of the 2nd Scottish Rifles at Neuve Chapelle who worked all day carrying in the wounded, and late in the evening reported himself to the Regimental Aid Post for treatment. It was then discovered that the big muscle in his back had been completely severed by a shell splinter. How he had carried on all day was a mystery; he had been carrying heavy stretchers in this state since shortly after the first attack, but would not spare himself while there were still others to save.

I have recorded Kennedy's story of the soldier who stayed with him all morning by the wire until he was collected by the medical orderlies, and I have also written of his sadness at hearing of the death of Private McHugh, killed trying to carry a wounded man out of danger while exposed to heavy fire. Many good men were lost in the First World War in this way. Officially it was frowned upon to risk the life of a fit man to save one who was damaged, but few soldiers took much notice of such rules. Besides, it was part of the tradition of the British Army that all ranks should run risks when necessary to save each other. As John Connell describes it:

This regimental tradition, however, was not solely, or even in considerable part, a celebration of victory; it was much more a

tradition of sacrifice within a brotherhood. The deeds it com-
memorated were not bloody and vengeful triumphs over a hated
enemy, but heroic though hopeless last stands, and the sacrifice of
brother for brother, officer for private soldier, private soldier for
officer.[16]

In the really important moral qualities I believe the Armies
in France were wonderfully rich. I am not blind to their faults,
but in trying to find out why battalions like the 2nd Scottish
Rifles were able to sustain such high morale one must look
first to the three virtues of sense of duty, kindness, and
unselfishness. Religion could help to provide them; on the
other hand a man could have them and be an atheist. Religion
was not an essential factor in morale, though a valuable help
in many cases. Whether a man fornicated, drank or cursed
mattered little, as long as he was not a constant drinker. My
thesis on the religious and moral aspects of morale is simply
this: A man who did his duty and loved his neighbour was the
hero of the trenches; no other moral values compared in
importance with these two.

Patriotism

We assumed that patriotism was one of the basic virtues, like courage, truth or unselfishness.

Mary Clive, THE DAY OF RECKONING[1]

IF MEMBERS OF the 2nd Scottish Rifles varied considerably in their religious convictions and their moral standards, similar variations did not exist in their attitude to their country. In common with nearly all other people living in Great Britain, and people of British stock all over the world, they were intensely patriotic. They had no doubt that Britain was the greatest country in the world, and the finest; they loved Britain, and its institutions, with a fierce, unquestioning devotion. Strong though these terms may sound, a weaker description would not do justice to the intensity of patriotism before 1914. However much these feelings might be cloaked beneath a contrived air of distaste for emotion the patriotism of that day had, in fact, a very emotional quality.

The first reason for this intense love of Britain was the fact that she was the most powerful nation in the world. She was not the richest, having been already overtaken by the United States, but her enormous Empire, backed by significantly the strongest Navy in the world, made her influence supreme in world politics. The position was still the same as it had been in 1892 when Kipling wrote:

> Hands off o' the sons o' the Widow,
> Hands off o' the goods in 'er shop,
> For the Kings must come down an' the
> Emperors frown
> When the Widow at Windsor says 'Stop'![2]

The writing may have been on the wall about the retention of this position, but very few Britishers could see it. The ordinary man simply knew that his country was on top, and he assumed it would always stay there. And very pleasant he found the situation, too.

It seems to me ridiculous to decry the patriotism of those days. Human beings enjoy being powerful and rich, and one can hardly expect the Englishman at the turn of the century not to have enjoyed belonging to a nation which was both. Even though a person lived a hard life, as long as not living too near the poverty line he or she could take a pride in Britain's greatness, and enjoy a little reflected national glory. At times this consciousness of national glory may have contributed to an arrogance which was not altogether attractive, but this is understandable. It is really more remarkable that there was so little chauvinism in the country. Fortunately the desire to appear restrained and diffident prevented displays of national pride being too obvious—to boast was bad form, even about one's country.

Another reason why patriotism was so strong in Britain was the beauty of the country, and the quality of life lived by much of the population. Naturally these things did not apply to members of the real lower classes in the big industrial centres. But they did apply to a point well down the social scale, certainly as far as the better paid echelons of the working class, and to life in the country, the villages, the small towns, and the pleasant parts of big cities.

Much of Great Britain was at its most beautiful in the early years of this century. The beauty of the British countryside, except for the wildest areas, has been much influenced by the hand of man. In 1914 a stage had been reached in the development of Britain where things were at their peak in terms of scenic beauty. All over the British Isles a pattern had been achieved which has already vanished in most parts. The market towns, with solid middle-class houses, rows of well-preserved cottages, tidy shops and clean streets, were welcoming and comfortable. Between the towns lay the big country houses with their spacious and beautiful parks. Dotted along the roads were neat villages, and the cottages in them, although possibly weak on plumbing, were generally most attractive to look at. The fields were a constantly changing patchwork quilt, whose efficiency and beauty were maintained by the four-year rotation of crops generally practised over most of the country. Apart from the poor areas of the big cities it was a very lovely land.

Patriotism flourished because it was well-driven home in almost everything that people read and were taught. The only methods of circulating ideas and information in the days we are considering were the written word, and the spoken word direct from person to person. On the whole most of the population read very little, and were not taught a great deal either. They thus had a few very simple and definite ideas about human affairs, which hardened as they grew older into unalterable convictions. One of these convictions was the importance of loving one's country.

To show how much the young Britisher was indoctrinated with patriotism by what he read, let us look quickly at the sort of things a young officer in 1914 would have covered in the reading of his youth.* Assuming he was born about 1890 in a well-to-do, upper-middle-class home, some of his earlier reading might have come from the pen of Juliana Horatia Ewing.† Two of the most successful were *Jackanapes* and *The Story of a Short Life.* The cover of the former is largely taken up by a picture of a Union Jack hanging on a frame-work of three poles, the main characters surrounding it including a magnificently attired cavalry officer. Both books are full of noble sentiments, glorious deaths, and fervid patriotism. In *The Story of a Short Life* the hero's mother 'came of an ancient Scottish race, that had shed its blood like water on many a battlefield, generations before the family of her English husband had become favourites at the Court of the Tudors'.[3] Another book of the same general tone was *Teddy's Button*

---

* *I have discussed this with my father and his sister (born 1886 and 1889 respectively). They produced many of the books they remembered as children for me to look at, and told me their views of them in retrospect. They agree that the intense patriotism of their younger days must have been strongly influenced by their reading.*
† *Mrs Ewing edited at one time* Aunt Judy's Magazine *(1866–1885) which had been founded by her mother, Margaret Gatby. She was a prolific writer for children.*

by Amy Le Feuvre, who wrote a number of successful children's books. The button in this story was that from the tunic of the hero's father, who had been killed saving the colours of his Regiment. One needs to beware of making fun of these books, however. They are well written, quite entertaining, and have much good sense in them as well as the more ridiculous parts.

Round about the age of twelve a boy might come to Henty. The colossal success of the books of G. A. Henty was due to his ability to write exciting stories in simple language about adventure in all parts of the world and at all periods of history.

The titles speak for themselves: *With Wolfe in Canda: Or the Winning of a Continent; Bonnie Prince Charlie: A Tale of Fontenoy and Culloden; By Sheer Pluck: A Tale of the Ashanti War; St George for England: A Tale of Cressy and Poitiers; The Bravest of the Brave: With Peterborough in Spain; For Name and Fame: Or, Through Afghan Passes.* These all have obvious connections with British history, but even when apparently remote from anything British, Henty always brought in a few choice sentiments about the Empire. For example, the Preface to *The Lion of St Mark: A Tale of Venice*, which starts 'My dear lads', includes the remarkable sentence:

The historical portion of the story is drawn from Hazlitt's History of the Republic of Venice, and with it I have woven the adventures of an English boy endowed with a full share of that energy and pluck which, more than any other qualities, have made the British empire the greatest the world ever saw.[4]

In his teens the young officer might well have read a good deal of Scott. He undoubtedly would have been made to read some of the Waverley novels, either by his family or at school. Whatever his feelings about them these would have extended his knowledge of British history. Another historical novel he was certain to have read was Charles Kingsley's *Westward Ho!*. First printed in 1855, it reached a thirteenth edition in 1876, and no young man growing up before 1914 could fail to have seen it, even if he had not struggled through its full 519 close printed pages. Apart from the content of the book, its dedication burns with patriotic fervour. It is dedicated to The

Rajah Sir James Brooke, K.C.B., and George Augustus Selwyn, D.D., Bishop of New Zealand, about whom Kingsley writes:

That type of English virtue, at once manly and Godly, practical and enthusiastic, prudent and self-sacrificing, which he has tried to depict in these pages, they have exhibited in a form even purer and more heroic than that in which he has drest it, and than that in which it was exhibited by the worthies whom Elizabeth, without distinction of rank or age, gathered round her in the ever glorious wars of her great reign.[5]

While reading Scott and Kingsley as a more serious diet, the boy in his teens would read Rider Haggard and Conan Doyle for his lighter moments. Getting a bit older, he would come to Marryat—*Mr Midshipman Easy*—and of course to H. G. Wells. All these writers in their own ways reinforced his ideas of the importance and value of Britain, her way of life, and her influence in the world.

Although probably not encouraged to read it, our young man would have enjoyed on occasions the *Boy's Own Paper*. This was written for, and bought by the lower rather than upper-middle-class youth, though both enjoyed it equally.* An immensely successful publication, it ran as a weekly from 1879 to 1912, since when it has appeared monthly. 'World-wide in scope, it was read not only by adventurous boys but by their equally adventurous sisters. Romance, adventure, school stories, all appeared there, including much of the work of Jules Verne, the first of the science fiction writers.'[7]

The author still to mention here is Kipling. Since he was writing during the time that the young officer we are considering was actually growing up, the latter might have not known many of Kipling's most famous later works. *Kim* for example came out in 1901, and the *Just So Stories* did not appear until 1902, when he would have been 12. It is likely that he would be more conversant with Kipling's earlier Indian stories and his *Barrack-Room Ballads* than with the works which now-adays are more readily connected with the name. In this earlier

---

* *A full study of the reading habits of all classes at this time, and the effect on their behaviour and opinions, would be fascinating.*

work Kipling's patriotism, and consciousness of Empire, was most marked.

Beyond the end of his school-days the average young officer read little. In the Mess of the 2nd Scottish Rifles would be found *Blackwood's Magazine* and *The Times*, and possibly a few sporting periodicals. The Mess library was small; a few military reminiscences and some Surtees comprised it, and it was rare for any officer to make much use of it.* One can say, in fact, that the officer had done his reading for life by the time he joined. What he had read was simple stuff, and he kept it in his head. Since it was mainly patriotic as well, it is fair to claim that he had been well indoctrinated with patriotism through the books he had read in his youth.

A further source of patriotism was the affection and respect felt by most of the population for the King and the Royal family. I say most of the population, and not all, because there was undoubtedly a small element in the country at the time which was anti-monarchy. Small though it was, and restricted to the industrial areas, it was probably stronger than any such element is today. Its influence was to grow during the War, and reach a peak in the 1920s before virtually disappearing altogether. But for the bulk of the British people the King and Queen were objects of deep devotion, and revered both as human beings and as symbols of the nation's greatness. Among the middle class, both upper and lower, this respect for Royalty was possibly strongest.

The final cause is one which might have been covered at the same time as Britain's greatness, namely the British Empire. But I want to look at it separately. Obviously the power of Britain rested mainly on the possession of her Empire, and pride in the nation's greatness was bound up with the satisfaction of seeing all the big red patches on a map of the world. However, it never applied to the ordinary individual only in that way. There was a sense of mission in the minds of most British people when they thought about the Empire. The cynic may say that Kipling's famous phrase 'the white man's

---

* The Life and Death of John Mytton, *by Nimrod, and the poems and stories about fox-hunting by Whyte Melville were as popular as Surtees at the time.*

burden' was part of a monstrous process of self-delusion by which lust for power tried to make itself respectable, and echo Blunt's lines:

> Their poets who write big of the
> 'White Burden'. Trash!
> The White Man's burden, Lord,
> is the burden of their cash.

But that would be wrong. My belief is that there was a strong national consciousness of the obligations of ruling the Empire, and a real faith in the value of Britain's civilizing role in the world. The concept of the 'Pax Britannica' was of deep significance to the thoughtful Englishman in the early days of this century. His feelings about the Empire are echoed in T. E. Lawrence's description of Allenby in Damascus in 1918. Lawrence describes how at last he was able to throw his problems on to someone else and to relax: '. . . in this dream-like confidence and decision and kindness which was Allenby . . .; Allenby, gigantic and red and merry, fit representative of the Power which had thrown a girdle of humour and strong dealing round the world.'[8] The average Britisher felt pride and satisfaction in this 'girdle of humour and strong dealing' and considered the maintenance of it to be a duty of the highest importance.

The country's powerful position in the world; the beauty of the land; the things people read and were told; the Royal family; the Empire: what did these mean to members of the 2nd Scottish Rifles in the trenches, and did they influence morale or not? Although all the officers and men I have questioned have agreed that patriotism meant a lot in 1914, much more possibly than today, they will not say a great deal about it. This springs not only from natural reticence, but also from the fact that love of Britain is so deeply imbued in them; it is so much part of them that they hardly recognize it.

It is simple to guess that thoughts about the greatness of Britain rarely entered the minds of the officers and men of the 2nd Scottish Rifles in a conscious form during the battle of Neuve Chapelle. Possibly in the moment of elation when they first surged up out of the trenches as the preliminary bombardment died away some of them may have found patriotic thoughts flashing through their minds, but I doubt if they returned again. At the same time the dogged persistence which held the survivors together right to the end of the battle was to some extent due to national pride, albeit subconscious. It helped them to know that they were soldiers in the Regular Army of the world's most powerful country. In the back of their minds was the knowledge that as such they must not fail in their duty. As representatives of a great nation they were bolstered up by the realization that for them to run away would be a terrible disgrace.

If thoughts of Britain's greatness were of doubtful importance, consciously at least, I am certain that memories of her beauty were not. For all those who had lived in the country, the small towns, or the pleasant part of the big cities, memories of their homes were a great source of strength. While enduring the worst moments of life in France the imaginative could lose themselves in dreams of home. For the well-to-do life in Britain before the War had been very good, and the young officer in particular trudging up to the front on the night of 9 March 1915, or lying-out wounded the next day waiting for the stretcher-bearers (as happened to so many), could recreate in his imagination a picture of the activities which abounded in a well-ordered upper- or upper-middle-class existence. Instead of seeing the filth and misery around him he could remember those moments which made up the joy of British country life. Standing at a window in the early morning on a summer's day when the mist was thick in the garden, and yet the faint glow of the sun gave promise of the mist clearing and a hot day ensuing; fishing a rough, hill stream on a spring day when clouds and rain alternated with bright sunny periods; standing at a butt on a grouse moor on a hot August day seeing the endless rolling hills covered in heather; coming home from a day's hunting on a wet winter night and seeing the lights of the house from the end of the drive with their promise of tea and fires and a hot bath: these sort of memories could dispel for a few minutes the horror of the battlefield. More than this, they could fill the person who had them with determination to win the War and preserve the life they were part of. If wounded, they could give him the will to survive. This was the flowering of patriotism into its finest form; the love of his country becoming a powerful personal motive for a man enduring and surviving danger and privation.

The feelings of the young man of the middle classes about his country in 1914 and 1915 were well expressed in Rupert Brooke's poem *The Soldier*. Becoming desperately hackneyed for many years, the poem is now much less well known. It starts:

> If I should die, think only this of me:

and goes on, a little too gushingly for modern taste perhaps, to describe the poet after his death as:

> A dust whom England bore, shaped, made aware,
> Gave, once, her flowers to love, her ways to roam,
> A body of England's, breathing English air,
> Washed by the rivers, blest by suns of home.
>
> And think, this heart, all evil shed away,
> A pulse in the eternal mind, no less
> Gives somewhere back the thoughts by England given:
> Her sights and sounds; dreams happy as her day;
> And laughter, learnt of friends; and gentleness,
> In hearts at peace, under an English heaven.[9]

Because officers had the best of life at home, these aspects meant most to them, and they wanted to preserve the British heritage most strongly. The following recollection from Lance-Corporal Smith of the 2nd Scottish Rifles illustrates this. He remembers the march up to the line on the night of 9/10 March: 'A particular incident on that occasion remains with me to this day. As I marched behind my company ('C'), I overhead a conversation by Captain Dodd with the Company Sergeant-Major; he was describing his last holiday in England, and remarked cheerily, "It's a lovely land, ours, Sergeant-Major, and worth dying for. What say you?" I must say I was not feeling that way myself. The Sergeant-Major politely agreed, however.' Dodd was killed within the first hour of the battle the next morning and his intense patriotism must have helped him in his last moments. However, many of the other ranks did share Captain Dodd's feelings. Commenting in 1905 on the patriotism of men in the ranks in the Boer War, Colonel G. F. R. Henderson wrote in an essay on 'The British Army':

To the fine spirit of the regular rank and file a brave enemy has offered a generous and graceful tribute. A certain section of his own people, as well as the majority of foreigners, preferred to regard the man who took the shilling as a mere mercenary possessing only the instincts of a hired bravo. Never was mistake more gross. The cottage homes of the British race, whether they stand in the long, unlovely streets of manufacturing cities, in villages old enough to have sent house-carles to Hastings and archers to Agincourt, in the Highland glens, or on the green hillsides of Wales, were not less loyal than the great houses. Britain, even among the lowest of her soldiers, is still a name to conjure with.[10]

The 'graceful tribute' referred to at the start of the passage came from a Boer General called Ben Viljoen. In a book of his reminiscences of the Boer War he wrote: 'Were it not that so many of my compatriots lacked that which is so largely characteristic of the British soldier, the quality of patriotism and the intense desire to uphold the traditions of his nationality, I would ask what people in the world would have been able to conquer the Afrikanders?'[11] This may sound a little fulsome, but it reinforces my point that the average soldier felt very strongly about his country.

The other rank who came from a middle-class background, or from a well-run working-class home where his parents had been in steady work, would have similar happy memories to give him strength as his officers. He would remember the joy of sitting down to meals as one of a big family in a warm kitchen; the excitement of going on holiday to the sea-side; the satisfaction of coming home with his pay at the end of a week's work. His memories would be very much tied up with other people, possibly in contrast to the officer who would think more about places and activities. The reason of this was that one of the particular qualities of lower-middle and working-class life at the turn of the century was community spirit. In villages and small towns this was very apparent, and indeed in many of the more prosperous sectors of the big cities.

Small towns in the North of England and Scotland were immensely conscious of their local identity. All the various members of the community were bound up with each other in a way that is rapidly disappearing today. Because they could not afford to move very far from their own immediate localities, people were closely dependent on their neighbours. They depended on each other for trade in their shops or at their crafts, for amusement, and for local government. Men were immensely proud to become Mayor or Provost of their towns, and of running the traditional functions and celebrations of their local communities. In small Scottish towns one can still see something of this, though the motor-car and the mobility of population will destroy it in time in the same way as it has already been destroyed in the South. The value of this local pride was, of course, that from pride in his own little town a man developed pride in the whole country. Human beings who are contented in one environment are the same in another; the man who loved his village loved his country.

Although it is easy enough to see that the officers of the 2nd Scottish Rifles had every reason to be patriotic, as had that percentage of the men who came of relatively prosperous origins, it is not so readily understandable why those who came from the worst sort of conditions described in Chapter 6 felt affection for their country. The first reason was that they were soldiers. It has been stressed again and again how much it meant to the boy reared in poverty to have a uniform, a secure job, however hard, and a definite place in the scheme of things, however lowly. It was from this pride in being a soldier that he grew to be proud of his country. At the bottom of his heart he felt deep gratitude to the nation which had given him a place in its Armed Forces. Nothing would drag an admission of such feelings from him, and he would laugh at anyone who tried to explain such emotions on his behalf. But I am sure that they existed. Often the coarsest and apparently most cynical 'old sweat' would show by a small action or unguarded word that he was a lot more sensitive and romantic at heart than he would ever care to admit. Because such a man would laugh at the idea of being patriotic it would be wrong to suppose that he was not; those who knew him well would understand why a protective shell of cynicism surrounded his real personality.

The second reason why the regular soldier from even the harshest home environment could be patriotic sprang from his overseas service. There might not be much to remember with joy about life in a Glasgow slum, but it stood comparison with conditions he saw around the world. The poor in Great Britain might be doomed to hunger and ill-health, but in the East the soldier saw human misery on a scale that made their fate enviable in comparison. At least in Britain people rarely died of starvation, and epidemics of disease did not sweep through huge areas of the country almost unchecked as they did in India. Children might beg for a penny in the streets of a British city, but they were not mutilated by their parents to make their case more convincing. Sanitation, as we have seen already, was not one of the best amenities of Glasgow in 1900, but in comparison with Calcutta its sanitary arrangements were princely. The British soldier noted these things, and realized that there was a lot to be said for life in Britain. The revelations of a Rowntree or a Booth are shocking enough when applied to poverty in Britain, but had someone made similar studies anywhere East of Suez the results would have been really horrifying. In much of the world problems of starvation, gross overcrowding, and ill-health on a massive scale are still to be found; fifty years ago, in spite of the monumental efforts of the administrators of the British Empire, they afflicted most of the foreign stations in which British soldiers found themselves to an even worse degree.

The third reason why men who came from the poorest classes were patriotic was due in part to their ignorance. Because they knew so little, and were in most cases apathetic, they followed the lead given by their officers and N.C.O.s very readily in matters of opinion as well as in the purely military field. The officers and N.C.O.s were strongly patriotic, and so the more simple soldiers echoed their sentiments unhesitatingly. This does not of course mean that they were in any way 'brain-washed' into patriotism, but simply that they joined an organization in which the general trend of opinion moved in certain definite directions, and they accepted this quite happily and went along with everyone else. Furthermore, there was no conscious attempt to instil pride of nationality into soldiers as was practised at the time in some Continental armies. Everyone assumed that soldiers were patriotic, and for the most part they were. Apart from being taught to stand to attention when *God Save the King* was played no outward display of patriotic fervour was required.

It is interesting to note the reactions of different people who fought in the War to the question I asked them: 'How much did belief in the Monarchy help, and in particular did visits by the Royal family to France mean anything?' As far as the officers were concerned, it would be fair to say that belief in the Monarchy helped a lot to preserve morale, and that visits by members of the Royal family to France were much appreciated. A typical answer to the question runs as follows: 'Belief in the Monarchy was a great help, and a visit was much appreciated by all officers and men, and boosted morale.' On the other hand, some did not feel quite the same. The answer of one officer, who collected a remarkable number of decorations in almost continuous service at the front, is less fulsome: 'Can't say. We only saw H. M. King George once and that a damn long way off.' Perhaps the best summing up of the position is by an officer who says first that belief in the Monarchy helped 'a lot', but as to whether visits meant anything writes: 'not so much, but we felt the interest taken, and if there had been no visits there would have been criticism'. One of the troubles no doubt was that the Royal visits were arranged with far too much pomp and circumstance. As another officer says: 'Visits by Royalty were much too formal and, in my view, had little meaning. They were much better arranged in World War II.'

Men who served in the ranks have answered the question differently. Just over half go along with this comment: 'I think it helped a great deal and the visit by the Royal family boosted up the Morale as it showed the troops the Royal Family was with them in all their duties.' But almost as many have opposite views. A sergeant of the 2nd Scottish Rifles who was wounded at Neuve Chapelle writes: 'Never gave it a thought. Heard about it when it was all over.' A Sergeant of the 1st Cameronians records: 'Not much. The visits of the Royal Family were matters of interest and no more,' while another Sergeant of the same battalion goes further and says: 'Not a lot, troops came out of the line had to clean up spit and polish for the parade, and the remarks made by the men was not very satisfactory.'

This last aspect is not to be taken too seriously. No soldier would ever admit to enjoying the spit and polish before a big parade, nor to going on the parade itself. On the other hand big ceremonial occasions undoubtedly do have an excellent effect on morale if not too frequent. My guess is that many of those who were most vociferous in their complaints about getting ready to be inspected by the King were really delighted when the parade actually took place, and that afterwards morale was high. Kennedy records, on this score, that he spent a few days in hospital in December 1914 at Estaires. He goes on: 'In less than a week I was back with the Battalion once more; but, while at Estaires, an event had taken place that had delighted the troops. This was the visit of His Majesty, the King, whose personal presence at a point so close to the front line made a great impression on officers and men alike.'

I think the answer to the apparent conflict of views about the influence of the Monarchy, the Royal visits, on morale is to look into 'the eye of the beholder'. For those who were romantic by nature and who enjoyed pageantry, the Royal family were a source of inspiration, and their visits were much appreciated. This element I would put at 80 per cent of the officers of 60 per cent of the men. For the others, the more prosaic and matter-of-fact characters, I doubt if the Monarchy meant very much. They were loyal subjects, but not to the extent of emotional involvement. On the other hand, I think all ranks were genuinely appreciative of one aspect of Royal interest, which was the sending of Christmas cards and presents to all members of the B.E.F. in 1914. Kennedy explains how: '. . . gifts had been sent to every officer and man in the B.E.F. In addition to pipes and tobacco for smokers, and writing-cases and packets of sweets for those to whom "the Indian weed" made no appeal, everyone received a postcard, on the face of which were the photographs of their Majesties the King and Queen. On the reverse side appeared the simple, kindly message, in a reproduction of their own handwriting: "With our best wishes for Christmas 1914. May God protect you and bring you home safe—Mary R. George R.I." The postcards, and the attractive little brass boxes with the portrait of Princess Mary embossed on the lid, meant much to their recipients.'

It is fair to claim that the Monarchy as an institution and the Royal family as people had a definite influence on the morale of the 2nd Scottish Rifles. They did not provide one of the strongest influences, nor did they mean much to quite a significant minority of the battalion. But to the majority they were important, and among this majority were found most of the leaders in the battalion. To return once more to the words of an N.C.O. of the Scottish Rifles: 'I think the Monarchy held a special place in all our hearts like loyalty to one's Regiment. We felt that the Monarchy was something to be proud of and worth doing our bit for.' Few N.C.O.s could have found such words to express these feelings, but many would have agreed with them.

From the Monarchy to the Empire. It would be ridiculous to claim that any officer or man consciously thought of himself as a guardian of the Empire when standing in a muddy trench in France during the winter of 1914–1915. His mind would be concentrated on much more immediate matters. The problems of survival, of the day-to-day round, of combating weariness, of getting enough to eat, and of the next 'show' or 'push'; these were what occupied the thoughts of fighting men. But at the same time I think that from the attitude of regular soldiers towards the Empire one can find another clue to their morale.

For the officer, the idea of service to the Empire had often been a major contributory factor in his choice of the Army as a career. If one remembers all the things he had read and been told as a boy it is easy to see how the dream of Empire must have coloured his adolescent years. His mind was full of romantic pictures, and he longed to go out on great adventures to the ends of the world and see for himself that:

Never was isle so little, never was sea so lone,
But over the scud and the palm-trees an English flag was flown.[12]

Later, as a commissioned officer, he had probably travelled widely, and seen the reality of British rule at work. Many of his dreams may have disappeared, but in the case of the thoughtful officer at least, the realities of imperial government and the preservation of law and order became an absorbing interest to replace the illusions of earlier years. He found his reward in playing his part in the civilizing mission of the Empire; the endless task of imperial policing and the conduct of minor campaigns were satisfying outlets for his energy and initiative. Between them the officers of the 2nd Scottish Rifles had an immense fund of imperial experience, which undoubtedly affected their approach to the First World War.

Among the older officers at least there had grown from their service in distant parts of the Empire a strong sense of the superiority of Britain, and things British, over the rest of the world. However much the modern mind may dislike this attitude, it cannot be disputed that it had a remarkably good effect on morale. Fortunately it was a sense of superiority which cloaked itself in as unassuming an air as was possible; it was an arrogance of spirit rather than of word, and conventional behaviour demanded that it should not be too openly displayed. As an aid to confidence and determination in action this sense of superiority was invaluable. Its great and obvious danger was that it often led to stubborn stupidity, and a refusal to admit mistakes. But that aspect is not one which really concerns me. At the level of the Regimental officer the imperial experience of most of the older men, and many of the younger as well, bred an assurance and certainty of victory which was invaluable. Though few of them were conscious of it, I believe that their tradition of power and dominion over much of the world was an important element in their morale.

Finally, I want to look at the concept of Empire in relation to the pre-1914 other rank. In his attitude to the Empire one can see expressed vividly the dichotomy of the old soldier's approach to his service. A realistic appraisal of his own lot was mixed up with a grudging pride in the power of his country and its imperial possessions. To return again to Kipling:

> We 'ave 'eard o' the Widow at Windsor,
> It's safest to let 'er alone:
> For 'er sentries we stand by the sea an' the land
> Wherever the bugles are blown.
> (Poor beggars!—an' don't we get blown!)
> Take 'old o' the Wings o' the Mornin',
> An' flop round the earth till you're dead;
> But you won't get away from the tune that they play
> To the bloomin' old rag over 'ead.
> (Poor beggars!—it's 'ot over 'ead!)
> Then 'ere's to the sons o' the Widow,
> Wherever, 'owever they roam.
> 'Ere's all they desire, an' if they require
> A speedy return to their 'ome.
> (Poor beggars!—they'll never see 'ome!)[13]

Although having few illusions about his own place in the scheme of things, the British private soldier could not avoid a certain satisfaction at the achievements of his country. He went about his duties throughout the Empire with a mixture of humorous scepticism and quiet pride. He laughed at the Raj, and he also rather admired it.

In the trenches in France in 1914 something of the same pattern developed in the soldiers' outlook. They grumbled and cursed, they made caustic jokes about everyone they could think of, they sang ribald and cynical songs, and the irony of their comments on life in general, and alleged British victories in particular, was as sharp and pointed as anything heard in a good music-hall. But in the same way that they had learnt to laugh at the Empire and admire it at the same time, they were able to balance this cynical frame of mind in the trenches with loyalty to their Regiment and their officers, and a real devotion to duty. Perhaps this was the special strength of the Regular soldier; this ability to combine discipline and sense of duty with a 'humorous acceptance of time and chance'.[14]

Patriotism was certainly an influence on the morale of the 2nd Scottish Rifles: not an influence of comparable importance to, say, loyalty to the Regiment, but one that it would be wrong to discount altogether. British people in 1914 were conscious of their country's power, of its Empire, and of its general influence for good throughout the world. Brought up from their earliest days to admire and love their country, they saw no reason to do anything else. Although it did not affect them in a very obvious way, for many the Monarchy was an important symbol of the unity and greatness of their nation. All the factors discussed in this chapter combined to create a significant if not vital influence on morale.

The High Command
and the Staff

*On the whole, as I have grown older, I find myself willing to
accept the general incompetence of human beings, and I no longer
expect a superman to emerge with a solution for every unforeseen
problem. I am inclined to think that the First War commanders
did pretty well, according to their lights, and the tendency to
blame them for the crimes and follies of a whole generation now
seems to be disingenuous.*

Charles Carrington, SOLDIER FROM THE WARS
RETURNING[1]

THE OFFICERS AND men of the 2nd Scottish Rifles did not
give a great deal of thought to the activities of the High
Command and the Staff. Probably only a handful of experienced officers realized that the lives of infantry units were in
fact deeply affected by those who worked at the higher levels
of command. The majority scarcely realized that the decision
of a General far from the front could mean the difference
between life and death for an infantry private. Before trying
to show why the work done by these unknown people in the
rear areas was so important, the terms Staff and High
Command must be defined.

At all levels above a company, commanders of military
formations have staff officers who issue orders and attend to
matters of detail in their name. The Commanding Officer of
the Scottish Rifles had as his two staff officers his Adjutant
and his Quartermaster. The term Staff, however, with a
capital 'S', is used to describe those who worked on the head-

quarters of formations above battalion level: at brigade, divisional, corps and army headquarters, and finally at the summit, General Headquarters or G.H.Q. The High Command were the individual officers who actually held command at all these levels. In the First World War (see Diagram on page 239), there were Brigadier-Generals commanding brigades, Major-Generals commanding divisions, Lieutenant-Generals commanding corps, Generals commanding armies and, over all, a Field-Marshal who commanded all the British forces in Europe. In writing about all these people one must make clear the sharp distinction between the commanders, the High Command, and the men who turned their orders and wishes into facts, the Staff. The interplay between the two, particularly higher up the scale, was very close. But one overriding factor divided them; the commanders were men responsible for their own decisions in their own right, while members of the Staff, however exalted, were always the mouthpieces of the commanders they served. This does not mean that a staff officer was not held responsible for his own work, but that outside his own headquarters he always spoke for the General he served and not himself.

The ways in which commanders and staff officers could influence morale were different. Although their work was closely linked, they must be judged by different standards.

The first duty of a commander was to win victories. In defining morale I pointed out that there is no better tonic for soldiers than to win a battle. Success indeed is the only criterion of a General; that he should achieve it as economically as possible in terms of casualties is important, but less so than the victory itself. If victory is not achieved in one battle, the commander must either persuade his men that he can be successful on another occasion, or else he must be replaced. Somehow the High Command in the First World War managed to convince their armies that they could win in the end, and eventually they did. Much of this was due to Field-Marshal Sir Douglas Haig.

The contribution made to morale by the Staff in 1914–1918 depended on more mundane things such as move tables being accurate, ammunition supplies being ready, the wounded being well cared for, and rations being adequate. Rations of course were vital; Socrates stated, it will be remembered. 'The general must know how to get his men their rations. . . .'[2] These comments of Ludendorff also are worth quoting: 'The work of the Army in the field depended to a high degree on their rations. That, next to leave, has the most decisive effect on the MORAL[E] of the troops. I thus had to give the food question my serious attention.'[3] The fact that the Germans were so short of food in 1918 may well have contributed to their defeat. In spite of Ludendorff's concern, the German soldier went hungry towards the end of the War, while the British remained reasonably well fed.

In looking at the higher control of the British Army one is tempted to wonder how well it worked. How good were the 'brass-hats' at their jobs? Two general points about the High Command and the Staff should be made before attempting to judge their efficiency.

The first is that sympathy is not one of the highest virtues in a commander in war. A brilliant American film, *Twelve O'Clock High*, was made some years ago on this subject. It showed a United States Air Force bomber group at work in the Second World War, and was concerned with the problem, using American service jargon, of 'over-identification with personnel'. This, in very general terms, means a military commander's tendency to become too fond of his subordinates, too conscious of their difficulties, and too anxious not to lose them. The film showed a popular, but tired, General commanding the group who had become too devoted to his pilots and too mixed up with their lives to drive them hard enough. The group was slowly losing efficiency, and being slightly less successful on each raid. In the end he was removed from his command. His successor arrived—hard, determined, and without sympathy. The film showed him gradually restoring efficiency after the initial resentment at his replacing his well-liked predecessor. Success followed success. Then gradually the new General started in his turn to weaken a little. The film closed with him beginning to go the way of his predecessor.

This theme has been elaborated upon because an understanding of its existence is essential if one is to see the problems of command in war in their true light. Above a certain level the leader must be rather remote from his subordinates or he will spare them too easily.

My second general point is that if the ability of the Staff had been as poor as certain writers would like one to believe, the morale of the fighting troops could not have been so good. I believe that battalions in the front line were well catered for in the way of direction and administration, and that they themselves felt that the Staff did an adequate job. There was a certain amount of muddle from time to time, but the normal pattern was one of efficiency. The truth is that had things been really bad the fighting troops could not, and would not, have gone on. Consider what the results of really bad staff-work on the lives of the fighting soldiers would have been if it

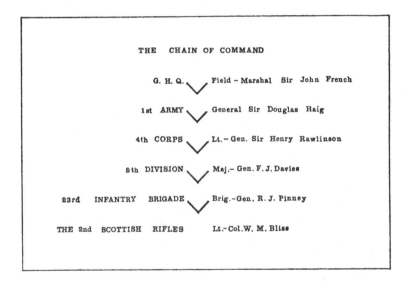

THE CHAIN OF COMMAND

G. H. Q.	Field – Marshal Sir John French
1st ARMY	General Sir Douglas Haig
4th CORPS	Lt.– Gen. Sir Henry Rawlinson
8th DIVISION	Maj.– Gen. F. J. Davies
23rd INFANTRY BRIGADE	Brig.–Gen. R. J. Pinney
THE 2nd SCOTTISH RIFLES	Lt.-Col.W. M. Bliss

had been a constant occurrence. Lack of food; lack of ammunition; being sent to the wrong places; no proper evacuation of casualties; poor treatment of the wounded; shortage of equipment; bad deliveries of mail from home; these are the results of incompetence by the Staff. Good battalions can take these sort of things in their stride on occasions. But if they happen too often morale suffers, and in the end the best of soldiers give up. The fact is that in the First World War the troops normally received good service.

At the time of Neuve Chapelle the senior British Commander in France was Field-Marshal Sir John French (see the Diagram). He was already a little insecure in his position, and in November 1915, some seven months later, he was to lose his command. Since my interest is with morale rather than strategy and tactics, I do not intend to comment on his skill as a director of operations. Apart from anything else I do not know enough about his ability in this field. But I am certain he was not a fool, in spite of his rather stupid appearance in his photographs, and of the efforts of almost everyone who has written about him since 1915 to damn him as one. It should be remembered that he was a very successful commander in the Boer War. He proved himself a forceful and imaginative leader of cavalry in South Africa, and between the Boer War and the outbreak of hostilities in 1914 reinforced his position in the estimation of the Army as the right man to command the British Expeditionary Force. One must remember that other Generals, many of great apparent promise, had not distinguished themselves in South Africa. French had met the test of battle there and had not been found wanting. It was only right in 1914 to choose a man to command the British Expeditionary Force who had already proved his worth in real war.

The problems that French had to deal with in the first year of the War would have taxed anyone. He may not have been up to the standard required for the task that faced him in France, but he was a good deal nearer it than most of his contemporaries. He seems to have been well respected, and his subordinate commanders from the rank of Major-General downwards do not seem to have doubted his ability. As far as I can see he had the trust of his armies to a reasonable degree, and certainly no strong case can be made against him on this score.

In the case of his successor, Haig, the trust of the Army was a much more positive matter. Throughout his time as Commander-in-Chief he retained the complete loyalty and confidence of the Army. Considering the set-backs that were suffered during his period in office, and the losses incurred, it was an amazing achievement. To show what those who actually came under his command thought about him I cannot do better than quote two officers who served under him in France for long periods. The first is General Jack. His diary for 16 December 1918 describes Haig's farewell to senior officers of the Army, and closes with these words: 'Before departing Sir Douglas said: "Thank you, gentlemen." Then passed from us a redoubtable, well-liked Chief, who for nearly four years had calmly borne a crushing load of responsibility.'[4]

Charles Carrington has this to say:

I wish to place it on record that never once during the war did I hear such criticisms of Sir Douglas Haig as now are current when his name is mentioned. There are channels of communication between human beings which the psychologists have not yet identified, and this silent man made himself known to his two million soldiers by telepathy. He was trusted, and that put an end to discussion.[5]

Haig's power to hold the trust of those under his command cannot be disputed in the face of comments such as these from men who spent years in the front line. Throughout all my investigations, and in all my reading about the War, I have been struck by the fact that criticism by fighting soldiers of every other senior General can be found somewhere, but never of Haig. Since Haig's power to retain the trust of his huge forces was obviously an important factor in maintaining their morale, its causes are worth examining. This power sprang in the first place from his calmness, and consequent ability to give the appearance of being completely unshakeable. Lord Moran has written of the importance of the 'durability of a General—his survival value', which he thinks depends more on character than capacity. His verdict on Haig and some other First World War commanders is that: '. . . as men they came from the old mould of their race, they wore well, they were built for great occasions. In the fundamental clash between great nations, when their existence is at stake, the issue is determined by moral and not by intellectual factors.'[6]

The second source was Haig's immense self-confidence. He has of course been accused of such boundless self-satisfaction and conceit that he verged on being a megalomaniac. This judgement is unfair, because it fails to take account of the enormous strain placed on a senior General in time of war, particularly when things are going against him. Lord Slim has written most eloquently of the anguish that can assail a military commander after his forces have been defeated in battle. Of his own feelings after the first Burma campaign in 1942 he has written:

In preparation, in execution, in strategy, and in tactics we had been worsted, and we had paid the penalty—defeat. Defeat is bitter. Bitter to the common soldier, but trebly bitter to his general. The soldier may comfort himself with the thought that, whatever the result, he has done his duty faithfully and steadfastly, but the commander has failed in his duty if he has not won victory— for that is his duty. He has no other comparable to it. He will go over in his mind the events of the campaign. 'Here', he will think, 'I went wrong; here I took counsel of my fears when I should have been bold; there I should have waited to gather strength, not struck piecemeal; at such a moment I failed to grasp opportunity when it was presented to me.' He will remember the soldiers whom he sent into the attack that failed and who did not come back. He will recall the look in the eyes of men who trusted him. 'I have failed them,' he will say to himself, 'and failed my country!' He will see himself for what he is—a defeated general. In a dark hour he will turn in upon himself and question the very foundations of his leadership and his manhood.

And then he must stop! For, if he is ever to command in battle again, he must shake off these regrets, and stamp on them, as they claw at his will and his self-confidence. He must beat off these attacks he delivers against himself, and cast out the doubts born of failure. Forget them, and remember only the lessons to be learnt from defeat—they are more than from victory.[7]

Haig had to face many defeats, and no doubt often had to shake off and stamp on his regrets. Whatever his failings he had the priceless quality of resilience, and to my mind the only possible thing to say about him is that he did his duty as he saw it, that he withstood all the strains placed upon him, and that in the end he was victorious. No great General could ask for a much better testimonial; if one adds that in doing all this he kept unbroken the trust, respect, and even affection of his troops, it seems sad that his reputation should have suffered such calumny during the past forty or more years.

As can be seen from the Diagram, there were three other high commanders above the 2nd Scottish Rifles at the time of Neuve Chapelle—Generals Sir Henry Rawlinson, Davies, and Pinney. As the Commander of the 23rd Brigade the last of these was the one best known to members of the battalion. He was a big man, and one of the senior officers who believed in going well up into the front areas. As a result he is well remembered by veterans of the battle of Neuve Chapelle, from whom the following two anecdotes are quoted.

Sergeant Noble remembers seeing General Pinney just before setting off on the march up to the line on the evening of 9 March 1915. He records that:

I was away from my platoon and in command of escort to bombers, but almost the last five minutes, General Pinney saw that I was a Sergeant and the N.C.O. in charge of bombers was a Corporal just returned from a school. He said 'Cannot have a Corporal commanding a Sergeant', so a lance-Corporal took my place and I rejoined Sergeant Hammond, No. 2 Platoon.

During the battle, on the second day, Pinney's appearance is remembered at a crucial moment by Corporal Bell of 'D' Company:

Major Carter-Campbell was wounded in afternoon again. Brig-Gen Pinney came along and said to Major Carter-Campbell he was to send along a Major from 2nd West Yorks to take charge of the 2nd Scottish Rifles. Major Carter-Campbell said 'No, tell Lieutenant Somervail and R.S.M. Chalmers what to do and they will do it alright.' By this time we were waiting to take Major Carter-Campbell down the line to go to hospital.

The 2nd Scottish Rifles certainly had no reason to complain about their Brigade Commander staying in the rear. He was obviously an active man who got around his battalions and was well known to the men in them. The majority of other commanders at his level in France at the time were of his type.

From the Staff in the First World War were expected efficiency and hard work. Described below are some of the things that had to be done by Headquarters 23rd Infantry Brigade before, during, and after the battle of Neuve Chapelle. The complications, as will become evident, were nearly as great as they would be today. The facilities for dealing with them were, on the other hand, primitive to a degree in comparison with the aids to staff work available nowadays.

In the preparations for Neuve Chapelle the 23rd Brigade Staff started by receiving orders for the attack from Headquarters 8th Division. They then had to re-formulate the orders for the attack as it applied to the battalions in their own Brigade. This entailed liaising with the Brigade already occupying the front-line trenches to plan the exact areas from which the attack would be launched, reconnoitring the routes up, working out a march table to get the battalions on the road at the right times and in the right order for the approach march, and choosing the site for the meal halt on the way. Next came the detailed orders for the attack itself. This involved considerable research and checking of small points before the exact deployment of the different waves of the assault could be decided. The planning of the supporting fire by the artillery followed decisions on deployment, and if one thinks how much fire-power there was available, it can quickly be seen that this was no easy task. The Staff had to know in detail the plans of the artillery and check with great care that every barrage tied in exactly with infantry movement. One battery being told to fire for two minutes longer than the correct time on a certain place might mean the advancing infantry running into the fire of their own guns.

Once the orders were ready it was the job of the Staff to see that they reached the right people in good time. Entailed in this were conferences, order groups, issue of written orders and confirmatory notes, and also ensuring that higher headquarters and flank formations were fully informed. Then there would be the provision of maps and air photographs to the infantry, and arrangements to be made for officers from the four battalions to go forward to visit the trenches from which they were to attack, as Kennedy did, on different days before the battle.

Once battle was joined, the Staff's work load was almost doubled. Information was the cry at every moment and from every quarter. All the commanders above the 23rd Brigade wanted to know what was happening, and so did those below, the battalions in the line, whose movements were dependent on knowing what was happening to other formations on their flanks. To deal with this endless demand for information there were only the minimum facilities: 'devices which required another twenty or thirty years to be invented and produced could not, of course, be used'.[8] The result was that the Staff were harassed almost beyond endurance in their endeavours to keep a flow of up-to-the-minute news of the battle travelling to and fro along the lines of communication. Whenever plans were changed, or fresh orders issued, it was the task of the Staff at each level to readjust them to their own particular formation and then send them forward. From the Headquarters of the 23rd Brigade these orders had to be carried right forward to the front, and be delivered, often in darkness, to battalions whose positions were constantly shifting.

The battle over, the Staff's work was far from completed. Reports had to be written, full particulars of casualties and losses of vital equipment had to be collected, War Diaries had to be entered up, the exact positions where everyone finished the battle had to be recorded and mapped, and boundaries had to be adjusted between battalions. At the same time, plans had to be made for future operations; the War never stood still, and as one battle ended arrangements were usually under way for the next.

This is a part of the full load of staff work, covering only the operational aspects—known as 'G', or General Staff, commitments in the British Army. There was also administration: supplies of every kind were required in abundance. Food, stocks of ammunition of all types for small arms and artillery, new weapons, spare parts, medical stores, forage for horses— the list is endless. All these commodities had to be moved up, stored, stacked, or issued, and accounted for as well. The

British Army dealt with such matters successfully; its supply system was its forte. Carrington describes the problem like this: 'The build-up for a battle required such masses of supplies and munitions, such elaboration of movements by road and rail, that it could not be concealed and, once set on foot, could change direction only at the cost of chaos. As a feat of organization the staff work of the B.E.F. was supremely efficient, far more so than in the armies of any of our allies.'[9]

But administration covers more than the supply of materials of war and food; it includes all the different aspects of the care of personnel. Men have to be moved up to the front, and taken out of the line for rests even if not actually casualties. When wounded or sick they have to be evacuated and treated in hospitals, and replacements have to be found for them. When they are killed they naturally have to be replaced in the same way, and also great care has to be taken to check reports of their death, and to notify their next of kin as quickly as possible. All these tasks, which have a way of endlessly complicating themselves, go to make up the burden of staff work in war.

Staffs in the First World War were far smaller than today. At the Headquarters of the 23rd Brigade there were four officers including the Brigadier-General. A modern brigade has about a dozen. And, as I have said earlier, the facilities in those days were so inadequate. General Jack described a scene when he was Staff Captain of a brigade in 1914: 'Johnson (Brigade Major), Churchill and I write the orders dictated by the brigadier in our small Field Service notebooks (6 by 4 inches), each making three carbon copies. These orders are shortly sent to battalions by their orderlies on pedal bicycles.'[10] Four years later, when Jack was himself a Brigadier-General, his Headquarters were visited by General Sir Herbert Plumer, commander of the Second Army: 'The General asks how the Brigade is getting on, and laughs—a little uncomprehendingly —when I put a typewriting machine as our first requirement. This is not so frivolous a request as it sounds. Our borrowed typewriter makes a noise like a travelling tank and mutilates the paper copies—and manuscript is too slow for the volume of office work. The Army Commander now laughs more genuinely and says he will do his best. . . .'[11] The borrowed typewriter in 1918 was better than the pocket-book and carbon copies in 1914, but even so the slowness with which such vital equipment became available is surprising. Only more surprising is the fact that such efficiency was achieved with so few aids to it.

My aim so far has been to explain the difficulties which faced the Staff in the First World War, and to suggest that on the whole they coped with them remarkably well. The men at the front understood these difficulties, and felt that they were looked after adequately; indeed, they would not have fought as they did had this not been the case. Why then was there undoubtedly a feeling of bitterness between the fighting men and those who worked behind the lines, the memory of which lives on even to this day?

In trying to trace the cause of this ill-feeling one must start by establishing the level at which it appeared. The vital place in the structure of command in this respect was Divisional Headquarters. Within a division units and individuals knew each other, but above that nobody was known. Divisions were self-contained and retained much the same composition throughout the War, but they were moved about frequently from corps to corps and army to army. The 2nd Scottish Rifles, for example, remained in the 23rd Brigade and the 8th Division throughout the whole War. The 8th Division, however, was shuttled backwards and forwards between corps and armies all the time. As a result: 'The remoteness and anonymity of a corps headquarters were such that the Corps Commander, inevitably, was blamed. Heaven knows, we grumbled and joked about brigade and division, but within reason. Knowing them, we made allowance. Corps we did not know and, since battles in France were mostly disastrous, the Corps Commander was rarely popular.'[12]*

Often enough corps and higher headquarters made remarkably little effort to encourage respect and affection. This story

* *This reflects on Haig's position. He was the one senior commander known to everyone, by name at least. His permanence at G.H.Q. and the fact that he was known of by everyone contributed to the esteem he was held in.*

from an officer of the Scottish Rifles shows what could happen. He came out of a hard battle, with heavy casualties, and then:

I was detailed to ride 10 miles back to Corps H.Q. to get pay for the troops from the Field Cashier. Having got the money we were informed by the M.P. that this beautiful untouched town was out of bounds for anyone not on the corps staff. We were not allowed to get even a cup of tea although the tea shops and cafés that abounded were full of staff officers and their clerks. We were all but put under arrest.[13]

It was not of course unreasonable that the big Headquarters should be billeted in comfortable quarters. A man doing a job on the Staff obviously did it better in comfortable surroundings than in cramped discomfort. What annoyed the fighting soldier so much was the way in which 'base-wallahs' tried to hog the good things for themselves. This feeling that there were two armies, one fighting and suffering in the trenches and one making itself comfortable well out of harm's way, was at the root of the bitterness between the front-line infantryman and his counterpart at the base or on the Staff which is caught so well in Siegfried Sassoon's famous lines:

> If I were fierce, and bald, and short of breath,
> I'd live with scarlet Majors at the Base,
> And speed glum heroes up the line to death.
> You'd see me with my puffy petulant face,
> Guzzling and gulping in the best hotel,
> Reading the Roll of Honour. 'Poor young chap,'
> I'd say—'I used to know his father well;
> Yes, we've lost heavily in this last scrap.'
> And when the war is done and youth stone dead,
> I'd toddle safely home and die—in bed.[14]

As I said before, the dividing line between these two armies came at the divisional rear boundary. I also believe that it was of more concern to the officers than their men that such a gulf existed. Although the men no doubt looked on 'base-wallahs' with a fair amount of contempt they never grew as bitter about them as their officers. One reason was that for many privates all officers other than their own particular ones were objects of some suspicion, and they were unlikely to see much difference between any of them.

To discover the roots of the almost instinctive distrust between regimental officers and the Staff we must look to the traditions of the old Regular Army. One of these was that to want to go to the Staff College, or to do a job on the Staff, was a bad thing. It was felt that a man who left his Regiment in this way was suspect; he was automatically branded as an ambitious self-seeker by many of his contemporaries. This attitude sprang partly from a sincere belief that by being a good regimental officer a man was doing the best he could for his country. But there is no doubt it was also in part an elaborate form of self-deception. As has been pointed out already, many officers lacked cultivation and intelligence. They knew that they were too ill-educated and mentally lazy to handle complicated staff-work, and they were not going to try. They thus fostered an anti-Staff spirit, largely through conversation, which in certain Regiments, particularly the expensive cavalry Regiments, became almost a fetish. On the whole the Scottish Rifles did not subscribe strongly to these ideas, largely no doubt because few of the officers were very rich, and the majority had to think reasonably seriously about making successful careers in the Army.

During the First World War another cause of distrust was the fact that staff officers wore red gorget patches on their uniforms and red bands around their hats in the way that only full Colonels and above do in the British Army today. The idea behind the use of these embellishments was to make a staff officer obvious when he came to visit units with the orders of the commander he served. Unfortunately its results in France were to highlight the staff officer's cleanliness and tidiness against the muddy disarray of the regimental officer, and to give the wrong sort of man an idea that he was rather a superior being because of his distinctive markings. In the trenches the red patches and hat-bands were always referred to as 'badges of shame', and soon after the War the practice of wearing them was abolished among junior officers, as it was realized what an unfortunate effect they produced.

It is fair to say that the bitterness which existed between different groups in the Army was mainly due to lack of communication. It was made worse by the sort of things I have mentioned—hogging the good conditions, red patches, and traditional contempt—but it need never have been as bad as it was had more effort been made by the Staff to show that they really cared about the lot of the fighting men, as most of them did, and to get to know them. On the other hand this was not easy. Corps were handling so many divisions, often for very short periods, that the chance of getting to know individuals even at the Divisional Headquarters level was rare. Furthermore, the problem of getting about was difficult, and trying to visit forward formations took time that often could not be spared from busy desks. Perhaps the only thing one can say is that many officers who were in senior positions in the Second World War remembered the bitterness they knew as young men in 1914–1918 and were successful in ensuring that it did not grow to anything like the same proportions again.

I am not prepared to bring this chapter to a close by trying to pronounce a positive verdict on the High Command and Staff in the First World War and their influence on morale. All that my knowledge of the subject permits me to do is to repeat the rather negative comment that I have made at different points in the book already, which is that armies do not fight well under bad commanders with poor staffs. With poor direction from their Generals and incompetence from the Staff, soldiers eventually give in. The only thing to do is judge those who ran the British Army in 1914–1918 for oneself against this standard. And at the same time it is right to remember the opinions of those who actually belonged to the armies which took part in the War. As General Jack wrote: 'I served in almost every battle on the Western Front in 1914–1918, and resent unjust, malicious slurs on my old commanders, despite any mistakes they may have made.'[15] The last word should remain with him.

Conclusions

What of the faith and fire within us
Men who march away
Ere the barn cocks say
Night is growing gray,
Leaving all that here can win us;
What of the faith and fire within us
Men who march away?

Thomas Hardy, *Men Who March Away*
(SONG OF THE SOLDIERS; 5 September 1914)

WE HAVE EXAMINED many of the elements of morale in the abstract; it is essential to return to flesh and blood. 'What of the faith and fire within' those members of the 2nd Scottish Rifles who set off from the French village of Estaires on the night of 9 March 1915 on their way to the front-line trenches opposite Neuve Chapelle. Let us try to see them once again in the mind as they trudge by. There are over seven hundred men, and they cover half a mile of road as they pass. They are living men: the knowledge that so many will be dead within a few hours gives the picture a bitter poignancy.

It is a raw, cold night, with the occasional gust of rain blown on a sharp, cutting wind. The mud on either side of the cobbled road is hardened by frost into rough ridges, and the puddles are iced over. The battalion marches in silence, without the pipers or the singing which normally help relieve the monotony. In this early stage the men are formed in fours, marching by platoons in company columns with a small party of bomb carriers at the rear of each company. Later in the journey, after a pause for a meal at about 1 a.m., they will shake out into single file for the last stretch across country to the trenches from which the assault is to be launched. Though not as heavily loaded as they would be if carrying out an ordinary relief in the line, the men are carrying a good weight each. They are wearing greatcoats with the skirts fastened back at the front, and besides a rifle and the standard hundred rounds of ammunition they have two extra bandoliers of one hundred rounds apiece. On the left hip hangs a haversack in which are rations for the following day, and an iron ration to be used only in an emergency; under the haversack, against the leg, is the old eighteen-inch bayonet, known always as a 'sword' in a rifle Regiment. On the right hip is a full water-bottle. One discomfort of marches later in the War the 2nd Scottish Rifles are spared, and that is the steel-helmet. All ranks are wearing the black Glengarry, which is light and comfortable, even though the steel-helmet would save a number of lives in the battle were it available.

Many of the characters met in this book are on their way to Neuve Chapelle. Bliss leads his battalion, with his new Adjutant, Gray-Buchanan, and the calm imperturbable Chalmers close beside him. With 'A' Company are Hayes and his Company Sergeant-Major, Culley, who are to fall side-by-side so soon after the attack begins tomorrow. With No. 2 Platoon is Sergeant Noble.

The other companies follow in alphabetical order. Immensely proud and elated, Ferrers is about to achieve all that 'he ever wished for': he is to go into an attack at the head of a company of the 90th with his sword in his hand. Also in his beloved ' "B" troop' are the two Kennedys; one to be killed before even going over the top, the other, Malcolm, to write in time the story of the battle on which I have drawn so heavily. In Malcolm Kennedy's platoon march Bryant, the Cockney Sergeant; Corporals Harrison and Forster; Privates Murray, Plank and the ever-reliable McHugh. The 'huge, gaunt' figure of Private Mason is at the rear of the company with the bomb carriers; a hideous, accidental explosion is to kill him before he gets to the end of this journey. Another

Platoon Commander in 'B' Company is Conway, who until a few months before was the Company Sergeant-Major, and is the first of many Warrant Officers of the battalion to be commissioned.

In 'C' Company, under Ellis, is Cameron the Pipe-Major, now working as a Platoon Sergeant, having insisted on leaving his beloved Pipes and Drums for a more active role in the trenches. Also with 'C' is a stretcher-bearer, Lance-Corporal Smith, listening to Captain Dodd talking of the beauty of England to the Company Sergeant-Major. 'D' Company brings up the rear, headed by Lloyd, who had thousands under his control in Egypt a year or two ago for each one man under his command now. Among his subalterns is Somervail, who is to be the lone survivor among the officers at the end of the battle, and is to bring out the unbroken remnant of the battalion in five nights' time.

Finally the long column passes, and another Regiment looms out of the darkness, for the road from Estaires is full of troops tonight. As the last man disappears from sight, and the picture fades back into its proper place in the past, one wants to know on what foundations the fortitude of this battalion was built. Can one pick out the main ingredients of its high morale? Out of the factors I have brought into this study I consider five to be the most important, which I have arranged in order of priority.

First, I would place Regimental loyalty; the pride in belonging to a good battalion, in knowing other people well and being known by them; in having strong roots in a well-loved community.*

Second, the excellent officer–other rank relationship; the high quality of the leaders, and the trust placed in them by their men; the mutual confidence and goodwill which developed in the harsh life of the trenches.

---

* *Liddell Hart has written of the British Army at 'First Ypres' (November, 1914) and the 'indomitable spirit which inspired their collective endurance'. He writes of their 'corporate sense': 'The family spirit was its keynote, and the key to the apparent miracle by which, when formations were broken up and requirements reduced to remnants, those remnants still held together.' This comment has helped me to decide to put Regimental loyalty in first place among the five most important factors. (Liddell Hart,* A History of the World War 1914–1918, *p. 177.)*

Third, strong discipline; the balance between self-discipline and the imposed sort.

Fourth, the sense of duty of all ranks; highly developed in the officer by his training and background; developed in the soldier both by his training and by the realization that someone else would have to do his job if he failed to do it properly himself.

Fifth, sound administration, so that in spite of many difficulties the battalion was well provided with the necessities of war such as rations and ammunition.

Here was the essence of the battalion's morale. Thus equipped, the 2nd Scottish Rifles marched up the line through the darkness to the Battle of Neuve Chapelle.

Appendix A

This appendix consists of four letters (edited) written by Major (later Lieutenant-Colonel) E. B. Ferrers, D.S.O., to Lieutenant M. D. Kennedy (later Captain M. D. Kennedy, O.B.E.) at different phases of the War, and just after it. The first one appears in Chapter 2 almost complete; being written so shortly after Neuve Chapelle is a most valuable record of one man's feelings at the time about the action.

1st letter

This letter was written by Ferrers from hospital about a week after the battle of Neuve Chapelle. It comes to a stop at the point where he fainted in the middle of writing it.

18.3.15.
No. 7 Stationary.

Dear Malcolm,

It was very kind of you to write, how well you do it. I make a queer old fist of it myself. My adventures were very like yours. I got through the wire and over their parapet just to the right of where your hedges ended. When I got there the cupboard was bare and someone shot me, as I thought in the right ankle, as I started for the next trench. This was really rather a relief as no one else was up and I was feeling exceedingly lonely. I couldn't walk so I lent up against the parapet and waved my sword and generally marked the distant point. I could see the lads all hung up in wire and I fancy some were firing half and quarter right but before I could appreciate the situation I took it again in the right thigh. As it came out very low down right in the middle of the stomach I accepted that as final and being fallen on my back partly on sand-bags and partly in a puddle I concluded to stay as long as I was and take stock of my worldly affairs. I doubted that I'd live very long but as I'd had all I'd ever wished for I didn't worry much over that. I calculated the lads would have finished with the wire and be coming over the parapet soon and I thought if I saw them started for the next trench that would do me very well. I made out that I had a bit of a chance if I could only keep absolutely still. Never did I feel the least doubt, but it was very lonely on my side of the parapet. I could see down towards the hedge for a few yards and by screwing round my head I could see toward the Bosches 2nd trench but that was about all. Presently someone I know quite well but I got so mixed I cannot remember who, tumbled through the fence, looked very lost for a moment but bucked up no end when he saw me. He started to Holla the rest on like a good 'un and when that produced no immediate result said to me 'It's no good Sir they won't come'. I said 'Don't you worry about the lads they'll come all right.' There was some sort of a frightful battle going on behind my head for he ran off there, and then Cpl Kennedy came over my gap and was hit and Harris & Plank and a few others cropped up and all got into action to the right. They were frightfully pleased about something I think they'd got some Bosches round a corner and were killing them; but I couldn't twist my head round to make sure. C Coy began to come up and built up a sort of a firing line about fifteen or twenty yards beyond me. Dodd was with them and presently I was told he was badly hit in the shoulder. Then I heard Snowden's voice

The letter goes no further. It is written in pencil on cheap lined paper which was presumably supplied by No. 7 Stationary Field Hospital.

2nd Letter

Ferrers and Kennedy were together in a convalescent home in Brighton, and this letter was written when Kennedy had gone off to the South of France for a chance to recuperate in a special home there. It may perhaps have a note of slightly forced gaiety in it.

140 Marine Parade,
Brighton.
23.3.16.

Dear Malcolm,

The North wind doth blow and we shall have snow which will be no change as it has been at it all the morning—the devil.

Do you realize that of all those who set forth to fight the Hun so gallant and so gay so many fell by the wayside that only Carter-Campbell, you and I remain to whom the crowning glory of seeing Neuve Chapelle with the 90th was vouchsafed?

Of the Regular Officers who had the fortune to be present besides ourselves only Conway is left. It is up to B Coy to keep alive the glorious traditions of the 90th. Surely we shall serve with them again.

Even Watkiss* now admits that I shall be fit for work within a reasonable period and then I can only hope.

Meanwhile I have so greatly improved that with a light cane I leap from point to point regarding distance as naught; to the West Pier and back without a halt the other day—but I never saw the flapper. So I am passed for Light Duty and am to go to town where I am to recruit conscientious objectors and recalcitrant Benedicts. And my last job was to lead B troop.† I shall live at the Caledonian and be strafed daily. . . .

I need not say that every one will welcome your return but I should stay in the sunshine. What I meant to say was having no news of our Gramophone arriving I have been and given the girl who sold it a good spanking, through her tears she has promised to pursue it and deliver it personally.

E. F.

3rd Letter

At this stage Ferrers was in France commanding a battle training school. He had managed to get back to the 2nd Scottish Rifles in February 1917, as described in Chapter 2, but was not really fit enough for service in the trenches. After a month or two with the battalion he had been forced to take a more peaceful job a bit behind the front-line.

24.7.18.

My dear Malcolm,

For years and years I have owed you a letter or letters. To begin with I must thank you for your Homeric and inaccurate account of Neuve Chapelle. But with what unusual truth do you say that the men were beyond praise. That first winter was an experience which ought to, and will, influence one's whole life. One did get to know the men and what men they were. Nowhere except in the front line could you find their like & the old B troop had peculiar virtues of its own. Now and again I meet an odd member of the

---

* *Watkiss was the Surgeon.*
† *At various points in his letters Ferrers calls 'B' Company 'B troop': it was one of his idiosyncrasies to do this.*

party. Hammond, Feeney & another whose name at the moment escapes me have been here recently. Nearly always they have been transferred to other Regiments which I consider a most cruel thing. Meanwhile the war goes on rather well. Our poor old town which received us on the night that we detrained from Le Havre was violently battered and passed into the wrong hands. I had been there for about five months with my school when they began putting 15 inch shells in and around the station. The billet in which Bn. H.Q. lay that night got a dud in the garden and a live one through the roof which was more than it could stand. Altogether they did surprisingly little damage and pulled off some marvellous misses. Then we were mobilized as an entrenching unit and went south for the tail end of the Somme battle. We got back for the Lys push which I just missed though being away for the night looking for a new home. The line is now as you know back to the forest in front of which we lay before Neuve Chapelle.

At that moment the situation was a little trying as the Bosche had far more troops than we had, but we always managed to find just enough. I was looking after reinforcements and found the job very trying. If the men hadn't been absolutely splendid things would have been difficult. But the old traditions held good and everyone was quite ready to do all that he could and that in the end did the Bosche in. The situation now is wonderfully different. I would not have thought it possible that such a change could take place in three or four months. The Americans have made a great difference, there are so many of them and they are first-class troops. Also they dislike the Bosche intensely and are quite clear as to what to do to him. . . .

I saw Croft* the other day who came down here fresh from a war fully content with life. Otherwise I have not met anyone for months, as I live a secluded life away back. It is a very good job if only there wasn't so much going on, one can only hope that one is doing something useful. . . .

All the news that I have of the 2nd Bn. is that Lee is going to get command, he has just come out again after a spell at home with the Tanks.

All good luck to you,

E. B. Ferrers.

---

* *Brigadier-General W. D. Croft, C.B., C.M.G., D.S.O. (and 4 bars) was an officer of the 2nd Scottish Rifles before the War. A Captain in 1914, a Brigadier-General in 1917 and a Major in 1919—a pattern followed by many Regular Officers.*

About the reference to Kennedy's account of Neuve Chapelle, Kennedy himself has written to me as follows:

The 'Homeric and inaccurate account of Neuve Chapelle' to which he refers was a poem I wrote about the battle. It indulged in a certain degree of poetic licence, one line using the words, 'bayonets glittering bright in the sun', which, of course, was quite incorrect, as there was no sun! But I was young and enthusiastic in those days!

4th letter

This final letter of the four I am reproducing has been edited a good deal, as there is a lot in it which would be of little interest to the general reader.

5.12.18.

Dear Malcolm,

A few words are due to you to wish you a joyful Christmas and to meditate generally on the armistice.

It is wonderful to reflect how little one is affected by the completion of a task which has been the sole object of one's existence for many years.

I can't fix an exact date for the time when I first really understood that the German Army had got to be overthrown and that there was no prospect of my getting anybody to stand between me and it. I rather think that it would be about 1908, before that one had allowed one's attention to be drawn off by Russians and Turks and the like.

As far as I can remember I never had a clear idea as to whether one would personally survive, everything seemed to indicate that one wouldn't but I cannot ever remember doubting that we should ultimately defeat them utterly and I can never remember feeling impressed by the respect that perhaps one ought to have had for so magnificent an organization. I rather think that they weren't really magnificent and that when we mocked at their Goose-stepping we were nearer the truth than we thought. As far as my experience went they fought correctly rather than well—whereas our little devils may have been good but I'm damned if they were correct. And they've done the blighters down proper. And look you, I don't care who says otherwise but the lad who goes in with a proper affection for the Old Battalion and damn all else is going to come out top dog in the long run. You can't surprise him because he's too beastly ignorant to be surprised, you can't sicken him with dark, or dirt or danger or disease or death or damnation because he's damned already and means to die for the Battalion anyhow so why not get on with the work and say Kamerad and let the Battalion get on to Berlin.

This however is a digression and just between ourselves.

I did not expect the war to end this way. To me it is rather horrible that the German Army should walk away behind a screen of poison-gas delay action mines and when that safe-guard looked like not keeping the enemy away should surrender everything it was told to and continue walking away saying that it was undefeated. I cannot picture our men doing that. It was well said while we were waiting for the definite announcement 'After all if we were in their position we should be at the top of our form'. Even in the darkest days in April there was no sign of anyone not sticking it out. The instructions were 'Find a wall to put your backs against', and men went forward to look for it more readily than they came back. I never heard that they found a wall but there were some damned stiff backs that managed very well without it.

We are to try to polish up the education of our men so as to send them back to civil life as little rusty as possible. I hope that they will be able to settle down to decent jobs, it does seem as if an effort is to be made to receive them properly and as far as I can see they mean to take advantage of the opportunities offered. It will be a big and a long job.

Meanwhile the Regular Battalions will probably resume their life abroad so as to relieve the Territorial and New Army Units that have been bearing the burden. I wonder if you and I will ever be fit to march with the 90th again. It would be a gap in one's life if one gave up hope but it would be horrible not to be up to the standard. Well we had our fun and led some damned brave men to a glorious victory.

E. B. Ferrers

Appendix B

COLONEL C. H. P. CARTER, Handed over to Colonel Bliss shortly after the photograph was taken.

MAJOR G. T. C. CARTER-CAMPBELL — Wounded at Neuve Chapelle. Returned to command 2nd Scottish Rifles for a short time before promotion. Ended the War in command of the 51st Highland Division.

MAJOR H. D. W. LLOYD — Killed at Neuve Chapelle.

MAJOR E. D. L. HAYES — Killed at Neuve Chapelle.

MAJOR G. A. ELLIS — Killed at Neuve Chapelle.

CAPTAIN E. B. FERRERS — Wounded at Neuve Chapelle. Came back to the battalion for a short time in 1917, but was not fit. Commanded 1st Cameronians in the 1920s.

CAPTAIN A. C. NORTHEY — Left 2nd Scottish Rifles to command Depot in early 1914. Later commanded 9th Scottish Rifles.

CAPTAIN W. H. MACALLAN — Went to Depot in 1914. Served with 3rd Battalion in the War.

CAPTAIN AND QUARTERMASTER T. FINN — Retired in 1919 as Lieutenant-Colonel Quartermaster.

[261]

LIEUTENANT R. N. O'CONNOR	D.S.O., M.C., nine Mentions in Despatches in the War. Lieutenant-General in the Second World War; Corps Commander in Africa and N.W. Europe. Retired 1947 as full General. Still living in 1966.
LIEUTENANT W. B. GRAY BUCHANAN	Killed at Neuve Chapelle.
LIEUTENANT AND ADJUTANT W. I. MAUNSELL	Killed just before Neuve Chapelle.
LIEUTENANT A. C. L. STANLEY CLARKE	Wounded just before Neuve Chapelle. Commanded 10th Scottish Rifles towards end of War for two years. Brigadier in Second World War. Still living in 1966.
LIEUTENANT R. D. HUNTER	Wounded at Aubers Ridge, May 1915.
LIEUTENANT W. J. KERR	Died of wounds in 1915.
LIEUTENANT H. R. CRAILSHEIM	Invalided home before the end of 1914.
LIEUTENANT R. V. CLERK	Killed at Gallipoli as Adjutant 7th Scottish Rifles.
LIEUTENANT J. P. KENNEDY	Killed at Neuve Chapelle.
LIEUTENANT L. WANLESS O'GOWAN	Posted early in 1914 to 3rd Scottish Rifles.
2/LIEUTENANT THE HON. J. DE BLAQUIERE	Killed at Neuve Chapelle.
2/LIEUTENANT D. C. FOSTER	Killed at Arras with 1st Cameronians in 1917.
2/LIEUTENANT T. E. D. DUNN	Killed in the trenches in January 1915.
2/LIEUTENANT J. F. EVETTS	Lieutenant-General in Second World War. Still living in 1966.

2/Lieutenant H. A. C. Sim   Killed at Aubers Ridge May 1915.

2/Lieutenant C. R. I. Hopkins   Killed in the trenches early in 1915.

2/Lieutenant T. L. Loder-Symonds   Killed at Aubers Ridge May 1915.

2/Lieutenant C. R. H. Stirling   Died in 1918 of wounds received when commanding the 2nd Scottish Rifles, at the age of twenty-five, in summer 1917. Won D.S.O. and M.C.

(One of the nastiest smears ever to come out of the First World War was that the officers of the old Regular Army 'looked after their own', i.e. that they avoided the danger of the trenches and stuck to safe and comfortable desk jobs in the rear. The facts above dispose of that theory.)

Appendix C

When a soldier joined the Regular Army before 1914 he was issued with a very neatly bound and well-produced book known as the *Soldier's Small Book*. Extracts from this book follow. One of the most interesting things about the copy from which I have taken these extracts is the meticulous care with which it was maintained, and the constant checking by officers. The book concerned belonged to Private (later Lieutenant-Colonel) Lucarotti, whose photograph follows page 106. It was verified and signed, or initialled, at frequent intervals, and all sorts of achievements such as obtaining education certificates and passing swimming tests are recorded in it. Between 28 September 1908 and 1 August 1913 no less than ten entries or verifications were made, each one signed by an officer. I labour this point to bring out again the care taken by officers of their men in the old pre-1914 Army.

The *Small Book* starts with:

GENERAL OBSERVATIONS

The Soldier's number, name, and corps should be distinctly written on the cover of this Book, and he is to communicate to his friends his regimental number, and to acquaint them that in all inquiries which they make after him, whether addressed to the Regiment or to the War Office, they are to state such number. He should advise them to communicate with his unit or his depot in preference to the War Office.

The principal object for which a Soldier is required to be in possession of this Book is to provide him with (1) certain information which he will find useful to him during his service, and (2) a record of his service in the Army.

It is therefore the Soldier's interest to take care of this Book and to see that it is correctly made up when he takes his discharge.

When a Soldier is discharged, he is to take this Book away with him; in the event of a Soldier dying in the service, this Book will be forwarded to the War Office for ultimate transmission to his representatives, if they desire it; and if it contain a record of Wounds received in action, or of distinguished acts of Bravery, it will remain an honourable memorial of his character and conduct.

As the particulars contained in this Book are liable to amendment, they do not confer on the Soldier the right to be subject to them during his whole service.

After two pages showing the soldier's name, description of attestation, personal particulars and next of kin, the text of the book continues.

Perhaps a little surprisingly, the first matter to be dealt with is:

Mode of Complaint by Soldier

'If any Soldier thinks himself wronged in any matter by any Officer other than his Captain, or by any Soldier, he may complain thereof to his Captain, and if he thinks himself wronged by his Captain, either in respect of his complaint not being redressed or in respect of any other matter, he may complain thereof to his Commanding Officer, and if he thinks himself wronged by his Commanding Officer, either in respect of his complaint not being redressed or in respect of any other matter, he may complain thereof to the General or other Officer Commanding the district or station where the Soldier is serving; and every Officer to whom a complaint is made in pursuance of this section shall cause such complaint to be inquired into, and shall, if on enquiry he is satisfied of the justice of the complaint so made, take such steps as may be necessary for giving full redress to the complainant in respect of the matter complained of.' (Sec. 43, Army Act.)

When a Soldier has any complaint to make, he should appeal to the Officer Commanding his Company; his tone and manner must be temperate and respectful; and he must be accompanied by a Non-Commissioned Officer, of his own Company if possible. No Soldier is on any account to presume to make a complaint to an Officer for another Soldier who conceives himself aggrieved; and not more than two Soldiers may approach an Officer to make a complaint at one and the same time. Anonymous complaints, or complaints through any channel other than that prescribed in the foregoing paragraph, are prohibited, and constitute military offences.

Page 7 is headed clearly 'OBEDIENCE IS THE FIRST DUTY OF A SOLDIER', and then come descriptions of four groups of offences. The first two groups are punishable by death. They read as follows:

NOTES FROM ARMY ACT

For the following offences a Soldier is liable, at all times, to the penalty of death, or of any less punishment:

Shamefully abandoning a post.

Shamefully casting away his arms, ammunition, or tools in the presence of the enemy.

Treacherously holding correspondence with or assisting the enemy.

Harbouring or voluntarily serving with the enemy.

Doing anything to imperil the success of His Majesty's Forces.

Cowardice before the enemy.

Mutiny.

Personal violence to a superior, or disobedience to his lawful commands, when in the execution of his office.

For the following offences, if committed on Active Service, a Soldier is liable to the penalty of death or any less punishment, and if committed not on Active Service, to imprisonment or any less punishment:

Deserting, attempting to desert, or assisting or persuading any other person to desert. (N.B.—A Soldier under orders for Active Service who deserts, or attempts to desert, is liable to the penalty of death.)

Leaving his Commanding Officer, or breaking into any house, in search of plunder.

Leaving his guard, picquet, patrol, or post without orders.

Forcing a safeguard or sentry.

Impeding, or when called on refusing to assist, the Provost Marshal or any of his assistants.

Doing violence to a person bringing supplies to the Forces, or detaining stores proceeding to the Forces, or committing any offence against the property or person of any inhabitant of, or resident in, the country in which he is serving.

Intentionally occasioning false alarms, or treacherously giving up the countersign.

When a sentry, sleeping or being drunk on his post, or leaving his post without orders.

Some general notes on punishments, saluting, guard duties,

and cleaning of weapons follow. There is also a paragraph on *How to Prevent Sore Feet*:

To prevent sore feet cleanliness and strict attention to the fitting of boots and socks are necessary. Before marching the feet should be washed with soap and water and carefully dried. The inside of the socks should be well rubbed with soft or yellow soap. After the march the feet must be again washed and clean dry socks put on. Soaking the feet in salt or alum and water hardens the skin. The nails should be cut straight across and not too close. A blister will probably be occasioned by an unevenness or hole in the sock, or an unevenness in the lining of the boot; the cause therefore should be ascertained and removed. The edge of a blister should be pricked with a needle and the fluid drained away by gently pressing the blister; a small pad of cotton wool or soft rag should then be applied, and kept in place by a small piece of sticking plaster. Men are cautioned against getting boots too small for them.

Some rather domestic points come next. First some comments on cleaning of clothes, and then some guides to cooking, and some recipes. There are nearly nine pages of recipes in the *Small Book*, but only a few are shown here:

RECIPES

FRESH BEEF OR MUTTON

1. *Plain Stew*—Ingredients: Meat, mixed vegetables, onions, flour, pepper, salt.

Peel or scrape clean and cut up the vegetables and onions, separate the meat from the bone, and cut it against the grain into pieces of 2 ozs. each, mix the dry flour, salt and pepper well together, place a little stock or water in the kettle, rub the pieces of meat in dry flour, and add to the stock, put in the vegetables and onions, barely covering the whole with stock or water; let it simmer gently for one and a half hours keeping the vessel closely covered till done.

2. *Irish Stew*—Ingredients: Meat, Potatoes, onions, pepper, salt, stock, or water.

Peel, wash, and slice the potatoes; peel, clean, and cut up the onions; separate the meat from the bones, and cut into small pieces, place a little stock or water in the kettle, and a layer of potatoes at the bottom, then a layer of meat and onions, season with pepper and salt, then another layer of potatoes, and so on alternatively until the vessel is nearly full, potatoes forming the top layer; barely covering the top with stock or water, and stew gently for one and a half hours, keeping the vessel closely covered, care being taken that it does not burn. The surplus fat must always be removed previous to cooking, as an Irish Stew should not be greasy.

3. *Curry Stew*—Ingredients: The same as for stew, with the addition of 5 ozs. of curry powder.

Mix the curry with the dry flour and proceed as for stew.

Finally, the *Small Book* covers furlough (or leave of absence), marriage, civil employment and soldiers' wills. The two short paragraphs on marriage are interesting:

MARRIAGE

A Soldier must not marry without first obtaining his Commanding Officer's sanction, otherwise, although the marriage is legal, he can never have any claim to be borne on the marriage establishment of his Corps.

A large proportion of Serjeants is allowed on the married roll, also a percentage, varying in different branches of the Service, of the Trumpeters, Drummers, and rank and file who have completed seven years' service, are in possession of at least two good conduct badges, and have at least £5 in the Army or Post Office Savings Bank. When a regiment goes to India the proportion of married men permitted to embark is increased.*

* *Squadron-Leader Victor Lucarotti has given me permission to use photographs and documents belonging to his father, the late Lieutenant-Colonel U. R. Lucarotti, M.B.E.*

Appendix D

Stuck in the back of Private Lucarotti's *Small Book* is a Memorandum by Lord Kitchener dated 1905 on the subject of venereal disease. It was written for the Army in India, and in terms designed to leave a soldier in no doubt as to the ravages of the various forms of the disease. Since the copy in Lucarotti's book was printed in Colchester it is fair to assume that it was reprinted especially for the 2nd Scottish Rifles before going to Malta, probably from a copy of the original Memorandum brought home from India. The most vivid paragraph must have scared the wits out of many a young soldier in its time:

The common women as well as the regular prostitutes in India are almost all more or less infected with the disease. It is rife in the country and in the villages as well as in the towns, and it is only by avoiding altogether the many facilities for indulgence which India affords that men can be sure of remaining safe from infection. The danger is not merely limited to the venereal diseases, syphilis, gonorrhea and chancre. Numbers of cases have occurred in which soldiers have died of plague and small-pox contacted from native women. Such diseases when contracted by Europeans from natives of Asia or Africa are almost invariably fatal, for diseases passed on from one race of men to another always increase in severity. Similarly, syphilis contracted by Europeans from Asiatic women is much more severe than that contracted in England. It assumes a horrible, loathsome, and often fatal form through which in time, as years pass by, the sufferer finds his hair falling off, his skin and the flesh of his body rot, and are eaten away by slow kankerous and stinking ulcerations; his nose falls in at the bridge, and then rots and falls off; his sight gradually fails, and he eventually becomes blind; his voice first becomes husky, and then fades to a hoarse whisper as his throat is eaten away by foetid ulcerations which cause his breath to stink. In the hospitals, and among the suicides, many such examples are to be found. Gonorrhea, again, although it begins as merely a scalding local inflammation, slowly spreads and infects other parts of the body and the blood, giving rise to other diseases, such as stricture (which causes excruciating pain), bladder troubles, and rheumatism of the joints. Though these diseases do not appear at once, they all follow in time and increase as the sufferer grows older.

Although the horror aspect seems rather overdone, it is worth remembering that quite a high percentage of the children in the poorer areas of Glasgow carried symptoms of hereditary syphilis—see Chapter 9, page 213.

Source Notes

INTRODUCTION

1. John Connell, 'Writing about Soldiers', *Royal United Service Institution Journal*, August 1965, p. 222.
2. Barrie Pitt, 'Writers and the Great War', *Royal United Service Institution Journal*, August 1964, p. 246.
3. Professor Cyril Falls, *War Books —A Critical Guide*.
4. Richard Hoggart, *The Uses of Literacy*, Preface to the Pelican Edition.
5. John Terraine, *General Jack's Diary 1914–1918*, p. 297.
6. Edmund Blunden, *Poems of Many Years*, p. 220.

CHAPTER 1

1. John Connell, *Wavell, Scholar and Soldier*, p. 74.
2. S. H. F. Johnston, *The History of The Cameronians (Scottish Rifles) Volume 1, 1689–1910*, p. 164.
3. Johnston, p. 296.
4. Field-Marshal Viscount Wolseley, *The Story of a Soldier's Life*, quoted in Volume 1 of the Regimental History, p. 266.
5. Correlli Barnett, *The Desert Generals*, p. 22.
6. Robert Graves, *Goodbye to All That*, p. 150.
7. R. Leggat, 'How It Was In The Army', *The Covenanter*, February 1963, p. 82.
8. Lord Moran, *The Anatomy of Courage*, p. 166.
9. Cyril Falls, in *Edwardian England 1901–1914*, p. 534.

CHAPTER 2

1. *General Jack's Diary 1914–1918*, p. 108.
2. Colonel H. H. Story, M.C., *History of The Cameronians (Scottish Rifles) 1910–1933*, p. 29.

3. Story, p. 30.
4. Story, pp. 32–33.
5. Story, p. 39.
6. J. H. Boraston and Cyril E. O. Bax, *The Eighth Division in War 1914–1918*, p. 19.
7. Alan Herbert, *The Secret Battle*, pp. 31 and 34.
8. Story, p. 41.
9. Alan Clark, *The Donkeys*, p. 51.
10. Story, p. 141.
11. C. E. Montague, *Disenchantment*.
12. Story, p. 47.
13. Told me verbally by Maj.-Gen. R. C. Money, C.B., M.C., in 1965.
14. *General Jack's Diary 1914–1918*, p. 107.

CHAPTER 3

1. Edmund Blunden, *Poems of Many Years*, p. 223.
2. Brig.-Gen. John Charteris, *At G.H.Q.*, p. 86.
3. Basil Liddell Hart, *A History of the World War 1914–1918*, p. 191.
4. Liddell Hart, p. 194.
5. John Terraine, *Douglas Haig: the educated soldier*, p. 113.
6. Sir Arthur Bryant, *English Saga 1840–1940*, p. 296.

CHAPTER 4

1. Moran, *The Anatomy of Courage*, pp. 16 and 81.
2. *The Concise Oxford Dictionary*, p. 737.
3. Wavell, *Soldiers and Soldiering*, p. 14.
4. Napoleon Bonaparte, *Observations sur les affaires d'Espagne*.
5. *General Jack's Diary 1914–1918*, p. 127.
6. Moran, p. 195.
7. Graves, *Goodbye to All That*, p. 113.
8. Joost A. M. Meerloo, *Mental Seduction and Menticide*, p. 278.

9. Meerloo, p. 280.
10. *Ibid.*
11. Meerloo, p. 274.
12. *Ibid.*
13. Meerloo, p. 281.
14. Montague, *Disenchantment*, p. 55.
15. Meerloo, p. 282.
16. Moran, *The Anatomy of Courage*, p. 166.
17. Meerloo, p. 271.
18. Moran, p. 153.
19. Brophy, *After Fifty Years* (Introductory essay in *The Long Trail*), p. 17.
20. Brophy, p. 18.
21. Story, *History of The Cameronians (Scottish Rifles) 1910–1933*, p. 141.
22. Herbert, *The Secret Battle*, p. 166.
23. Shakespeare, *Henry V*, Part 1, Act 4, Scene 3.

CHAPTER 5
1. John Connell, *Wavell, Scholar and Soldier*, p. 74.
2. General Ludendorff, *My War Memories 1914–1918*, p. 391.
3. *General Jack's Diary 1914–1918*, p. 226.
4. Field-Marshal Earl Wavell, *Soldiers and Soldiering*, p. 155.
5. C. E. Montague, *Disenchantment*, p. 155–157.
6. Colonel G. F. R. Henderson, *The Science of War*, p. 409.
7. *General Jack's Diary 1914–1918*, Foreword by Sidney Rogerson, p. 13.
8. *General Jack's Diary*, p. 170.
9. *General Jack's Diary*, p. 22.
10. Cyril Falls, 'The Army' in *Edwardian England 1901–1914*, p. 524.
11. *John Betjeman's Collected Poems*, p. 43.
12. Margery Perham, *Lugard, The Years of Adventure 1858–1898*, p. 643.
13. *General Jack's Diary*, p. 144.
14. Sir Charles Petrie, Bt., *Wellington: A Reassessment*, p. 127.
15. John Arlott, 'Sport', in *Edwardian England 1901–1914*, p. 474.

16. Sir Winston Churchill, *Great Contemporaries*, p. 10.
17. Alan Clark, *The Donkeys*, p. 174.

CHAPTER 6
1. Field-Marshal Earl Wavell, 'The Soldier as Citizen', in *Soldiers and Soldiering*, p. 124.
2. Seebohm Rowntree, *Poverty, A Study of Town Life*, p. 259.
3. Rudyard Kipling, 'Gentlemen-Rankers', *Barrack-Room Ballads*, p. 63.
4. Wavell, p. 125.
5. Printed in *The Covenanter*, March 1965, p. 18.
6. Sir William Robieson kindly made inquiries through Glasgow University on my behalf in 1965, but without discovering any similar sources to Booth or Rowntree, nor evidence of any study of the same nature.
7. Charles Booth, *Life and Labour of the People in London* (Final Volume—Notes on Social Influences and Conclusion), p. 429.
8. Rowntree, p. 356.
9. Rowntree, p. 207.
10. Rowntree, p. 212.
11. Rowntree, p. 224.
12. Rowntree, p. xix.
13. Booth, p. 89.
14. Rowntree, p. 310.
15. Booth, p. 20.
16. Averil Stewart, *Alicella*, p. 95.
17. Marghanita Laski, 'Domestic Life' in *Edwardian England 1901–1914*, p. 206.
18. Laski, p. 181.
19. Rowntree, pp. 256–260.
20. Booth, p. 89.
21. Booth, p. 86.
22. *Ibid*
23. *Ibid.*
24. Booth, p. 87.
25. Cyril Falls, 'The Army', in *Edwardian England 1901–1914*, p. 525.
26. Rowntree, p. 464. Appendix D.
27. Rudyard Kipling, 'The Incarnation of Krishna Mulvaney' from *Life's Handicap*.

28. Cyril Falls, 'The Army', in *Edwardian England 1901–1914*, p. 520.
29. Falls, p. 537.
30. Major-General H. Essame (British Army [Rtd.]) 'Second Lieutenants Unless Otherwise Stated', *U.S. Military Review*, May 1964.
31. Booth, p. 84.
32. Story, *History of The Cameronians (Scottish Rifles) 1910–1933*, p. 410, and Rowntree, p. 310.
33. Booth, p. 88.
34. Charles Carrington, *Soldier From the Wars Returning*, p. 98.

CHAPTER 7
1. John Connell, 'Writing About Soldiers', *Royal United Service Institute Journal*, August 1965, p. 223.
2. *Ibid.*
3. Averil Stewart, *Alicella*, p. 94.
4. *Edwardian England 1901–1914*, p. 110.
5. P.-H. Simon, *Portrait of an Officer* (translated by H. Hare), pp. 86–87.
6. *General Jack's Diary 1914–1918*, p. 127.
7. Robert Browning, *The Lost Leader*.

CHAPTER 8
1. Graham, *A Private in the Guards*, p. 1.
2. Graham, p. 17.
3. Henderson, *The Science of War*, p. 189 (quoted from *Battles and Leaders of the Civil War*, Vol ii, p. 662).
4. Graham, p. 2.
5. *Ibid.*
6. Gibbon, *The History of the Decline and Fall of the Roman Empire*, Vol. 1, Chapter 1 and Chapter 3.
7. Carrington, *Soldier from the Wars Returning*, p. 248.
8. Nimrod, *The Life and Death of John Mytton*, p. 32.
9. Nimrod, p. 33.
10. Nimrod, p. 40.

11. Falls, in *Edwardian England 1901–1914*, p. 542.
12. *Manual of Military Law*, Sixth Edition, Feb. 1914. These rules were made under the authority of the Army Act of 1881.
13. Shaw, 'Preface to St. Joan', p. 33.
14. John Brophy, 'After Fifty Years', Introductory essay in *The Long Trail*, p. 14.
15. *General Jack's Diary*, p. 307.
16. *General Jack's Diary*, p. 106.
17. Graves, *Good-bye to All That*, p. 156.
18. Field-Marshal Viscount Slim, *Defeat into Victory*.
19. Kipling, 'Back to the Army Again'.
20. *British Army Review*, April 1965, pp. 10 and 11. The article is by Lt.-Col. A. A. Hanbury-Sparrow, D.S.O., M.C.

CHAPTER 9
1. Siegfried Sassoon, 'The Redeemer', from *Collected Poems*.
2. Rowntree, *Poverty*, p. 406.
3. *General Jack's Diary*, p. 116.
4. Robert Graves, *Goodbye to All That*, p. 157.
5. Graves, p. 158.
6. The story of the Rev. T. B. Hardy, V.C., D.S.O., M.C., has been told me by the Warden of the Royal Army Chaplains Department (R.A.Ch.D.) Depot, and is also recorded by Montague in *Disenchantment*, p. 67.
7. Percy Croney, *Soldier's Luck*.
8. Graves, p. 158.
9. Suggested as a possibility by the Warden of the R.A.Ch.D. Depot.
10. C. E. Montague, *Disenchantment*, p. 76.
11. Graves, p. 158.
12. Report of the Medical Officer of Health, City of Glasgow, 1913.
13. *Ibid.*
14. Told me by Lt.-Col. D. A. Foulis, D.S.O., O.B.E.
15. Carrington, *Soldier from the Wars Returning*, p. 224.

16. John Connell, *Wavell, Scholar and Soldier*, p. 74.

CHAPTER 10

1. Mary Clive, *The Day of Reckoning* p. 97.
2. Rudyard Kipling, 'The Widow at Windsor', *Barrack-Room Ballads*, p. 39.
3. Juliana Horatia Ewing, *The Story of a Short Life*, p. 9.
4. G. A. Henty, *The Lion of St Mark*, Preface.
5. Charles Kingsley, *Westward Ho!*, Dedication.
6. 'Children's Literature', an article in the *Encyclopaedia Britannica*, Volume 5, p. 523.
7. Wilfred Scawen Blunt, from 'Satan Absolved'.
8. T. E. Lawrence, *Seven Pillars of Wisdom*, p. 682 (3.X.18).
9. Rupert Brooke, 'The Soldier', from *The Collected Poems of Rupert Brooke*.
10. Colonel G. F. R. Henderson, *The Science of War*, p. 421.
11. Quoted by Henderson.
12. Kipling, 'The English Flag', *Barrack-Room Ballads* (Other Verses), p. 174.
13. Kipling, 'The Widow at Windsor', *Barrack-Room Ballads*, p. 41.
14. Wavell, 'The Soldier as Citizen', in *Soldiers and Soldiering*, p. 124.

CHAPTER 11

1. Carrington, *Soldier from the Wars Returning*, p. 11.
2. Wavell, *Soldiers and Soldiering*, p. 14.
3. Ludendorff, *My War Memories 1914–1918*, p. 349.
4. General *Jack's Diary 1914–1918*, p. 301.
5. Carrington, p. 107.
6. Moran, *The Anatomy of Courage*, p. 208.
7. Field-Marshal Viscount Slim, *Defeat into Victory*.
8. John Terraine, *Douglas Haig: the educated soldier*, p. 113.
9. Carrington, p. 105.
10. General *Jack's Diary*, p. 29.
11. General *Jack's Diary*, p. 265.
12. Carrington, p. 104.
13. Told me by Lt. Col. D. A. Foulis D.S.O., O.B.E., one-time Commanding Officer of the 10th Scottish Rifles.
14. Siegfried Sassoon, *Base Details*.
15. General *Jack's Diary*, p. 309.

Bibliography

ADAMS, W. S. *Edwardian Portaits.* Secker and Warburg, 1957.

ANON. *A Soldier's Diary of the Great War.* Faber and Gwyer, 1929.

BARNETT, CORRELLI. *The Desert Generals.* William Kimber, 1960.

BEAVERBROOK, LORD. *Men and Power 1917–1918.* Hutchinson, 1956.

BELHAVEN, THE MASTER OF. *The War Diary of the Master of Belhaven.* John Murray, 1924.

BLUNDEN, EDMUND. *Undertones of War.* Cobden-Sanderson, 1928.

— *Poems of Many Years.* Collins, 1957.

BOOTH, CHARLES. *Life and Labour of the People in London* (Final volume—Conclusion). Macmillan, 1902.

BONHAM–CARTER, VICTOR. *Soldier True: The Life and Times of Field-Marshal Sir William Robertson, Bt., G.C.B., G.C.M.G., K.C.V.O., D.S.O., 1860–1933.* F. Muller, 1963.

— *In a Liberal Tradition.* Constable, 1960.

BORASTON, J. H. and BAX, CYRIL, E. O. *The Eighth Division in War 1914–1918.* The Medici Society, 1926.

BROPHY, JOHN and PARTRIDGE, ERIC. *The Long Trail: What the British Soldier Sang and Said in the Great War of 1914–1918.* A. Deutsch, 1965.

BRYANT, SIR ARTHUR. *English Saga 1840–1940.* Collins with Eyre and Spottiswoode, 1940.

CARRINGTON, CHARLES. *Soldier from the Wars Returning.* Hutchinson, 1965.

CAREW, TIM. *The Vanished Army.* William Kimber, 1964.

CHARTERIS, BRIG.-GEN. JOHN. *At G.H.Q.* Cassell, 1931.

CHURCHILL, SIR WINSTON S. *Great Contemporaries.* Odhams Press, 1949.

— *Thoughts and Adventures.* Macmillan, 1943.

CLARK, ALAN. *The Donkeys.* Hutchinson, 1961.

CLIVE, MARY. *The Day of Reckoning.* Macmillan, 1964.

COLLIER, BASIL. *Brasshat: A Biography of Field-Marshal Sir Henry Wilson 1864–1922.* Secker and Warburg, 1961.

CONNELL, JOHN. *Wavell, Scholar and Soldier.* Collins, 1964.

CUMMING, BRIG.-GEN. H. R. *A Brigadier in France.* Jonathan Cape, 1922.

DUFF COOPER (VISCOUNT NORWICH). *Haig.* Faber and Faber, 1935.

EDMONDS, CHARLES. *A Subaltern's War.* Peter Davies, 1929.

[275]

EX-PRIVATE X. *War is War.* Gollancz, 1930.

FALLS, CYRIL. *War Books—A Critical Guide.* Peter Davies, 1930.

— *The Gordon Highlanders in the First World War 1914–1919.* Aberdeen University Press.

GRAHAM, STEPHEN. *A Private in the Guards.* Macmillan, 1919.

GRAVES, ROBERT. *Goodbye to All That.* Jonathan Cape, 1929. (*Revised edition,* Cassell, 1957).

HAIG, FIELD-MARSHAL THE EARL. *The Private Papers of Douglas Haig 1914–1918* (edited by Robert Blake). Eyre and Spottiswoode, 1952.

HENDERSON, COLONEL G. F. R. *The Science of War.* Longmans, Green & Co., 1916.

HERBERT, A. P. *The Secret Battle.* Methuen, 1919.

HERBERT, THE HON. A. *Mons, Anzac, and Kut.* Hutchinson, 1919.

JOHNSTON, JOHN H. *English Poetry of the First World War.* Princeton University Press, 1964.

JOHNSTON, S. H. F. *The History of The Cameronians (Scottish Rifles)* Volume 1, 1689–1910. Gale and Polden, 1957.

KIPLING, RUDYARD. *Barrack-Room Ballads.* Methuen, 1892.

— *Soldiers Three.* Macmillan, 1895.

LAWRENCE, T. E. *Seven Pillars of Wisdom.* Jonathan Cape, 1935.

LIDDELL HART, B. H. *A History of the World War 1914–1918.* Faber and Faber, 1930.

LUDENDORFF, GENERAL. *My War Memories 1914–1918.* Hutchinson, 1921.

MACGILL, P. *The Great Push.* Jenkins, 1916.

MANNING, F. *Her Privates We.* Peter Davies, 1930.

MARK VII. *A Subaltern on the Somme, 1916.* Dent, 1927.

MAXWELL, FRANK. *Frank Maxwell—Brigadier-General, V.C., C.S.I., D.S.O. A Memoir and Some Letters.* John Murray, 1921.

MEERLOO, J. A. M. *Mental Seduction and Menticide.* Jonathan Cape, 1957.

M. O. H., GLASGOW. *Report of the Medical Officer of Health, City of Glasgow, 1913.*

MORAN, LORD. *The Anatomy of Courage.* Constable, 1945.

MONTAGUE, C. E. *Disenchantment.* Chatto and Windus, 1922.

NOWELL-SMITH, SIMON (EDITOR). *Edwardian England 1901–1914.* Oxford University Press, 1964.

OFFICIAL HISTORY OF THE WAR. *Military Operations: France and Belgium, 1915—Vol. 1.* H.M. Stationery Office.

PARSONS, I. M. *Men Who March Away* (An Anthology of Poems of the First World War). Chatto and Windus, 1965.

PERHAM, MARGERY. *Lugard, The Years of Adventure 1858–1898.* Collins, 1956.

PURDOM, C. B. *Everyman at War.* Dent, 1930.

REMARQUE, ERICH MARIA. *All Quiet on the Western Front.* Translated A. W. Wheen. Published in U.K. 1929.

RIFLEMAN, A. *Four Years on the Western Front.* Odhams Press, 1922.

ROSKILL, S. W. *The Art of Leadership.* Collins, 1964.

ROWNTREE, B. SEEBOHM. *Poverty—A Study of Town Life.* Longmans, Green and Co., 1901.

SASSOON, SIEGFRIED. *Memoirs of a Fox-hunting Man.* Faber and Gwyer. 1928.

— *Memoirs of an Infantry Officer.* Faber and Faber, 1930.

SCOTT, RALPH. *A Soldier's War Diary.* Collins, 1923.

SIMON, P.-H. *Portrait of an Officer* (Translated H. Hare). Secker and Warburg, 1961.

SLIM, FIELD-MARSHAL VISCOUNT. *Defeat into Victory.* Cassell, 1955.

STEWART, AVERIL. *'Alicella', a Memoir of Alice King Stewart and Ella Christie.* John Murray, 1955.

STORY, COLONEL H. H. *The History of The Cameronians (Scottish Rifles) 1910–1933.* Printed by Hazell, Watson and Viney, 1961.

TAYLOR, A. J. P. *The First World War—an illustrated history.* Hamish Hamilton, 1963.

TERRAINE, JOHN. *Douglas Haig: the educated soldier.* Hutchinson, 1963.

— *The Western Front 1914–1918.* Hutchinson, 1964.

— *General Jack's Diary 1914–1918.* Eyre and Spottiswoode, 1964.

WAVELL, FIELD-MARSHAL THE EARL. *Soldiers and Soldiering, or Epithets of War.* Jonathan Cape, 1953.

WOLF, LEON. *In Flanders Fields.* Viking Press, New York, 1958 (Pan, 1961).

Magazines and Journals

CONNELL, JOHN. *R.U.S.I. Journal.* 'Writing About Soldiers', August, 1965.

ESSAME, MAJ.-GEN. H. *U.S. Military Review,* 'Second Lieutenants Unless Otherwise Stated', May 1964.

HANBURY-SPARROW, LT.-COL. J. A., D.S.O., M.C. *British Army Review,* 'Discipline or Enthusiasm', April 1965.

HORNE, CPL. J. C. *The Covenanter*, 'A Salute To Malta', March 1965.

LEGGAT, R. *The Covenanter*, 'How It Was In The Army', February 1963.

PITT, BARRIE. *R.U.S.I. Journal*, 'Writers and the Great War', August, 1964.

Index

Adjutants, 19, 22–3, 44, 71, 82, 112–13, 196, 236
administration, sound, 238–40, 244–7, 254
Aisne, battle of (1914), 196
Aldershot, 17, 25
Alicella (Stewart), 142
Allenby, Viscount, 23, 100, 224
amateurism, 109, 125–6
Anatomy of Courage, The (Moran), 8, 43, 92
Angus, Earl of, 20
Animal Transport section, 47, 94
Arlott, John (quoted), 130
Army Chaplain, The (Middleton), 206n
Aubers Ridge, 9, 82, 262, 263

Baddesley Common, Romsey, 51
'badges of shame', 249
Bandmaster, 36
Barnett, Correlli (quoted), 26, 27
Barrack-Room Ballads (Kipling), 222
'barrack-room lawyers', 161
batmen, 28
battalion commanders, 110–11, 112–13, 122–3
Battalion Headquarters, 19, 22–4, 65
battalion training, 48
battalions: command of, 19–20; Home and overseas postings, 15, 17, 20, 149; size and structure, 18–19, 20; Special Reserve, 19
battle, compulsory return to, 105–6
behaviour, 95, 119
belief in cause, 99–100
Bell, Corporal (quoted), 243
Betjeman, John (quoted), 128
Blackwood's Magazine, 223
Blaquicre, 2/Lieut. the Hon. J. de, 262
Bliss, Lieut.-Colonel W. M., 21, 22, 58, 71, 73, 112–13, 187, 192, 252, 261
'bloody-mindedness', 97, 98, 100
Blunden, Edmund (quoted), 14, 83
Blunt, Wilfrid Scawen (quoted), 224
Boer War, 17, 52, 115, 227, 240

Bomber Command, 8
Booth, Charles, 138; quoted, 138, 140–1, 142, 143, 144, 146, 147, 155, 158
boxing, 33, 34
Boy's Own Paper, 171n, 222
Brigades: 22nd Infantry, 27; 23rd Infantry, 51, 57, 58, 60, 66, 77, 78, 80, 81, 244, 246, 247; 24th Infantry, 76; 25th Infantry, 58; Highland, 32; Household, 32; Rifle, 17
'British Army, The' (Henderson), 227
Brooke, Rupert (quoted), 226
Brophy, John (quoted), 105, 191
Bryant, Sir Arthur (quoted), 89
Bryant, Sergeant, 37–8, 136, 252
bugle calls, 44
'bull', 45
bullying, 193
Burma campaign, 194, 242

'cadres', 47
Cameron, Pipe-Major, 37, 253
Cameronians (Scottish Rifles), 18–19, 201; formation of, 16–17; 1st Battalion, 16, 17, 20–1, 82, 149, 261, 262; 2nd Battalion, *passim*; 3rd Battalion, 82, 261; 4th (Special Reserve) Battalion, 51–2, 82
Cardwell, Edward, Viscount, reforms of, 15, 16, 17
Carrington, Charles (quoted), 160, 184, 215, 236, 241
Carter, Colonel C. H. P., 261
Carter-Campbell, Major George, 21–2, 23, 73, 74, 75, 77, 80, 112, 184, 187, 243, 256, 261
casualties, 73–4, 75–6, 84; heavy, as cause of high morale, 100–1; officers, 75–6, 84, 177–9, 261–3; other ranks, 73–4, 84; unnecessary, 97
cause, belief in, 99–100
cavalry regiments, 30n, 32, 249
celibacy, 150, 210–11, 212

[279]